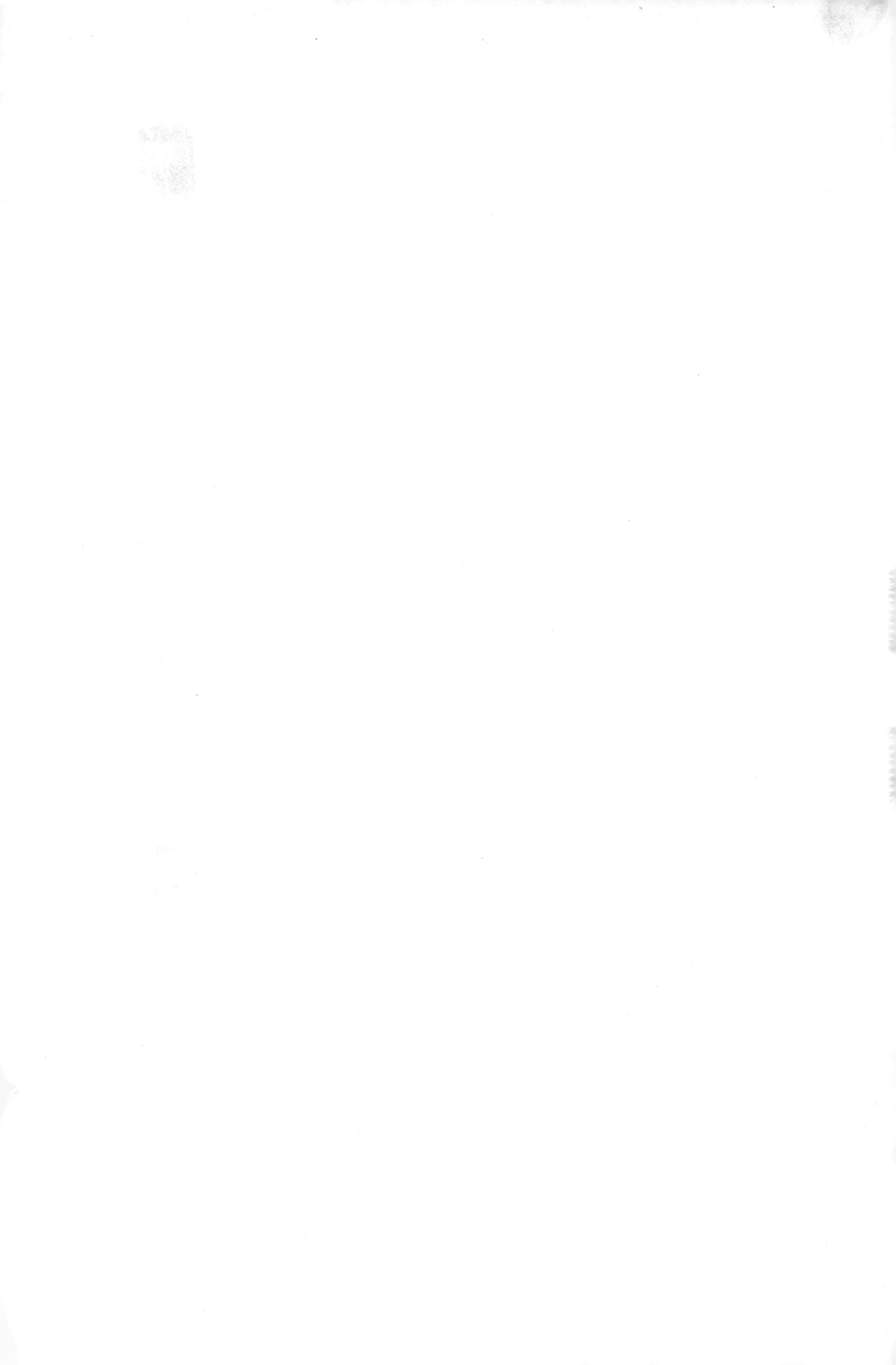

The Book of the
BLACK FIVE
LM CLASS 5 4-6-0s
Part 2, 45075-45224

By
Ian Sixsmith

5224, which emerged from Armstrong Whitworths on 10 December 1935, was the final locomotive built with a vertical throatplate boiler and was allocated to Newton Heath from new until 1962. Two minor changes can be seen when compared with the early engines in the batch – the LMS insignia on the tender are spaced wider and the builder's plate is on the front frames instead of above the steam pipe. The access covers on the cylinder wrappers were added after a few years in service.

Irwell Press Ltd.

ISBN 978-1-906919-50-4

First published in the United Kingdom in 2012
by Irwell Press Limited, 59A, High Street, Clophill,
Bedfordshire MK45 4BE
Printed by Konway Press

Contents

	INTRODUCTION AND ACKNOWLEDGEMENTS	**Page 5**
1.	**A 'UNIVERSAL' TYPE OF ENGINE**	**Page 7**
	Buying from the Trade	
	Leading Features of the Design	
2.	**HERE, THERE AND EVERYWHERE**	**Page 13**
	Taking over	
	Highland Division	
	On the Southern Region	
	The end of steam	
3.	**THE DEVIL IN THE DETAIL**	**Page 21**
	Boilers	
	Smokebox door	
	Spark arresters	
	Frames	
	Wheels and axles	
	Cylinders and inspection covers	
	Combination levers	
	Carriage warming pipes	
	Tablet exchange apparatus	
	Snowploughs	
	BR days	
	Tenders	
	Liveries	
	Names	
4.	**ON THE RECORD**	**Page 35**
	Health Warning	
	Sheds...	
	Repairs and Maintenance	
	Works...	
	Mileages	
	'Improvements, Etc'	
	Crosshead Driven Vacuum Pumps	
	Steam sanding	
	Speed Indicators	
	Modification and Modernisation	
	AWS equipment	

A Crewe South Black 5, 45093 heads through Manchester Exchange a mixed freight with a motley collection of wagons headed by wooden ex-private owners. It was fitted with AWS in February 1959 and moved to 5B in September 1963 and was withdrawn in w.e. 6/11/65. Photograph www.rail-online.co.uk

Introduction and Acknowledgements

Those of you in possession of Part 1 will recall how this series came about; just how could a tome on the LMS Black 5s in the *Book Of* series be arranged? The first question to be answered was how many volumes, on the grounds that even the mighty Irwell machine would struggle to cope with a thousand pager! After much discussion over sausage sandwiches and pints we came up with – five. Part 1 covered the background to the design, the first fifty locomotives from Vulcan Foundry and the 1935 engines built at Crewe, and this part deals with the similar 1935 Vulcan Foundry and Armstrong Whitworth locomotives. Part 3 will describe the 'Mark 2' 1936 Armstrong Whitworth locomotives and will sweep up the remaining pre-war engines. Part 4 will deal with the war-time and immediate post-war LMS batches leaving Part 5 for the Caprottis and the final LMS and BR-built locomotives.

As we will discover, the Black 5s were not all the same – far from it – and I trust the reader will follow through the story in the approximate chronological sequence which seemed at the time to make sense. So the books are arranged in the order in which the locomotives were introduced, with an added twist that particularly in matters such as boilers and tenders there is a certain amount of back and forward cross-referencing. Some details are covered in more depth in the earlier books and only summarised in the later parts.

The core of the material by weight is from the Engine History Cards and Engine Record Cards aided and abetted by information begged and borrowed from a number of sources, and backed up by a very large pile of photographs.

I would record my thanks especially to Paul Chancellor, Peter Groom, Michael Mensing, Norman Preedy, Rail-Online and The Transport Treasury for allowing me to use their pictures. I have also consulted magazines including *The Railway Gazette, SLS Journal, The Railway Observer* and the *LMS Journal*.

Finally, and in this case it is definitely last but not least, I could not have produced this book without the help of John Jennison of Brassmasters fame (Brassmasters – purveyors of exquisite etched brass kits of LMS prototypes including the Black 5s; PO Box 1137, Sutton Coldfield, West Midlands, B76 1FU; www.brassmasters.co.uk). He helped interpret the History and Record Cards and made available his extensive photograph collection, allowing me to fill in many gaps in the story.

45182 on shed at Edge Hill was a Patricroft engine from 3/11/56 until 14/11/64 when it was transferred to Trafford Park. This picture was taken between its fitting with AWS in November 1959 and September 1963 when the shed's code was changed from 26F to 9H. Photograph www.rail-online.co.uk

Vulcan Foundry were first off the mark in delivering the 1935 Black 5s which was not surprising since theirs was a follow-on order whereas Armstrong Whitworth were starting from scratch. 5078 seen at Crewe North on 3 March 1935 had arrived from Vulcan the previous day. This batch of engines differed from 5020-69 in a number of minor details but, more importantly, had a boiler with increased superheating, identifiable by the domed covers on the firebox shoulders.

1. A 'UNIVERSAL' TYPE OF ENGINE

In 1939 the *Railway Gazette* under the heading L.M.S.R. GENERAL UTILITY LOCOMOTIVES observed: *The ideal locomotive, dreamed of and longed for by the operating departments of large railway systems everywhere, is one that could 'go anywhere and do anything.' This, indeed, was the definition put forward, perhaps only half seriously, by the late Mr. J. H. Follows, then Chief General Superintendent of the L.M.S.R., when we discussed the subject with him in his office at Derby shortly after his appointment to that position in 1923. As we stated in the editorial columns of our issue of February 19, 1932, when recording his retirement, he pleaded for something in the nature of a 'universal' type of engine to dispose of the majority of the operating problems with which he had to deal.*

The fact that Follows was still looking for this ideal may make one wonder what the LMS had been doing in the intervening years. It appeared not to have caught up with the other three companies, who had all developed successful mixed traffic designs and produced them in quantity. In fact it had not been idle in the decade since the 1923 grouping, building over 2,000 new locomotives to eliminate large numbers of inadequate and inefficient pre-grouping classes, but it had only produced one design likely to match the 'go anywhere, do anything' ideal, the 245 Hughes-Fowler 'Crab' 2-6-0s.

There had been a number of proposals for a mixed traffic 4-6-0 between 1924 and 1931 but it was not until 1932 that approval was given for ten of these in the 1933 Locomotive Renewal Programme. They were referred to as a 'superheated converted Prince of Wales' with outside Walschaerts valve gear, and 'having regard to the heavy Passenger stopping trains now worked by Prince of Wales type engines, these engines are heavy on coal and are falling due for re-boilering. It is suggested that they be replaced by a similar engine of modern design'. However the Programme was amended in May 1933 before construction began, since it would not be possible to complete the design work 'to ensure their being built this year'. They were accordingly deferred to the 1934 Programme.

There was also a growing motive power crisis in Scotland as the Northern Division's pre-grouping designs were ageing and struggling to cope with traffic demands. The only new engines which had been introduced north of the border were Class 2P and Compound 4-4-0s and the 4F 0-6-0s, plus ten Crab 2-6-0s which went to the Highland Section during 1928/29 but were restricted from many of the far-north lines. The LMS even seriously considered re-boilering some of the 4-6-0s it had inherited before finally deciding to build a new lightweight 4-6-0 especially for use north of the border, ten of which were approved in the 1934 Locomotive Renewal Programme.

Only a few months later came the decision to initiate a 'scrap and build' policy approved at the October 1933 LMS Board Meeting. This had recommended that 121 locomotives, the boilers of most of which would require to be renewed shortly or which otherwise would not in the ordinary course be broken up for some years, be replaced by one hundred engines. Fifty of these would be 'Improved Claughtons'; that is, Jubilee]s and fifty the 'Improved Prince of Wales', or Black 5. This, it was estimated, would result in an 18% saving in coal consumption and a 25% saving in cost of repair, per mile. It was agreed that 'the Locomotive Trade' should be asked to 'submit alternative tenders for each type in lots of twenty-five and fifty locomotives'.

As described in Part 1 the fifty 2-cylinder mixed traffic engines were duly ordered from the Vulcan Foundry and another twenty from Crewe under the 1934 Renewal Programme. The Scottish design was not to see the light of day as bridge strengthening and other civil engineering improvements made it unnecessary. In April 1934 Stanier and the Chief Operating Manager recommended that twenty

Under a five year special 'investment' programme covering the replacement of locomotives of obsolete design by locomotives of up-to-date design the LMS placed orders in 1934 for 100 4-6-0 mixed traffic engines 'which would allow for the displacement of 108 19in Goods locomotives' such as no.8834 seen here at Willesden. The 100 new engines were Black 5s 5125-5224 purchased from Armstrong Whitworth and delivered by the end of 1935. Photograph www.rail-online.co.uk

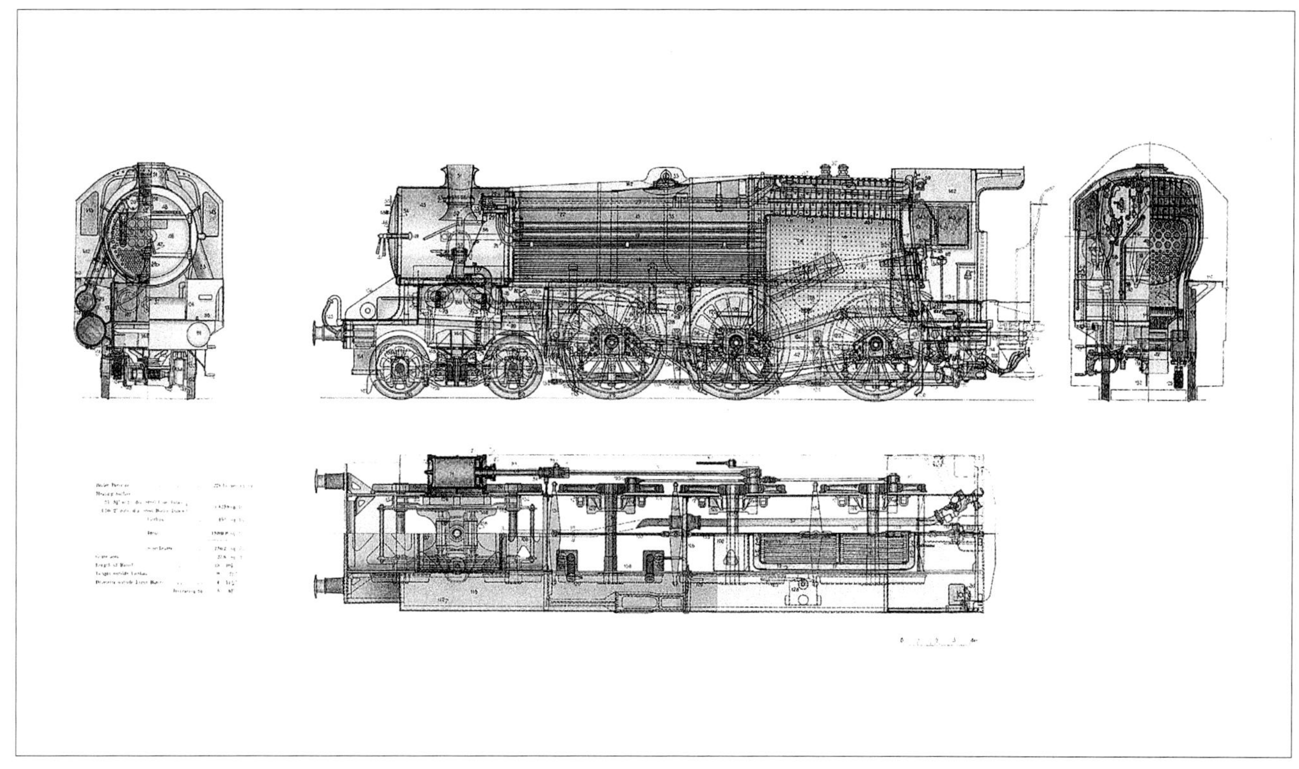

Cut-away general arrangement diagram of the 21 element superheater Black 5.

4-6-0 engines and tenders of a new type suitable for mixed traffic work both in England and Scotland be built in the Company's workshops in place of the ten improved 4-6-0 'Prince of Wales' type and the ten 4-6-0 engines and tenders for the Northern Division authorised (as part of) the Locomotive Renewal Programme for 1934.

Buying from the Trade

Even before the first Black 5 had been delivered from Vulcan Foundry in August 1934 the 1935 Locomotive Renewal Programme, adopted in June 1934, included another 55 mixed traffic 4-6-0s and tenders at a cost of £338,250. However, before these were ordered there had been a further and significant acceleration in the programme of new building. Reports on 'locomotive construction policy' were presented to the LMS Board on 29 November 1934 which approved 'a five year special investment programme covering the replacement of 902 locomotives of obsolete design by 772 locomotives of up-to-date design'. The Chairman stated that under this programme, orders had been placed as an addition to the 1935 locomotive renewal programme *for 100 4-6-0 mixed traffic engines, at an approximate cost of £511,882, which would allow for the displacement of 108 19 inch Goods locomotives, and that it was proposed to withdraw, without replacement, 120 locos rendered surplus as a result of various improvements in the use of stock*. At their meeting on the previous day, the Mechanical & Engineering Committee was asked to formally approve *The purchase from the trade of 50 mixed traffic two-cylinder 4-6-0 engines out of the 55 authorised under the ordinary 1935 renewal programme*. These were 5075-5124. Stanier reported to the meeting that an order for the latter had been placed with the Vulcan Foundry Limited at a price of £5,500 each (compared with £5,540 for the first lot); the other five (5070-5074) were to be built at Crewe.

Behind the small reduction in Vulcan's price since the 1933 order lay another tale. Ten firms had tendered in July 1934 and prices ranged for 30 locomotives from £5,395 (Armstrong-Whitworth, with welded tank) to £6,575. As there was a good case for increasing the number of mixed traffic engines and in order to test Armstrong-Whitworth's tender, supplementary enquiries were sent out for 50, 75, 100 and 150 locomotives. The new tenders were received from the ten firms in August, 1934, and the prices ranged as follows:

50 = £5,365 to £6,575
75 = £5,353 to £6,350
100 = £5,343 to £6,350
150 = £5,335 to £6,350

The lowest price for each quantity in both the July and August tenders was from Armstrong Whitworth. However they had received no previous orders for LMS locomotives (their last delivery to one of its constituents was a 4F to the Midland Railway in 1922), and in the meantime the company had undergone an extensive re-organisation. Since their prices were much lower than those of other firms, they were informed that before discussing orders the LMS required to be satisfied:

- *that their tender was not based on an*
- *unremunerative cut price,*
- *that no question of extras arose,*
- *that their facilities and inspection*
- *arrangements were adequate.*

Recent work done by the firm (a batch of K3 2-6-0s for the LNER) settled the second and third points, and an LMS representative was duly despatched to Tyneside to 'enquire into the basis of Armstrong-Whitworth's estimate'. He reported back that the firm's estimating and costing system was sound, which dealt with the first point. The five lowest tenders were then considered. These were:-

	For 50	For 100
Armstrong Whitworth	£5,365	£5,343
R.Stephenson	£5,600	did not tender
Vulcan Foundry	£5,668	£5,608
Hawthorn Leslie	£5,770	did not tender
North British	£5,790	£5,790

It was decided to order 100 from Armstrong Whitworth at £5,343 (5125-5224) and 50 from other firms. As in the previous year, the decision came down to a combination of price and delivery; of the four with the lowest prices Stephenson and Hawthorn Leslie were quickly ruled out with delivery times for 20, 30 and 50 locomotives of 41, 49 and 65 weeks and 56, 69 and 95 weeks respectively. So it was back to Vulcan and North British who were each offered 25 at the price of £5,500, or £168 and £290 respectively below their tenders. In the meantime, Beyer Peacock

& Co. Ltd. who had tendered at £6,550 (20), £6,525 (30) and £6,400 (50) pressed their claim, but not surprisingly it was considered that their prices ruled them out of consideration. North British refused the offer and Vulcan Foundry who were next seen agreed, 'after some demur' (i.e. arm-twisting) to supply 50 at £5,500 (5075-5124), which were delivered within less than five months, immediately following on from 5020-5069.

Armstrong Whitworth's 100 engines were churned out in eight months, from April to December 1935, and production was generally about fifteen a month, with as many as eighteen or nineteen in two particular months. They were hauled away to Crewe three and four at a time (via Carlisle to minimise the LNER's haulage charges!) to have the some parts of the motion refitted and be put into traffic.

Matters had indeed moved swiftly on; within three years of Follows' retirement and William Stanier's appointment as Chief Mechanical Engineer in 1932 the LMS had fifty new mixed traffic 4-6-0s in service, 25 under construction and had ordered another 150 (table below).

Lot	Nos.	Works nos.	Built at	Dates
123	5075-5124	4618-4667	Vulcan Foundry	Feb 1935 - Jul 1935
124	5125-5224	1166-1265	Armstrong Whitworth	Apr 1935 - Dec 1935

Leading Features of the Design

The 1939 *Railway Gazette* article summarised the design features: *The boiler is designed with taper barrel and has a Belpaire firebox with sloping throatplate. Mounted upon it are two Ross pattern safety valves 2½ in. diameter, which blow off at a boiler pressure of 225 lb. per sq. in. With a view to reducing weight, 2 per cent, nickel steel plates have been used for all plates with the exception of the smokebox tubeplate, dome and its cover; the inner firebox is of copper. The feed water is supplied through top feed valves on the second barrel plate with water distributing trays. The main regulator is of the grid type, and is situated in the dome on the second barrel plate immediately behind the feed water casting. A Davies & Metcalfe exhaust injector is fitted on the right-hand side and a Gresham & Craven live steam injector on the left-hand side of the engine respectively. The cylinders are fitted with 10 in. dia. piston valves, which have a travel of 6½ in., lap 1½ in., and exhaust clearance 1/16in. They are actuated by Walschaerts gear. Particulars of the valve events are given in the accompanying tables, for both forward and backward gear. A twelve-feed mechanical lubricator supplies lubrication to the following points: Valve spindle and piston packing, cylinder barrel, top and bottom, and front and back ends of the steamchest; the latter feeds are passed through an atomiser of the company's standard design.*

The coupling and connecting rods are of high-tensile, fine-grain steel. The wheel centres are steel castings with triangular section rims and retaining rings of Gibson type for fixing the tyres. The balance weights for the coupled wheels are built up of steel plates on both sides of the spokes and riveted, the requisite weight being provided by filling in between the plates with lead; 50 per cent, of the reciprocating parts are balanced. For the coupled wheels, steel axle-boxes are used, having pressed-in bronze alloy bearings 8½ in. dia. by 11 in. journal, with a white-metal crown. A thorough distribution of oil to the horizontal centre of the journal is fed from a groove at the back of the bearing through a series of 3/16 in. dia. holes. All axleboxes are arranged so that the oil pads can be examined by sliding out the underkeep while the axlebox is in position. Each of the axleboxes is provided with a dust shield carried on the inside face of the box.

A separate eight-feed mechanical lubricator supplies the coupled axleboxes, *each with an independent oil feed to the top of the box, and a standard back-pressure valve and flexible oilpipe connection. The*

The engines built by Armstrong Whitworth were delivered in groups of three or four to Carlisle, the nearest point on the LMS to the manufacturer's works on Tyneside. This was done to minimise the charges from the LNER for the journey over their metals.

four-wheel bogie is of the L.M.S.R. type in which the weight is taken through side bolsters; bogie check spring gear is provided to ensure smooth riding. All the laminated bearing springs for engine and tender are made of silico-manganese steel, and the plates are of ribbed section having wedge and wedge key type fixing in the buckle. The spring links are of the screwed adjustable type.

The cab is commodious, with the rear window on each side of the footplate arranged for sliding, and in addition small hinged glass wind screens act as draught protectors for the enginemen when looking out. Articulated brake blocks are fitted to all the coupled wheels, and are coupled up through crossbeams and centre pullrods to the steam brake cylinder operated by the driver's vacuum brake valve. A steam manifold with main shut-off valve is mounted on the top of firebox doorplate in the cab, and to this are attached the necessary valves for the ejector and steam brake, injectors, carriage warming, whistle, and the pressure gauge. Two sets of water gauges are fitted on each side of the regulator rod stuffing box and quadrant; the top and bottom cocks are actuated simultaneously through a link coupling, and are operated by a handle fixed to the top cock. A sand gun is mounted immediately above the sliding firehole door, and is intended to be used about every 75 miles to keep the tubes clear; this automatically receives its charges by suction from a sand hopper (capacity five charges) fastened to the front cab panel plate on the fireman's side. In connection with the use of softened water, a continuous blowdown valve is mounted on the fireman's side. These several mountings are of the company's standard design.

The tender is of the six-wheel type and carries 4,000 gallons of water and 9 tons of coal. The coal bunker has been carefully arranged so that as far as possible the coal will be self-trimming. Both the water pick-up and tender hand-brake handles are arranged vertically (i.e., with shaft axis horizontal), bevelled wheels being provided for transferring the motion to their respective

gears. The steam brake can be applied simultaneously with the steam brake on the engine to each of the six tender wheels.

The tender axleboxes are of an outer steel casting, with alloy bearings containing inserts of white metal. For the purpose of removing the alloy bearing without taking the wheels from underneath the tender, a mild steel liner ^! in. thick is inserted between bearing and outer steel casting, which when removed allows the bearing to be withdrawn. A cast iron spring pad to take the axle load rests on the top of the axlebox (located in position by the spigot on the end of the spring buckle). A cast iron cover on the outside face of the steel casting encloses the axle journal, and a felt pad dust shield rebated into the inner face ensures a clean journal.

5126 was the second engine from Armstrong Whitworth delivered at the end of April 1935. The main difference from the Vulcan Foundry batch was the welded tender in place of the riveted pattern and the only indication on the engine were the rectangular works plates instead of oval ones.

Edge Hill allocated 5118 at Rugeley in August 1935 with a very mixed parcels train. It was to move to the Northern Division at the end of the following month, firstly to Carlisle and then to Perth in July 1936.

2. HERE, THERE AND EVERYWHERE

The first deliveries from Vulcan Foundry began in February 1935 and from Armstrong Whitworth in April, with the Western Division the main recipient; the intention was to displace large numbers of ex-LNWR locomotives, although the other Divisions also benefitted. In autumn 1935 the original ten engines, 5020-5029, together with 5000-5006, were transferred from Scotland to the Western Division and were replaced by thirty of the later 21-element superheater engines, 5081-5087 from Crewe North and 5157-5179. These were allocated to Perth (North and South sheds), St.Rollox, Kingmoor and Inverness with two of the latter normally outstationed at Wick, two at Helmsdale and two at Aviemore.

The final 25 engines from Armstrong Whitworth (5200-5224) all went to the Central Division, shared between Bank Hall, Low Moor, Newton Heath, Wakefield and Farnley Junction. An examination of their Engine History Cards reveals that many of these were stored, some within weeks of entering traffic, and while it is understandable that some were hastily stored in September 1939 as the country went to war, it is not obvious why they were not required in 1935 and 1936 when new engines were still being delivered. The only explanation I have come across is that it was a continuation of the old L&Y practice of storing new or recently overhauled engines when there was little or no work for them to do, when existing ones were coping with the traffic demands and those engines being replaced could see out their remaining mileage. Thus the new ones were held in reserve, and only released when needed. Bank Hall's 5200-5203, delivered in October 1935, were all stored during December and 5200 and 5203 remained in store until May 1936. Low Moor's 5206-5209 delivered in November 1935 were also stored during December 1935 while 5206 remained in store until March 1936 and 5208 until May 1936; 5210 was stored from April to December 1936 and 5221 was stored in October/November 1936. Even Blackpool's 5220, delivered in November 1935, was stored during October and November 1936, and two years later, Newton Heath's 5222-5224 were stored from October-December 1938. (Note the periods of storage were not all continuous and some of the engines returned to traffic for a week or two before going back into storage).

By the end of 1935 there were 225 Black 5s in service, working from a steadily increasing number of sheds, with around a third on the Western Division and the balance spread roughly equally between the other three Divisions. The sheds with the highest allocations were Crewe (North and South) with 34 engines, followed by Perth (22), Patricroft (14) and Inverness and Newton Heath each with 13.

Taking Over

In Scotland, the large influx of Black 5s enabled almost all the express workings in the Highlands to be taken over from the ten Crab 2-6-0s, which had been at Perth since they were built, and the ex-Highland Railway 'Clans', which were moved to the Oban line. The engines from Perth North shed worked complicated rosters, at least one of which extended over ten days and involved the engine spending successive nights at Inverness, Carlisle, Inverness, Helmsdale, then four nights at Inverness during which it worked to Wick and back and spent Sunday on Inverness shed, then Wick again and finally Perth. The express freight turns between Perth South and Carlisle Kingmoor which had been worked by the CR '179' class superheated 4-6-0s were taken over by the Black 5s. In the 'Far North', two of them were stabled at Wick overnight and worked the two morning trains to Inverness; these changed from day to day and Glasgow Balornock (St.Rollox) and Perth engines took their turn with those from Inverness.

It was not only in Scotland where they transformed the motive power scene: the effect in North Wales was equally dramatic as the new engines

The Western Division used its new mixed traffic engines on express duties such as the Birmingham-Euston trains. 5163 was hauling one of these through Kilburn in a picture taken in the brief period when this engine was shedded at Crewe between 3/8/35 and 4/10/35, after which it was transferred to Perth. 5163 was one of thirty of the later 21-element superheater engines sent to the Northern Division in exchange for original low superheat Class 5s, presumably because the workload in Scotland was generally more demanding than on the Western Division.

replaced many LNWR 4-4-0s and 4-6-0s. They were now the commonest type to be seen there and worked most of the expresses except for the Irish Mails. One of the jobs for the Llandudno Junction allocation was the Llandudno-Manchester 'Club Train' which up to that time had been worked by one of the shed's 'Claughtons'. The 4-4-0s were relegated to the local services between Chester and Bangor or Llandudno and only had one or two regular express turns while Prince of Wales 4-6-0s virtually disappeared. The new 4-6-0s at Llandudno Junction worked complex rosters which involved freight trains formerly worked by 0-8-0s; Holyhead's engines were used mainly on freight and cattle trains although they were also involved in passenger work.

At the end of 1936 there was another re-shuffle with thirty of the 1936 Armstrong Whitworth series going to the Midland Division to replace their earlier, mainly Vulcan Foundry built, engines, which moved to the Western Division.

Highland Division

Between 19 and 29 January 1937 tests were carried out at the request of the Chief Operating Manager 'with a view to ascertaining to what extent accelerations in passenger services were possible'. The engine tested was 5159 of Inverness shed which had run 91,055 miles since new and 13,047 miles since its last service repair. It was considered that the engine was well handled and its steaming was good although this was only attained when working at late cut-offs by very careful operation of the exhaust steam injector.

On 19 January with the 8.35am from Inverness, timekeeping to Slochd Summit was not maintained despite the engine being worked continuously at 35%-45% cut-off with full regulator opening, although time was regained down the banks. When working the 4.00pm Perth-Blair Atholl local, sectional running times could not be maintained and on three occasions the engine had to reverse before a start could be made on rising gradients. Returning from Blair Atholl next day timekeeping in general was maintained due to the falling ruling gradient. Going north with the 11.45am from Perth to Inverness, times were maintained, and times were kept on the southbound run on 21 January. On the Inverness-Wick line, sectional timekeeping was generally well maintained but on the level and easier gradients the engine had to be worked at a cut-off of 25%-30%.

The overall conclusion from the tests was that, while in general the timekeeping and steaming of the engine was satisfactory, the test workings involved the engine being operated 'beyond the point where economy is secured and therefore an acceleration of trains with the loadings of the test could not be recommended'. If the Chief Operating Manager desired to reduce the existing scheduled timings, it 'would be necessary for the booked loads of these trains to be reduced to, say, 150-200 tons'.

The Highland Division saw a rapid and marked increase in traffic during the war with freight train-miles operated almost 90% higher in 1942 compared with 1939. Ordinary passenger traffic was down, but this was more than offset by the number of troop and special military passenger workings. To cope with the extra work 23 more Black 5s were transferred to the Northern Division from England, most of them going to Kingmoor, Perth or Inverness.

On the Southern Region

Working of Black 5s over the Central Section of the Southern Region began in 1950 with summer excursions to the South Coast a regular feature over the next few years. An interesting development in 1953 was the rostering of a Longsight Black 5 to work through to Brighton on Friday nights with the 11.40pm from Manchester London Road to Brighton, Eastbourne and Hastings. The Longsight engine returned from Brighton on Saturday with the 12.30(SO) from Hastings to Manchester. The through working from Manchester to Brighton ceased after 1959 when, due to electrification work on the West Coast main line, the Fridays Only train to Hastings was routed from Manchester via Woodhead and the GCR line through Leicester Central, the engines changing at Kensington. The class also reached the Eastern Section in the summer of 1956 with the first of what were to

Edge Hill's 5124 was the last Class Five built by Vulcan Foundry, in July 1935. It received a domed boiler and 1936 livery in June 1938 and was photographed at Manchester London Road on 7 September of that year in the MSWJR platforms. Photograph E.R. Morten.

Above. The Black 5s were the largest engines allowed north of Derby over the Peak Forest route to Manchester until bridge reconstruction work was completed so 'Jubilees' could take over from the start of the 1938 Summer timetable. Trafford Park and Kentish Town engines amassed very high mileages on this route over which the LMS accelerated passenger services from the start of the Winter 1937 timetable. 5093 departs southwards from Manchester Central on 28 May 1938; it had been allocated to Trafford Park from 11/9/37 but was transferred away on 3/9/38. It received a domed boiler in November 1937 when it also acquired the 1936 livery. Photograph S. Dewsbery.

Middle. Crewe South was primarily a freight shed and 5148 was one of its large stud of Class 5s seen here with a WCML freight in the late 1940s. It is in LMS 1946 livery with high positioned cab numbers and had received a domed boiler in December 1947. It was not renumbered until March 1951. Photograph www.rail-online.co.uk

Bottom. Newton Heath's 45104 at Norwood Junction on 8 October 1952 with a transfer freight via Crystal Palace. The Class became regular visitors to the Southern Region in the 1950s on these workings and also on excursion trains to the coastal resorts.

Seven Black 5s were loaned to the Southern Region when it had to withdraw its 'Merchant Navy' Pacifics with axle problems, and then all of its 'West Country/Battle of Britain' Pacifics for examination. 45223 arrived from Newton Heath on 23/5/53 and returned there on 27/6/53. It has headcode discs on SR-style lamp brackets, with an extra lamp iron on the right hand side of the smokebox door between the hinge straps.

become regular incursions into Kent, and after that they appeared on almost the whole of the Eastern Section main lines except between Tonbridge and Hastings.

In May 1953 the Southern Region had to withdraw its 'Merchant Navy' Pacifics with axle problems, and then all of its 'West Country/Battle of Britain' Pacifics for examination to check for the same defect. Amongst the substitutes hastily drafted in for the light Pacifics were seven Black 5s, including 45130 from Mold Junction, 45216 from Bank Hall, 45222 from Huddersfield and 45223 from Newton Heath. They were fitted with SR-style lamp brackets, an extra lamp iron on the right-hand side (as viewed from the front) of the smokebox door between the hinge straps. The footsteps had to be moved in an inch or two and the injector overflow pipes cut back to fit within the tighter loading gauge. 45216 was noted at Waterloo on 20 May and again the next day working the 10.30am to Bournemouth, returning from there on the train due in Waterloo at 6.24pm. 45223 hauled both these trains the following day and on 23rd 45130 took a boat train from Waterloo to Southampton Docks. A week later on 30th this engine worked another boat train, returning light to Nine Elms. On 24th 45222 went to Aldershot with a troop train while on 25th 45130 was at Waterloo again, this time on the 7.10am stopping train from Yeovil before working the 2.54pm to Basingstoke. From then on the Black 5s were mainly used on Salisbury semi-fast duties, on trains between Waterloo and Basingstoke and on Bournemouth reliefs until they were returned to the LMR the following month. Apart from this brief period, Black 5s were only occasionally seen on the ex-LSWR lines, but in the 1960s they became more common, on a variety of both passenger and freight duties, even working regularly into Waterloo again.

The End of Steam

Black 5s featured prominently during the dying days of BR steam in 1968 as the remaining members of the class were corralled into a small pocket of north west England to meet their inevitable fate. By the end of May there were only six operational steam sheds and still a few steam hauled parcels and freight trains in the Preston area, hauled by either Stanier 4-6-0s or 2-8-0s, and the Black 5s also deputised when diesels failed on passenger trains. Former 'namer' 45156, which became a celebrity and was kept in immaculate condition, was used as stand-by for heating the Royal Train when it was stabled overnight at Lowton on 16 May 1968. During June, it spent most of its time as Manchester Exchange station pilot.

Bolton, Newton Heath and Patricroft sheds were closed to steam at the end of June, leaving Carnforth, Lostock Hall and Rose Grove. Only two passenger trains were still booked for steam haulage, the 20.50 (SO) from Preston to Blackpool South and 21.25 (SO) Preston to Liverpool Exchange, although the latter was sometimes diesel powered. However, during July some holiday relief trains were steam hauled. On 12 July 45156 was used for the first leg of a Colne-Newquay service and a week later it worked through to Stockport on the 23.35 Accrington to Euston train.

On Saturday 3 August enthusiasts from all over the country descended on Preston station and an unusually long queue formed at the booking office with a great rush for tickets to Blackpool South or Liverpool Exchange. The platforms were crowded with all manner of enthusiasts in the guise of passengers, photographers and tape recordists, whilst two bearded figures wearing funeral top hat and tails arrived with a coffin draped with slogans on the impending demise of the steam locomotive. They were all waiting for the arrival of the 17.05 from Euston

Top. On 31 August 1955 45113 from Edge Hill drifts through the countryside between Melton Junction and Asfordby Tunnel with the afternoon Northampton-Nottingham (via Kettering). Whether this was a planned diagram for the Liverpool engine or it had been 'borrowed' by Northampton is not known. Photograph Peter Groom.

Middle. Bread and butter West Coast Main Line work for Longsight's 45150 as it passes through Harrow on 15 August 1959 with a typical Black 5 express working. It was one of those engines which moved around over the years, though remaining on the Western Division until 1964. Photograph www.rail-online.co.uk

Bottom. Inverness allocated 45098 on 3 September 1958 at Boat of Garten with the 11.54am to Glasgow. The paint on its smokebox is still gleaming following a Light Intermediate overhaul completed the previous week. This station was on the Highland Railway's original main line to Inverness, via Grantown on Spey, Dava Moor and Forres. The line was closed under the Beeching cuts but the section from Broomhill to Aviemore via Boat of Garten has since been brought back into use by the Strathspey Railway Company. Photograph M.N. Bland, www.transporttreasury.co.uk

which divided there and when the front portion had departed for Carlisle headed by a Brush Type 4 diesel, Lostock Hall's 45212 backed on to the rear seven coaches which were for Blackpool, and then the penultimate main line steam hauled passenger train was soon on its way. (The final train was for Liverpool and was pulled by another Black 5, 45318). Early the next day 45212, which had returned to Preston from Blackpool, was used to shunt the sleeping cars off the 23.45 from Euston into the bay platform at Preston station which gave it the distinction of being the last steam engine to haul passengers in a normal service train, even though it was only a shunting movement.

After that the only passenger trains were the final 'End of Steam' special trains and on Sunday 4 August no less than six toured Lancashire to commemorate the final day of BR steam hauled passenger trains. They were hauled by thirteen different locomotives over various parts of their routes; ten of them were Stanier Black 5s. Unsurprisingly these included 45156 which worked throughout the 'GC Enterprises' eight coach special from Stockport to Carnforth and return via Denton, Manchester Victoria, Bolton, Darwen, Blackburn and Hellifield.

It was fitting that three Black 5s were involved the following weekend on the final steam hauled train operated by BR on standard gauge track which ran on 11 August 1968 from Liverpool and Manchester to Carlisle via Blackburn, Hellifield and Ais Gill, returning by the same route. 45110 took the train as far as Manchester Victoria, and it worked the final leg back to Liverpool, taking over from two of its classmates for the 31-mile journey, before working 'light' to Lostock Hall shed. It was to join 45163 and 45212 in preservation; 45156 did not make it.

Right. **Three Black 5s were involved in the final steam hauled train operated by British Railways on standard gauge track. 45110, watched by young and old on the crowded platforms, is ready to depart from Liverpool Lime Street with the '15 Guinea Special' on 11 August 1968. It took the train as far as Manchester Victoria where it handed over to Britannia 70013. Later in the day 45110 brought the return working back to Lime Street from Manchester, taking over from 44871 and 44781. It survived the cutters torch and was preserved on the Severn Valley Railway and has since enjoyed a renaissance on the main line, although currently not certified for operation. Photograph F. Ward, collection J. Suter.**

Above. **Shrewsbury shed had a number of Black 5s for many years and while their most well-known work was over the Central Wales line they were also used on local passenger and longer distance freight work. 45190 passes through the ex-GWR station at Birmingham Snow Hill on 19 February 1963 with a northbound iron ore, probably from the quarries at Wroxton nearBanbury. It was a Shrewsbury engine from 1947 until transferred to Annesley in October 1964. Photograph colourrail.co.uk**

Top right. **Black 5s had a regular working with an Eastern Region Pullman express on the Bradford portion of the 'Yorkshire Pullman' as far as Leeds. Low Moor's 45208 was only a few months from withdrawal and in typical run-down condition as it departs with the Pullman from Bradford Exchange on 1 June 1967.**

45208

1T57

The second Vulcan Foundry order had a number of detail differences compared with the first (5020-69). There were domed covers on the firebox shoulders indicating the 21-element superheater boiler, the chimney was lower, the plain combination lever was now fluted, the top feed pipes were recessed and the tender axlebox covers had cruciform strengthening ribs. The worksplates were still above the steam pipes, the LMS on the tender was close-spaced and the stiffening webs at the rear of the four spokes adjacent to the crankpin were retained. All of these were changed part-way through the batch.

3. THE DEVIL IN THE DETAIL

Some of the notes herein are necessarily repeated from the equivalent section in Part 1; this is not déjà vu!

The two batches of Black 5s delivered by the end of 1935 were to all intents and purposes of uniform design and appearance and the differences found in the first 75 engines were not perpetuated, except for very minor details. Like their predecessors they received the same progressive modifications and improvements in answer to both design weaknesses and changing operational and maintenance conditions. On top of this, exchanges of tenders, boilers and later even frames became part of the normal repair processes in an effort to minimise the time spent in the workshops.

Boilers

The ability of the boiler to produce sufficient steam when required is a major determinant of the success or otherwise of a steam locomotive and although the early Black 5s did not suffer the same problems as the Jubilees, design changes were made before all of the second batch had been completed. The LMS had realised that the relatively low level of superheat brought by Stanier from Swindon was inadequate in the different setting that was the LMS and the domeless 14-element superheater boilers fitted to 5020-5069 and 5000-5006 were redesigned to accommodate 21 elements. These were used on 5007-5019 and 5070 onwards. The only difference in external appearance was the addition of two washout inspection doors with small domed covers on each shoulder of the firebox on 5010 onwards. When boilers were exchanged and an original 14-element boiler replaced a later type, blanking plates had to be fitted over the holes left by the doors in the firebox clothing.

Formal recognition of this came in the approval, in May 1935, of £63,831 for increased superheating. 'In order to obtain reduced maintenance costs', up to this time 167 Princess Royal, Jubilee and Black 5s had been built with a reduced degree of superheat, 'but work experience has shown that this went too far and a higher degree of superheating will result in an increased operating economy, which will more than meet the additional maintenance cost of improved superheating'. On the Black 5s the rebuilding increased the superheating from 14 to 24 elements, and at the same time problems experienced with the smokebox mounted regulators were addressed by fitting dome mounted regulators, positioned just forward of the firebox. The top feed covers were also modified and the dome-like central portion was replaced by a transverse fairing and since the smokebox regulator lubricator was no longer needed, the streamlined cover over the atomiser on the smokebox side was reduced in size. The work was done during heavy repairs between March 1937 and October 1940 leaving the 21-element boilers as the only ones to remain domeless.

Under the LMS system of progressive repairs, a pool of spare boilers was created to allow locomotives requiring boiler repairs to be returned to service without waiting for the original boiler to be repaired, which could take much longer than the rest of the engine. When more Black 5s were built in 1936/37 they had 24-element domed boilers and also a larger grate and sloping throatplate to improve combustion, and naturally the spare boilers built as the first heavy general repairs became due on the class were of this design. It was therefore necessary to modify some of the early locomotives with vertical throatplate boilers to accept the sloping throatplate type. In all 13 of the engines covered in this volume were converted; 5097 and 5142 in 1937, two in the 1940s, five in the 1950s, and four in the 1960s; of these

The final type of Black 5 boiler had the top feed positioned further forward on the first ring of the boiler and a low positioned atomiser without the large cover of the earlier boilers. 45177 had this type from March 1957 to November 1961, having been converted to sloping throatplate configuration in 1953 from a domeless boiler. Pictured at Perth when shedded at 65B St Rollox, where it remained until October 1960, 45177 also has a part-welded tender, fitted in May 1958, and AWS, which dates the photograph as either 1959 or 1960.

The Vulcan Foundry built Black 5s all had riveted pattern 4000 gallon tenders. 45080 at Farnley Junction in the late-1950s with tender no.9173 originally paired with 5079 but transferred to 45080 in March 1955 when they exchanged tenders. Photograph www.rail-online.co.uk

45216 at Stockport on 12 February 1960 ran with tender no.9000 from 23/1/59 to 15/2/61. This was one of the three prototype 4,000 gallon tenders built in 1933 for the first two 'Princess' 4-6-2s and for the USA tour of 6100 'Royal Scot'. Their original flat sidesheets were rebuilt with curved upper sides and they were first paired with Crewe-built Black 5s Nos. 5000/73/74. From this angle the shallower curved cut-out at the top of the side panelling and different rivet pattern compared with the standard 4000 gallon tender can be seen. Photograph D. Forsyth, Paul Chancellor Collection.

After World War 2, the LMS built two tenders to allow coal consumption to be accurately measured for test purposes. They had the standard 4,000 gallon tender frames and running gear with a smaller 3,750 gallon water tank and modified bunker, which was a separate entity that could be suspended on shafts running along each side and the weight transmitted by levers to a steelyard at the rear. Its weight could be measured with the steelyard by means of a sliding weights system. By 1960, with the onset of dieselisation, they were no longer needed and the steelyards and their covers were removed. 45081 was paired with one of these tenders from 1/12/63 until 25/1/64. Photograph R.K. Blencowe.

only 5124 and 5169 were subsequently reconverted to the vertical throatplate type.

The final changes in boiler design came in 1947 when the top feed arrangement was changed to reduce the build-up of scaling on the superheater flues. This allowed the top feed to be moved further forward, to the first ring of the barrel away from the dome, and from 1948 they had a raised fairing over the main cover to accommodate a further modification to eliminate problems with the valves. In 1956 45082 was converted with one of these boilers and was followed between 1957 and 1960 by 45087, 45151 and 45177, which had been already been fitted with sloping throatplate boilers; 45082 received the earlier sloping throatplate type in 1962.

The domeless boilers had dome-like top feed covers whereas the domed boilers had transverse covers. The covers were interchangeable and they were sometimes swapped around. This seems to have occurred more often in Scotland where St.Rollox produced numerous combinations of dome and top feed covers, including some examples having both the separate top feed cover and the cover intended for the dome giving the effect of a double domed engine.

Smokebox Door

From 5225 onwards a counter weight was fitted to the left-hand side of the smokebox door/ring to help carry the weight of the door when closed. As boilers and smokeboxes were changed, these could also be seen on the earlier locomotives.

Spark Arresters

Some Scottish Region Black 5s without self-cleaning smokeboxes were fitted with spark arresters, presumably for working to Fort William; 45166 and 45173 of Corkerhill were noted during September 1954 with the letters 'SA' painted on the smokebox door below the shed plate.

Frames

In order to keep the weight down and achieve maximum route availability the frames were of lightweight construction, only 1 inch thick and lightly stayed, and after a few years in service this came back to bite the LMS as extensive cracks developed, especially at the top corners of the horn gaps, which then had to have sections cut-out, and new pieces welded in and trimmed to shape. As the problem got worse a spare set of frames of the later type designed to accept sloping throatplate boilers was made at Crewe in 1943 to allow engines to be returned more quickly from repair. When the first locomotive requiring major frame repairs arrived, it was stripped and rebuilt on the new frames and once these frames had been repaired they became the spare set. This resulted in many inter-changes of frames, both between the vertical throatplate engines and the later sloping throatplate locomotives, and between locomotives from each builder. Since the builders plates normally stayed with the frames, this could result in engines that had been built at Crewe or Vulcan Foundry appearing with Armstrong Whitworth plates and vice versa. The original styles and position of the plates differed between batches: Crewe-built locomotives had oval plates fitted to the front framing at both sides; Vulcan Foundry 5020-5069 and 5075-5106 had the same pattern but fitted on both sides of the smokebox directly above the top of the steam pipe and above the ejector pipe, although from 5107 onwards they were attached to the front framing instead. The first six engines built by Armstrong Whitworth (5125-30) had rectangular pattern plates on the smokebox in the same position as the earlier Vulcan Foundry locomotives and on the remainder the plates were

attached to the front framing. The plates included the works numbers which were 4618-4667 for 5075-5124 and 1166-1265 for 5125-5224 respectively.

Wheels and Axles
To save weight, the coupled wheels had a three inch hollow bore through the axles and the bogie wheels on the first fifty Vulcan Foundry locomotives (5020-5069). The first four from Crewe (5000-5003) also had hollow axles; all the other engines had a small turning centre machined in the solid axle. The wheels on the first twenty engines from Vulcan Foundry (5075-5094) and the first seventy locomotives (5000-5069) had stiffening webs at the rear of the four spokes adjacent to the crankpin. Over the years wheelsets were swapped during works visits and all sorts of combinations resulted.

Cylinders and Inspection Covers
The cylinder lagging sheets originally had a small circular cover plate with four bolt fixing, to provide access to the steam chest drain pipe instead of removing the complete cylinder lagging sheets. In the late 1930s/early 1940s larger covers were fitted and all locomotives eventually carried the later pattern. Two rectangular covers at the top of the lagging sheets were fitted to 5225 onwards and both types of cover plate were gradually fitted to the earlier locomotives.

Combination Levers
The Horwich design of combination lever used on 5000-5069 was plain rectangular in section, offset below the spindle guide and forked at the lower end. It was changed from 5070 onwards and used on 5075-5224. The combination levers were now straight and fluted with a slight offset, still forked at the bottom pin, allowing use of the same union link and crosshead arm secured to the crosshead by two bolts as with the earlier locomotives.

Carriage Warming Hose Pipes
Crewe-built engines had a front steam heating valve and pipe fixed to the bottom edge of the buffer beam just to the right of the vacuum pipe dummy. Those from Armstrong Whitworth did not, although in some cases these appeared later, probably as a result of frame changes. The flexible hoses were usually taken off during the summer months when not needed, and were sent into works for examination, pressure testing and renewal or repair as necessary.

Tablet Exchange Apparatus
Black 5s used on the Northern Division single lines had to have automatic tablet exchange apparatus which was attached to the rear left-hand cabside at about footplate height. When not in use, the jaws were held upright against the side plate and as the tablet was to be exchanged they would be swung downward through 90 degrees to project the required distance from the engine to make the exchange. Engines working on other single line routes that used train staffs had holders fitted to the cab sides about a foot below the windows.

Snowploughs
As the primary motive power in the Highlands for around thirty years many of the Scottish-based locomotives were equipped in the winter with small snowploughs fixed to the front bufferbeam with two heavy steel angle uprights held by three fixing bolts about a foot in board from the buffers. With these the engines could run through small drifts whilst hauling normal trains, or as patrolling light engine, preventing the build-up of snow drifts which would otherwise cause a complete blockage if traffic ceased. Most engines fitted with ploughs were based at either Inverness or Carlisle Kingmoor, but a small number allocated to sheds such as Northampton, Springs Branch, Preston and Patricroft were also modified.

BR Days
In addition to the various 'improvements' described in the next chapter the class saw a number of minor changes in the early 1960s. The two most noticeable perhaps were the repositioning of the steam lance

Tenders were exchanged frequently during works visits because repairs to them were usually completed in less time than the locomotives they arrived with. Hence the part-welded tank tenders introduced in 1944 with the wartime Black 5s soon found their way onto the earlier engines. The Scottish based engines seem to have exchanged tenders more frequently than those in England and 45168, pictured at Craigentinny on 4 September 1956, had two part-welded examples, from April 1956 to July 1957 and then again from November 1958 until February 1959.

5113 was one of almost twenty of the 1935 built engines repainted in the short-lived 1936 livery with sans serif insignia in place of the scroll pattern. A full repaint would only have been carried out at a HG repair, and 5113 was in works from 24/3/38-7/6/38 when it was fitted with a domed boiler ex 5053 which had been rebuilt with a 24 element superheater in place of the original 14 element type which it had been built with.

Wakefield allocated M5101 in mid-1948 regularly worked the Sheffield-Bradford part of the 'South Yorkshireman', taking over from a B1 at Sheffield. On completion of a Heavy General repair on 5/2/48 it had emerged with a domed boiler and one of the early BR livery variations, essentially the LMS 1946 style with an M-prefix on the smokebox numberplate and above the cab number and the sole indication of new ownership, BRITISH RAILWAYS on the tender. It was not renumbered to 45101 until March 1950.

equipment and the top lamp bracket. The former was originally low down near the base of the right-hand side of the smokebox, although many were moved just above the top of the steam pipe when boilers were changed and smokeboxes renewed. When the original internal pipes corroded the BR type was fitted which were in the low position with a long external steam feed pipe from above the handrail.

With the onset of electrification from around 1960 'electric overhead' warning flashes, white enamel plates with the symbolic warning sign of forked lightning (in red) were fixed to those parts of the locomotive where footplate crews could come into contact with overhead wires. Also, from late 1963 the upper lamp bracket was for safety reasons moved down to the right of the central door fastening, and the central lamp iron above the bufferbeam was also moved to the right to remain directly under it.

Tenders

Although the initial diagram, ED 177, showed a Fowler pattern tender with 3,500 gallon water and 5½ tons coal capacity, by the time the first Black 5s were built the LMS had decided to equip them with the new Stanier 4,000 gallon coal design carrying 9 tons of coal. The tanks of the original tenders built with Vulcan Foundry 5075-5124 were assembled with snap head rivets like those of 5000-5074, but when the Armstrong Whitworth batch (5125-5224) appeared they had welded tanks which reduced the weight of the tender by over a ton. However, problems were experienced with the seams and a hybrid type with part-welded tanks was introduced in 1944. The three types soon interchanged between engines because the tenders took less time to repair than locomotives and after a works visit an engine would take the next spare available tender, not necessarily the one it arrived with.

Crewe-built 5000, 5073 and 5074 were originally paired with the three prototype 4,000 gallon tenders which had been built in 1933 for the first two 'Princess' 4-6-2s and for the 'Turbomotive' 6202, although this one was actually used for the USA tour of 6100 ROYAL SCOT. Their original flat sidesheets were rebuilt with curved upper sides and they were subtly different from the standard 4,000 gallon tender, with a different rivet pattern and curved cut-out at the top of the side panelling, and two of them had Timken roller bearings, identifiable by their complex axlebox covers. Over the years these three tenders moved around the class, appearing behind 5144, 5146, 5147, 5198 and 5216. One other tender type which ran with one of the engines covered in this volume was a former coal-weighing tender, briefly paired with 45081 from December 1963 until January 1964.

Liveries

With only three exceptions (to be covered in Part 4) the class was always painted black. Insignia and lining-out naturally followed the fashion of the day, with lots of small variations to keep the engine-picker happy.

When built, the engines carried the standard LMS black livery lined with vermillion, with the lining around all four edges of the cab side sheet and below the cab windows; on repainting it was carried straight to the cab roof in the 'Crewe style'. The serif insignia were gold leaf shaded red to the right and lake below; the cab numbers were 12 inches, with the power classification (5P with 5F below) in 3 inch numerals and a scroll pattern front numberplate. The 14 inch LMS letters on the tender were spaced at 40 inches on Vulcan Foundry 5075-5111 and Armstrong Whitworth up to 5136 (and possibly 5137); those following had the same standard 60 inch spacing used on the Crewe-built locomotives.

In February 1936 the LMS brought in fashionable new sans serif insignia to replace the serif characters, and these were applied to all of the 1936/37 built Black 5s from Armstrong Whitworth (which will form the subject of Part 3). The size of the cab numbers was reduced to 10 inches but the letters remained 14 inches high. The change was short-lived and in mid-1937 the LMS reverted to the serif style, albeit with cheaper yellow rather than gold insignia. Earlier locomotives repainted in the 1936 style included 5091, 5093, 5097, 5113, 5114, 5122, 5124, 5125, 5131, 5154, 5180, 5182, 5187, 5188, 5191 and 5200; some of these did not receive the livery until mid-1938 as stocks of transfers were slowly used

45090 in one of the interim liveries which were applied while BR was deliberating on its standard styles. The picture was taken in July 1948 when it was renumbered, although the new smokebox numberplate has yet to be fitted. It is in plain black and the tender has the full BRITISH RAILWAYS without crest and the cab numbers are still LMS 1946 pattern, positioned high to clear the Manson tablet exchange apparatus. Photograph R.K. Blencowe.

Before the final BR scheme for mixed traffic locomotives was chosen three Black 5s were painted during January 1948 in experimental green liveries at Crewe and one in black, with grey/cream/red lining in LNWR style. 45217, pictured at Polmadie in August 1948, was one of three Black 5s selected for further experimentation. It emerged from Horwich during April 1948 in the same style of lined black with 8in Gill Sans numbers, although still with BRITISH RAILWAYS and no crest on the tender and smokebox number cast with LMS 1946 pattern numbers.

Newly outshopped from the works after a Heavy Intermediate repair, 45150 at Crewe North in October 1949 sports the new BR crest and Gill Sans smokebox numberplate but has been given a new coat of plain black devoid of lining. Photograph www.rail-online.co.uk

up. During the war, all full re-paints were plain black although many engines were never fully repainted and probably kept traces of their original lining for many years – even though it was invisible under the layers of grime. The numbers themselves were mostly in 12 inch characters and the power classification if used at all was abbreviated to 5. After the war plain black continued and most re-paints had scroll and serif characters in yellow (plain or red-shaded), usually with the cab numbers in the 'high' position.

It was not until 1946 that wartime austerity was replaced by a new style which had pale straw sans serif characters with inset maroon lining. The lettering was 14 inches and numbers were either 10 inch or 12 inch. Engines known to have received 10 inch numerals were 5084, 5156, 5159 and 5165. Those with 12 inch numerals included 5075, 5088, 5114, 5116, 5148, 5166, 5176, 5190, 5202, 5209 and 5217.

Nationalisation in 1948 brought more livery confusion. Although all the Black 5s repainted in the first part of the year were plain black, there were many variations of insignia. While the new British Railways was deliberating matters an M-prefix was applied to the LMS numbers for a short time, although even this was inconsistent. 5081, 5082, 5101 and 5112 had 12 inch numbers with a 6 inch high M above and a small figure 5 below. The M was added to the smokebox plate on 5101 and 5114, which had a small extension piece riveted to the end ahead of the numbers. Others including 5077 and 5099 had the M below the cabside number and the power classification above. Northern Division engines 5117, 5127, 5161 and 5165 had the M added ahead of their existing numbers. All had BRITISH RAILWAYS on the tender sides in 8 inch cream Gill Sans letters and all retained their LMS smokebox number plates.

The M prefix was dropped by mid-March 1948 and ex-LMS locomotives had 40,000 added to their numbers. Many engines remained for a time in plain black livery. Smokebox door number plates varied between scroll and serif, Gill Sans or 1946 style, and some engines ran for a time with no plates. Cab side numbers were in 10 inch 1946 style characters, 8 inch Gill Sans or 10 inch Gill Sans in various positions and different spacings with power classification figures also in differing positions. A few had a small 4 added in front of their existing LMS numerals. Some tenders still had serif L M S on their sides, others had BRITISH RAILWAYS in 8 inch or 10 inch Gill Sans characters, and a few were devoid of any insignia.

Before the final BR scheme for mixed traffic locomotives was chosen four late-built Black 5s were painted during January 1948 in various experimental liveries at Crewe: three were in the greens of the SR, GWR and LNER and the fourth was in black, with grey/cream/red lining in LNWR style. 5217 was one of three Black 5s selected for further painting in experimental liveries, emerging from Horwich during April 1948 in the same style of lined black. This livery was soon selected officially for all non-Pacific mixed traffic locomotives and although Black 5s started to appear in this livery quite soon after its adoption, many retained their immediate post-war plain black with BR insignia applied for several years. It wasn't until the mid-1950s that all were lined out.

The lettering and numerals were cream Gill Sans edged with a narrow black band. Locomotives repainted in England had 8 inch numbers positioned in line with the tender lettering or emblem whereas St.Rollox started using 10 inch numerals, only changing to the 8 inch type in the mid-1950s. The latter mostly were positioned slightly further down so that their lower edges or even centrelines were in line with the main running plate. The power classification 5 was either immediately above or below the numerals in the same style, although when it changed to 5MT, it usually appeared above the numbers. The smokebox door number plates cast at St. Rollox initially had 1946 LMS style characters whilst those produced at Crewe and Horwich were Gill Sans throughout.

Initially the tenders carried BRITISH RAILWAYS in full, but this was replaced by the larger size of early BR 'lion on a wheel' emblem from around August 1949. From 1957, BR crests approved by the College of Arms replaced the emblem, at first with forward facing lions on each side, but after complaints

45080 in an official works photograph shows off the BR mixed traffic livery finally selected. The background has not been whitewashed out very well, especially around the front end and the top of the tender!

In final condition on 3 March 1966 at Mirfield 45139 has AWS, fitted in August 1961, external pipework on the smokebox for the steam lance and the upper lamp iron has been moved down to the centre right of the smokebox away from the live wires when working on electrified lines. The tender has the post-1957 pattern crest and there are overhead warning flashes on the firebox and front frames.

5154 received the name LANARKSHIRE YEOMANRY on 8 April 1937. The curved nameplates were cast at St.Rollox and attached to backing plates riveted to pieces of angle iron that were riveted to the platforms. They also had crests on separate plaques which were attached by studs from the rear.

Right. A specially posed official – probably one of those cases where the same engine is renumbered to allow a picture to be taken of another – 5157 was certainly captured in the same pose by the official photographer on 7 April 1936. Neither is recorded in the History Cards as visiting the works until 1937.

Bottom right. 5157 became THE GLASGOW HIGHLANDER on 6 March 1936. Unlike the other three, its crest was above the name.

Below. 5156 was named AYRSHIRE YEOMANRY on 19 September 1936. It had a separate, straight plate with EARL OF CARRICK'S OWN in small lettering underneath the plaque.

YEOMANRY
5P
5F
5158
L M S

THE GLASGOW HIGHLANDER

from the College of Arms all lions faced left.

From December 1963 all locomotives receiving a full repaint were to be painted in plain black. However this does seem not to have been applied by every works and engines outshopped from St.Rollox in early 1964 were still being lined out. Engines repaired at Cowlairs had their shed allocations painted in LNER style on the front buffer beams.

Names

Four Northern Division Black 5s received names, 5154 and 5156 from Carlisle Kingmoor, both transferred to St.Rollox in 1943, and 5157 and 5158 at St.Rollox. The curved nameplates were positioned over the middle coupled wheels with crests on separate plaques, 5157's above the name and the other three below. In 1957 45154 and 45156 were transferred to Newton Heath and the latter survived right up to the end of steam on British Railways in August 1968. Needless to say it lost its nameplates in the early 1960s and ran for several years with the name painted on the backing plates but these, too, had been removed by July 1968, only to be refitted on the day it was withdrawn and adorned with painted names and crests.

Another of those wonderful unsolved mysteries is whether or not a fifth Black 5 was named in the late 1930s. The surviving evidence is unclear although it seems that there was an intention to name 5155 as QUEENS EDINBURGH. It was referred to in several internal LMS memoranda during 1937 and 1938,as well as in one LMS-backed publication and there has been the usual conjecture in the enthusiast press over the years, but no-one has managed to produce any definitive photographic proof.

Loco	Date Fitted
5154 LANARKSHIRE YEOMANRY8	April 1937
5156 AYRSHIRE YEOMANRY	19 September 1936
5157 THE GLASGOW HIGHLANDER	6 March 1936
5158 GLASGOW YEOMANRY	22 May 1936

Right. **45156 waiting at Manchester Exchange has a painted smokebox number and 9H Patricroft shedcode and a blank backing board on which the name and badge would be restored for its final day in service. It had been stored during January and February 1968 and was allocated briefly to the Manchester shed from w/e 11/5/68 before moving to Rose Grove in July when Patricroft was closed. Photograph www.rail-online.co.uk**

After it had been transferred from Scotland to Newton Heath In 1957 45156 lost its nameplates in the early 1960s and ran for several years with the name painted on the backing plates. By July 1968 these had also been removed but were they were refitted on the day it was withdrawn and adorned with painted names and crests.

5158 was named GLASGOW YEOMANRY on 22 May 1936. Its plates had a noticeably sharper radius than the other three. The inscription 'Field Brigade R.A.T.A.' was below the crest.

Inverness allocated 45124 leaving Kyle on an up goods. The picture was taken in early 1955 before the sloping throatplate boiler fitted in June 1951 was replaced by a domeless example and the welded tender exchanged for a part-welded one during a Heavy General repair at St Rollox completed in June 1955. Photograph RAS-TG Hepburn

4. ON THE RECORD

Health Warning

As pointed out in earlier volumes of this series the LMS/LMR Engine History Cards and Engine Record Cards, while containing much useful and even fascinating information, should be regarded as a guide to what happened to the engines, not an unimpeachable document to be afforded the status of gospel. It seems to be stating the obvious that the Cards only show what was written on them at the time but the temptation to read and interpret too much should be resisted. Even so, the Cards are a marvellous, fascinating, invaluable record of what happened. Yet they are often infuriatingly silent on events that we enthusiasts half a century or more later consider of vital interest and importance. They were filled in, by hand, by clerks and naturally enough contain errors of omission (quite a few) and commission (a few).

Dates of leaving and entry to works were of course to some extent nominal and a day or two either side should always be assumed. Worse, the works were not above 'fiddling' dates slightly at the beginning or the end of a month to enhance the monthly figures, either of engines 'in' or engines 'out'. It was thus not entirely unknown for a locomotive to be out on the road with the figures showing it still in works and vice versa, for a few days at least. As with all BR steam locomotives, the record fades from about 1959-60 as the people involved realised their charges were on the way out. No-one responsible for the Cards bothered to record the last 'seeing out' mileages on the LMR or other Regions where the Black 5s ended up.

Although History Cards for those engines which were withdrawn from the LMR survive at the NRM, the picture is less complete for the remainder, and especially those which succumbed north of the Border. With a handful of exceptions the post-1950 Cards for these no longer exist and so there are no details of annual mileages or boiler changes from that date, although the works visits on the Record Cards do indicate when a boiler would have been changed. For the very small number of engines which served out their time at WR or NER sheds the ink runs out in the late-1950s, usually around 1957.

Sheds...

The same was true of allocations and many shed moves at the end did not find their way onto the History Cards. However the Chief Accountant's Statistics Office at Derby kept going to the bitter end of BR steam and beyond, and so the LMR shed allocations from 1963 onwards were taken from the weekly Locomotive Stock Book Alteration Lists produced there. Final gaps were filled for the locomotives allocated to the ScR and NER from the Engine Record Cards which were maintained after the History Card entries ended. The shed descriptions used are as written on the Cards and therefore translation is needed for some of the LMS sheds: Carlisle M = Durran Hill, Carlisle N = Kingmoor, Carlisle W = Upperby; Leeds = Holbeck; Sheffield = Millhouses. Transfer dates were for the week ending, although a few ScR moves can only be tied down to the period ending date.

One of the justifications for the wholesale scrapping of pre-grouping engines when the Black 5s were authorised was the standardisation of parts which would reduce the spares stock needed at each depot. However this was not necessarily achieved in practice as John Dunn, the running shed foreman at Bangor, recalled. He was dismayed to discover that such items as cab fittings and buffer beam connections varied between members of the class, depending on where they were built. It seems that the LMS, in the interest of keeping costs down, allowed contractors to use their own "off the shelf" components.

45123 on 7 April 1961 near Garve on an Inverness-Kyle train. It was allocated to Inverness from 1941 until 1962, hence the tablet catcher and brackets for a snowplough. Photograph RAS-DMC Hepburne-Scott

Repairs and Maintenance

Under the LMS motive power organisation most sheds carried out minor running repairs and adjustments, including boiler wash-outs etc. Jobs which required the engine to return to Works or to one of the larger sheds, such as Rugby, were usually designated under one of the 'Classified Repair' codes. These were either 'Heavy, (H) or 'Light' (L), further sub-divided into 'Casual' (C), 'Intermediate' (I). 'Overhaul' (O), 'Service' (S) or 'General' (G). Occasionally engines were sent to Main Works for other reasons, such as modifications (e.g. fitting of AWS if this did not coincide with a normally programmed visit) and in these cases the code 'NC' (Non-Classified) was used. The other code which appears from time to time on the Engine Repair cards is 'TRO', which stands for 'Tender Repair Only'. Suffixes, usually after 'NC' were '(EO)', which signified 'Engine Only' and 'Rect.', or 'Rect. (EO)' which was used when an engine had to be returned to Works soon after a works visit for 'rectification', i.e. tightening up bits that had come loose and loosening bits that were too tight.

According to the classification prescribed by the Board of Trade a heavy repair was any one during which an engine was reboilered or had its boiler removed from the frames. It was also when any two of the following were carried out:

- *Fitting new tyres to four or more wheels.*
- *Fitting new cylinders.*
- *Fitting new axles.*
- *Re-tubing or otherwise repairing the boiler whilst still in the frames with not less than fifty firebox stays renewed.*
- *Both turning wheels and refitting axleboxes.*
- *Stripping and renewing both motion and brake gear.*

Intriguingly, light repairs often involved major work such as fitting new axles, replacing cylinders, partially retubing or patching the boiler in situ, or refurbishing the motion, axleboxes, frames, etc. As long as only one of these items was involved, however, the repair was still regarded as light.

Most heavy repairs were 'generals' whilst most light repairs were 'intermediates'. General repairs were carried out either at set time intervals or at predetermined mileages beyond which it was deemed that an engine could not safely remain in service and were designed to return it virtually to 'as new' condition. Intermediate repairs were normally undertaken when some major component reached the stage where it had to be attended to before the engine was due for general repair, but the aim was to carry out as few intermediate repairs as possible. Thus HG repairs were usually done at approximately 3 to 4-yearly intervals with, typically, two Intermediate repairs (either Light or Heavy) between. The opportunity was often taken to carry out modifications at the Heavy Works visits, though special programmes, such as installation of ATC/AWS in the late 1950s and early 1960s sometimes required engines to be called in specially.

Works...

Visits to works followed a typical railway ritual: the owning shed would submit a Shopping Proposal, usually some time before it was expected an engine would achieve a mileage or condition beyond which it would be uneconomical or unsafe for it to continue in service. What happened next depended on what was said on the form; either the engine would be called in by the Regional Shopping Control Office, or a Mechanical Inspector would be sent to verify its condition and make his recommendations. The Control Office had to balance between maintaining works loading and keeping the number of engines under or awaiting repair within budgeted targets. This was one of the reasons for the figures being fiddled from time to time.

The LMS Engine History Cards did not record which particular workshop carried out the repairs, although the BR cards and the Engine Record Cards do show this information. The latter dutifully carried on right to the bitter end and so for most locomotives there is a complete list of works visits from cradle to grave. One regional variation which the studious reader will quickly observe is that the Scots appear to have recorded all the minor works visits for rectification rather more conscientiously than their English counterparts. Maybe

45081 from Carlisle Kingmoor at Newton Heath during the two months, in December 1963 and January 1964, when it was paired with a former Coal Weighing tender. It has AWS, although the date of fitting is not recorded, and a domed boiler. 45081 was, apart from its first six months, always allocated in the north and was based at one of the two Carlisle shed from 1944 until withdrawn in October 1965. Photograph www.Rail-online.co.uk

their engines broke down more often or perhaps this type of attention was given in England at the sheds instead.

Crewe Works was responsible for heavy repairs to Black 5s on the LMS Central, Midland and Western Divisions, and St.Rollox (Glasgow) for those allocated to the Northern Division, although it was noted in 1942 that in most weeks two of its allocation of Black 5s and Jubilees were being sent to Crewe for these repairs and this continued until the mid-1950s.

A Heavy General (HG) repair at Crewe in the LMS period usually took between 25 and 40 weekdays: this was insufficient time to do the necessary work on the boiler, so engines undergoing HG repairs invariably left Works with a different boiler from that with which they had entered. Matters continued after 1948 in a similar vein until about 1962 with Crewe maintaining the LM Region engines and any others allocated at various times to the Southern Region (S&DJ), Western Region (mainly Shrewsbury) and the North Eastern Region (after transfer of the Yorkshire sheds). St.Rollox looked after the Scottish based engines, including those at Carlisle Kingmoor. From around 1963 St.Rollox and Crewe started to run down their steam activities at least as far as Black 5s were concerned and Cowlairs began to repair Black 5s from both Regions. After Cowlairs closed in 1966, Crewe did a few final Heavy repairs to L.M. engines; by this time repairs to Scottish engines seem to have ceased. 45222 was even repaired at Eastleigh in December 1966 when its leading wheelset was removed for attention to the axleboxes.

Mileages

Total annual mileage was recorded on the History Cards, but only up to around 1960 and, because the Cards have been lost, is not available for most of the ScR engines after 1950. In any event it was an estimation, a minor miracle of paperwork and not mechanically recorded. Having said that a few snippets can be extracted to show how the early Black 5s compared with the engines they displaced.

In 1936, the first year in which all the engines covered in this volume were in service for a full twelve months, the average mileage was 55,167, with Northern Division 5176 the highest at 75,453 and Springs Branch's 5126, which spent two months in the works, far behind with only 34,821. The average compared favourably with 20-28,000 miles for the LNWR 'Precursor' and 'George V' 4-4-0s and the Highland 4-6-0s, 33,000 miles for the Caledonian 4-6-0s and 37,000 for the LNWR Prince of Wales as reported for the years 1933-35. The new Black 5s were generally not affected by regular works visits in their first twelve months or so in service, and these would account for at least one month in each year as the class fell into the normal ongoing repairs regime.

As more of the engines came into service and the class worked lesser duties as well as the longer distance services on which they were originally used, the average mileages reduced. The cumulatives to 31 December 1950, the last date up to which figures survive for every engine, show a fall to an average of around 41,000 a year. The Scottish engines were generally worked harder than many of their English counterparts, led by 5086 which reached 845,672 miles, an annual average of 52,855. Its fellow Northern Division engines, 5081-5083, 5085 and 5087, 5163-5165, 5167, 5170, 5171 and 5173-5175, also achieved over 800,000 miles in the same period. The wooden spoon went to Wakefield's 5206 and Farnley Junction's 5080 which managed only 516,218 and 521,429 respectively during the same sixteen years; this was typical of the locomotives based on the Central Division with their shorter route mileages.

'Improvements, Etc'

The History Cards had a section headed 'Improvements, Etc.' that recorded brief details of modifications or improvements applied to the engines. What was recorded varied from major work such as the fitting of speed indicators or AWS right down to apparently trivial jobs costing a few pounds. The clerks responsible for the cards did not always record changes which must have taken place such as the removal of the crosshead vacuum pumps which was done on all the pre-war engines, nor were they necessarily consistent with the descriptions and Works Order numbers used as a shorthand for this purpose. That said, it is possible with a little detective work to get a reasonably accurate picture of what was done, and when. This book uses the relevant 'off works' date for each particular modification rather than the 'period ending' date which was actually written on the Improvements section of the cards because clearly this makes more sense.

Tabulated in the following pages for each engine are the most significant 'Improvements' together with boiler and tender changes. The main boiler types, as discussed in the previous chapter, are indicated on the individual engine histories which follow, as are changes in tender type. Where a boiler or tender change is known to have occurred or a modification applied but the date is not recorded a '?' is shown in the tables. To help interpretation, if a change from the as-built type occurred then this has been indicated, e.g. a locomotive built with a domeless boiler and riveted tender receiving a domed boiler or a welded

INDIVIDUAL COSTS OF LOCOMOTIVES - THREE YEARS 1933 – 1935

Operating Class	Wheel Type	Type	No. of Locos. in service at Dec. 1935	Average annual mileage	Average mileage between 'General' Repairs	Weekdays not in service
5MT	4-6-0	Mixed Traffic (Standard)	225	55,310	-	81
Passenger Classes						
5	4-6-0	L&Y Old Class 8	40	32,265	88,472	115
4	4-6-0	Prince of Wales	131	37,055	117,174	82
4	4-6-0	Caledonian	32	33,482	103,114	80
4	4-6-0	Highland	8	33,052	121,179	116
4	4-4-0	Standard Compound	240	47,589	125,396	87
3	4-4-0	L.N.W. 'Precursor'	55	27,813	109,865	124
3	4-4-0	L.N.W. 'George V'	76	20,754	102,021	160
Freight Classes						
4	4-6-0	L.N.W. 19'	75	21,241	92,881	98
4	4-6-0	Highland - Superheated	8	26,243	115,349	99
4	4-6-0	Highland - Non-Superheated	7	25,021	-	79
4	2-6-0	Standard (Tapered)	40	39,652	-	67
4	2-6-0	Standard (Parallel)	240	38,022	138,356	63
4	0-6-0	Standard	727	27,590	111,372	58

tender. Note that the History Cards stopped recording boiler changes before the end, when a locomotive clearly may have had at least one more boiler after that shown.

Crosshead Driven Vacuum Pumps
The crosshead pump, which was attached to the bottom of the lower left-hand slide bar, was intended to maintain the vacuum in the train pipe when running. Enginemen were instructed to use the small ejector to maintain the vacuum when standing in a station, or just before starting, but as soon as the engine was running fast enough for the pump to maintain the vacuum, the small ejector should be shut off to conserve steam. In service, the pumps proved to be unreliable and costly to maintain and were not used, the crews preferring to use the small ejectors to maintain the vacuum, and they were removed between 1938 and 1941.

Steam Sanding
Sand was originally applied to the rails by gravity from six sandboxes supplying the six coupled wheels but this method proved unsuccessful and by 1938 steam sanding was introduced. It is uncertain when this work was actually carried out on some of the Northern Division engines because many of their History Cards show it dated either 19/5/45 or 20/5/45; this was simply a housekeeping exercise with the modification actually done some years earlier.

Speed Indicators
The LMS experimented with speed indicators and recorders on a number of classes right up to the time of nationalisation, the M&EE Committee approving in October 1937 the recommendation that, 'with a view to enabling engines accurately to observe speed restrictions... 998 locos working express passenger trains be fitted with electric speed indicators'. Between 1938 and 1943 a number of Black 5s were fitted with British Thomson Houston speed recorders which had the alternator mounted on a bracket suspended from the running plate alongside the left-hand trailing wheel. It was driven by a pin on the end of a small return crank from the driving wheel crankpin with a voltmeter in the cab graduated to indicate the speed. The equipment proved unreliable and, with wartime spares being in short supply, its removal was ordered in 1944.

Further trials with modified BTH and Smith-Stone speed indicators began in 1949 but slow progress was made until 1957, when the ex-LMS Pacifics were fitted with the latter type. In May 1959 authority was given for the widespread fitting of this equipment and though 99 Black 5s were scheduled, initially, to be so fitted, the scheme was cancelled in 1964 with only a few of the class

equipped. These included 45158, 45186, 45198, 45215, 45217, 45221 and 45223. These indicators were again electrically operated, with the speed calculated from the voltage produced by a generator mounted directly on and driven from a return crank on the rear left-hand crankpin. An armoured flexible cable led via a rheostat box into the cab.

Modification and Modernisation

The continuing problem of frame fractures caused much head-scratching and prompted several abortive solutions before it was finally solved in the 1950s. In December 1938 the M&EE Committee was informed that, 'During the course of repairs to Class 5 4-6-0 MT engines, it had been found that several of the frames had been bent inwards near the leading axlebox'. To eliminate this trouble Stanier recommended that cross stretchers be fitted in the region of the axlebox guides to the 472 engines concerned. Unfortunately this only seemed to increase the incidence of cracks, and the cause was eventually traced to the transmission of the racking stresses between the frames which resulted in further loosening of the guides and stays. Attempts to repair the frames by chipping away vee-shaped grooves along the cracks with an air caulking gun and then welding them up, were not successful and the cracks duly reappeared at the edges of the welds.

The underlying weakness of the frame design meant that none of these modifications cured the problems, although eventually the cause was beginning to be understood, largely as a result of trials and experiments carried out by the Research Department. In a paper read to the Institution of Locomotive Engineers in 1946, E.S. Cox stated that these investigations had shown 'the overwhelming importance of a tight connection at the bottom of the horn gap'. He went on to say that the types of axlebox guides and hornstays used on the Black 5s prevented this from being achieved. The results bore fruit, however, in the Black 5s built during 1946. These had two features which significantly improved things: firstly manganese steel liners were fitted on both the axleboxes and horns. These hardened in use so that after a short time the rate of wear slowed down giving a major improvement, the clearances and alignment of the boxes with the frames being maintained to within very close limits over much higher mileages than previously experienced. Secondly, adoption of Horwich pattern hornstays as used so effectively for many years on the Crab 2-6-0s. Problems with the screwed spring links were also dealt with by the use of flat section links with large box-section brackets through which were inserted interchangeable flat cotters, by which means the weight was adjusted on the coupled wheels.

The early engines were therefore fitted with manganese steel liners, Horwich hornstays and cottered links as they underwent general repairs from 1947 onwards, although financial authority was not given until 1951 when Job No. 5597 to WO/E 1173 was issued to Modernise (or Modify as some of the History Cards describe the work) the 643 locomotives which had not already been dealt with informally. Although the costs were over £600 per engine the results were certainly impressive and the interval between periodic repairs rose from an average of just under 57,000 to over 97,000 miles. However, with the end of steam approaching not all the engines received the modified spring links, many retaining the screwed type until withdrawn.

AWS

From 1959 onwards most of the class were fitted with the BR Automatic Warning System (AWS) which was also recorded on the History Cards as Automatic Train Control (ATC). The main visible features were a cylindrical vacuum reservoir on the right-hand running plate immediately in front of the cab with a smaller timing reservoir on the left-hand side. An extra frame stretcher was added to the front of the bogie to which the AWS receiver was fixed with a guard plate attached to the buffer beam to prevent the screw coupling damaging the receiver.

Snowplough fitted 45117 May 1961 on the 10.45am Kyle-Inverness soon after leaving Achanalt; perhaps more snow was expected. It also has AWS, probably fitted in early 1960. Photograph RAS-WJ Verden Anderson

45075 from Farnley Junction pilots a Jubilee on a Liverpool-Newcastle express out of Manchester Exchange. It has Overhead Line Warning flashes but its AWS was not fitted until December 1960, which dates this picture as mid-1960. 45075 had been at the Leeds shed from 1935 and moved down the road to Holbeck in September 1964. Photograph www.rail-online.co.uk

45075

Built as 5075 at Vulcan Foundry 23/2/35
Renumbered 45075 w.e. 11/6/49

Improvements and modifications

29/6/38	Removal of vacuum pump
24/12/42	Steam sanding
20/12/56	Modification
15/12/60	Fitting BR ATC equipment

Repairs

19/3/36-3/4/36	LS
3/3/37-24/3/37	HS
11/5/38-29/6/38	HG
15/12/39-4/1/40	HS
18/6/41-7/7/41	LS
5/12/42-24/12/42	HG
13/5/44-27/5/44	LS
1/2/46-20/2/46	LS
14/7/47-19/9/47	HG
19/5/49-9/6/49	LI
4/9/50-2/10/50	LI
12/3/51-7/4/51	LC
8/3/52-15/5/52	HG
26/7/54-20/8/54	HI
30/8/55-30/9/55	LC
12/11/56-20/12/56	HG
22/2/57-19/3/57	LC(EO)
12/12/58-8/1/59	LI
8/8/59-6/10/59	LC(EO)
23/11/60-15/12/60	NC(EO)
7/6/61-29/7/61	HI
7/2/64-28/3/64	G

Boilers

New	9005
9/6/38	8924 from 5144
24/12/42	8914 from 5077
19/9/47	8957 from 5001
15/5/52	8959 from 45037
20/12/56	9033 from 45074
?	9037

Tenders

New	9169
27/5/44	9524 (welded)
20/12/56	9562 (welded)

Mileage/(weekdays out of service)

1935	42,469 (58)
1936	44,383 (68)
1937	37,558 (64)
1938	39,289 (90)
1939	37,124 (59)
1940	28,608 (57)
1941	30,241 (60)
1942	23,676 (80)
1943	42,367 (33)
1944	35,732 (49)
1945	33,312 (43)
1946	36,681 (53)
1947	24,775 (114)
1948	41,888 (46)
1949	41,034 (38)
1950	38,643 (59)
1951	37,417 (69)
1952	32,898 (80)
1953	32,922 (51)
1954	35,786 (60)
1955	29,838 (108)
1956	36,254 (68)
1957	42,895

Mileage at 12/36: 86,852
Mileage at 31/12/50: 577,780

Sheds

Newton Heath	23/2/35
Farnley Jct	17/8/35
Holbeck	6/9/64
Normanton	25/6/67

Withdrawn w.e. 9/9/67

5075, the first of the second Vulcan Foundry batch, was allocated to 25G Farnley Junction from August 1935. There are numerous differences from the first batch – standard height chimney, front platform cover, recessed top feed pipes, domed covers on firebox, bogie axles not hollow and cab roof gutter. In this photograph it still has the crosshead vacuum pump which was taken off in June 1938.

45076

Built as 5076 at Vulcan Foundry 2/3/35
Renumbered 45076 w.e. 24/4/48

Improvements and modifications

28/1/39	Steam sanding
28/1/39	Removal of vacuum pump
23/2/57	Modernisation
24/3/62	Fitting BR ATC equipment

Repairs

8/6/36-24/6/36	**LS**
13/7/37-9/8/37	**HS**
5/12/38-10/1/39	**HG**
22/7/40-3/8/40	**HS**
8/8/42-22/8/42	**HS**
25/10/43-9/11/43	**HG**
3/8/45-25/8/45	**LS**
11/1/47-31/1/47	**HS**
15/3/47-2/5/47	**HO**
17/3/48-21/4/48	**NC**
14/1/49-8/2/49	**LI**
2/9/50-3/10/50	**LI**
19/6/51-13/7/51	**LC**
20/3/52-14/5/52	**HG**
26/5/52-16/6/52	**NC(Rect)**
18/3/54-6/4/54	**LI**
19/1/55-16/2/55	**HI**
18/2/55-22/2/55	**NC(Rect)(EO)**
8/1/57-2/2/57	**HG**
6/11/57-21/12/57	**LC**
21/9/59-30/10/59	**HI**
18/1/62-2/3/62	**HG**
9/4/62-19/4/62	**NC(Rect)**
30/12/64-23/1/65	**LI**

Boilers

New	9006
10/1/39	9007 from 5077
9/11/43	9042 from 5106
2/5/47	8970 from 5137
14/5/52	8670 from 45128 (domed)
2/2/57	8677 from 45060 (domed)
?	9058

Tenders

New	9170
24/8/64	10446 (welded)

Mileage/(weekdays out of service)

1935	41,033(52)
1936	39,808(62)
1937	35,770(66)
1938	41,174(78)
1939	43,268(62)
1940	26,886(75)
1941	31,290(51)
1942	32,426(77)
1943	37,037(55)
1944	36,440(30)
1945	25,191(54)
1946	31,509(58)
1947	33,654(104)
1948	28,268(72)
1949	35,370(43)
1950	25,838(55)
1951	29,524(64)
1952	30,343(84)
1953	38,220(38)
1954	33,794(51)
1955	33,005(88)
1956	30,615(50)
1957	34,066(81)
1958	41,068(38)
1959	29,499
1960	37,768

Mileage at 12/36: 80,841
Mileage at 31/12/50: 544,962

Sheds

Newton Heath	23/3/35
Farnley Jct	17/8/35
Wakefield	@24/6/36
Newton Heath	8/9/56

Stored
11/9/39-27/9/39

Withdrawn w.e. 29/6/68

45076 with a train of ex-LNER stock at Low Gill in the mid-1950s. It was shedded at 26A Newton Heath from September 1956 onwards. 45076 had a domed boiler between May 1952 and March 1962 and kept its original riveted tender until 1964. Photograph N.E. Preedy.

45077

Built as 5077 at Vulcan Foundry 2/3/1935
Renumbered 45077 w.e. 29/4/50

Improvements and modifications

4/11/38	Steam sanding
4/11/38	Removal of vacuum pump
11/10/61	Fitting BR ATC equipment

Repairs

4/4/35-29/4/35	LO
17/4/36-12/5/36	LS
29/5/37-4/6/37	LO
16/6/37-14/7/37	HS
26/9/38-4/11/38	HG
9/8/40-24/8/40	HG
26/10/42-14/11/42	HG
14/8/44-2/9/44	LS
8/12/45-12/1/46	LO
11/7/46-17/8/46	LS
23/1/48-6/3/48	HG
31/3/50-25/4/50	LI
13/2/52-13/3/52	LI
21/10/53-21/11/53	HG
17/1/55-15/2/55	LC(EO)
11/4/56-14/5/56	HI
11/3/57-6/4/57	LC(EO)
14/10/58-13/11/58	HG
17/8/59-23/10/59	LC(EO)
7/11/60-9/12/60	LI
20/9/61-11/10/61	NC(EO)
22/1/63-15/2/63	HI

Boilers

New	9007
4/11/38	8914 from 5134
14/11/42	8825 from 5179
6/3/48	8943 from 5101
21/11/53	9041 from 45089
13/11/58	9059 from 45146

Tenders

New	9171

Mileage/(weekdays out of service)

1935	37,010 (73)
1936	38,932 (89)
1937	36,765 (77)
1938	38,893 (84)
1939	39,534 (55)
1940	27,241 (71)
1941	36,484 (45)
1942	33,847 (69)
1943	38,550 (29)
1944	32,343 (61)
1945	19,597 (86)
1946	28,747 (88)
1947	29,736 (78)
1948	38,227 (67)
1949	30,767 (61)
1950	39,608 (41)
1951	29,321 (67)
1952	33,449 (63)
1953	27,901 (68)
1954	43,364 (40)
1955	35,420 (63)
1956	39,207 (49)
1957	42,938 (48)
1958	35,589 (59)
1959	35,588
1960	26,977

Mileage at 12/36: 75,942
Mileage at 31/12/50: 546,281

Sheds

Farnley Jct	23/3/35
Blackpool	2/10/48
Wakefield	8/12/51
Farnley Jcn	12/4/52 (loan)
Wakefield	24/5/52
Blackpool	21/6/52
Rose Grove	23/5/53
Blackpool	13/6/53
Southport	25/9/54
Blackpool	25/6/55
Bank Hall	17/11/56
Blackpool	5/1/57
Fleetwood	23/11/63
Rose Grove	5/12/64
Patricroft	13/2/65
Newton Heath	19/6/65

Stored
13/10/36-9/11/36

Withdrawn w.e. 14/8/65

45077 on 16 June 1957 at Preston was always domeless and retained its original riveted tender until withdrawn in August 1965. It was always a Central Division engine and had been transferred to Blackpool in January 1957 from Bank Hall.

45078

Built as 5078 at Vulcan Foundry 2/3/35
Renumbered 45078 w.e. 9/4/49

Improvements and modifications

25/8/38	Removal of vacuum pump
19/6/43	Steam sanding
24/2/62	Fitting BR ATC equipment

Repairs

28/11/35-23/12/35	LS
23/3/37-13/4/37	HS
27/7/38-25/8/38	HG
15/7/40-31/7/40	HS
7/10/41-25/10/41	LS
5/6/43-19/6/43	HG
18/10/43-5/11/43	LO
19/8/44-1/9/44	LS
7/12/45-5/1/46	HS
2/7/47-26/8/47	HG
28/1/49-9/4/49	HG
7/5/49-13/5/49	No repairs
30/11/50-5/1/51	LI
27/3/52-25/4/52	HI
18/11/53-19/12/53	HG
10/8/54-25/8/54	LC(EO)
28/5/56-23/6/56	LI
1/9/58-3/10/58	HG
4/7/60-23/8/60	HI
10/4/61-13/5/61	LC(EO)

Boilers

New	9008
25/8/38	8649 from 5032 (domed)
19/6/43	8669 from 5114 (domed)
26/8/47	9017 from 5199
9/4/49	8671 from 5092 (domed)
19/12/53	8650 from 45034 (domed)
3/10/58	8912 from 45031

Tenders

New	9172

Mileage/(weekdays out of service)

1935	39,265 (64)
1936	44,184 (66)
1937	31,512(108)
1938	28,834(147)
1939	25,328(152)
1940	30,837(70)
1941	31,840(62)
1942	28,024(53)
1943	32,692(72)
1944	49,504(53)
1945	42,464(76)
1946	37,068(60)
1947	32,080(77)
1948	35,270(44)
1949	28,521(103)
1951	30,417(33)
1952	34,514(47)
1953	33,726(58)
1954	42,933(41)
1955	32,272(37)
1956	33,058(48
1957	36,228(60)
1958	33,697(76)
1959	31,175
1960	34,765

Mileage at 12/36: 83,449
Mileage at 31/12/50: 548,209

Sheds

Farnley Jct	23/3/35
Wakefield	23/12/35
Blackpool	24/7/43
Farnley Jct	12/10/46
Southport	25/10/52
Huddersfield	23/5/53
Southport	4/7/53
Accrington	19/6/54
Blackpool	9/1/60
Warrington	5/9/64

Stored
7/10/36-8/11/36

Withdrawn w.e. 30/10/65

45078 at Farington south of Preston in 1962. It was allocated Blackpool from January 1960 and received AWS in February 1962. The domeless boiler was fitted in October 1958 and it kept its first riveted tender until withdrawn in October 1965. Photograph www.rail-online.co.uk

45079

Built as 5079 at Vulcan Foundry 9/3/35
Renumbered 45079 w.e. 8/5/48

Improvements and modifications

13/7/38	Removal of vacuum pump
?	Steam sanding
8/4/61	Fitting BR ATC equipment

Repairs

23/4/36-14/5/36	LS
25/1/37-1/2/37	LO
3/4/37-11/5/37	HS
26/5/38-13/7/38	HG
26/3/40-12/4/40	HS
1/4/41-22/4/41	HS
18/3/42-25/4/42	LS
23/3/43-10/4/43	LS
19/10/43-11/11/43	LO
26/6/44-15/7/44	LS
20/2/45-3/3/45	LO
25/4/45-12/5/45	LO
25/8/45-15/9/45	HG
25/11/47-17/1/48	LS
17/3/48-6/5/48	NC
26/8/48-25/9/48	LO
12/1/50-16/2/50	HG
17/2/50-3/3/50	TRO
1/1/52-26/1/52	HI
29/7/53-29/8/53	HI
10/8/54-3/9/54	LC(EO)
10/3/55-7/5/55	HG
25/5/57-21/6/57	LI
27/12/58-24/1/59	LI
27/2/61-8/4/61	HI
8/5/62-26/5/62	HC
18/11/64-12/12/64	INT

Boilers

New	9009
17/6/38	8662 from 5045 (domed)
22/4/41	8990 from 5210
15/9/45	8949 from 5043
16/2/50	8642 from 5215 (domed)
7/5/55	8641 from 45204 (domed)

Tenders

New	9173
19/3/55	9174

Mileage/(weekdays out of service)

1935	42,449 (35)
1936	45,567 (70)
1937	39,999 (91)
1938	46,109 (108)
1939	38,695 (102)
1940	30,602 (51)
1941	33,554 (42)
1942	40,703 (60)
1943	35,849 (72)
1944	45,456 (69)
1945	28,061 (100)
1946	41,954 (34)
1947	25,195 (73)
1948	24,980 (120)
1949	33,844 (60)
1950	34,450 (67)
1951	26,409 (25)
1952	34,105 (53)
1953	31,846 (54)
1954	33,288 (52)
1955	31,049 (104)
1956	38,131 (38)
1957	32,250

Mileage at 12/36: 88,016
Mileage at 31/12/50: 587,467

Sheds

Farnley Jct	23/3/35
Low Moor	17/8/35
Farnley Jct	14/11/36
Southport	13/2/37(loan)
Southport	27/3/37
Low Moor	30/10/37
Wakefield	21/10/39
Sowerby Bridge	6/6/42
Blackpool	14/11/42
Farnley Jct	12/10/46
Newton Heath	22/11/47
Farnley Jct	18/11/50
Huddersfield	11/10/52
Farnley Jct	7/2/53
Holbeck	5/1/64

Stored
19/10/36-9/11/36
31/10/38-22/12/38
2/1/39-27/3/39

Withdrawn 8/3/67

Super power on a Trans-Pennine express as 45079 pilots a Jubilee in the mid-1950s. The Class 5 spent its life on the Central Division alternating between various sheds and was in its fifth spell at Farnley Junction from February 1953 when this picture was taken. It was domed until February 1950 and always had a riveted tender.

45080

Built as 5080 at Vulcan Foundry 9/3/35
Renumbered 45080 w.e. 22/5/48

Improvements and modifications

4/8/38	Removal of vacuum pump
27/1/45	Steam sanding
17/1/61	Fitting BR ATC equipment

Repairs

2/3/36-17/3/36	LS
4/8/36-7/8/36	LO
17/3/37-16/4/37	HS
28/9/37-2/10/37	LO
26/11/37-22/12/37	HO
10/6/38-4/8/38	HG
5/4/40-22/4/40	LS
1/2/41-22/2/41	HS
23/9/42-14/10/42	LS
25/11/43-18/12/43	LS
10/1/45-27/1/45	HG
9/4/47-26/5/47	HS
8/4/48-21/5/48	LO
8/12/48-31/12/48	LS
3/5/50-8/6/50	HG
30/1/52-20/2/52	LI
28/4/53-1/6/53	HI
2/4/54-10/5/54	HC
16/7/55-20/8/55	HG
29/1/57-22/2/57	LI
10/9/58-13/10/58	LI
10/8/59-26/9/59	HC(EO)
5/12/60-17/1/61	NC(EO)
30/5/61-26/6/61	HG
1/4/64-7/5/64	INT
1/2/65-9/3/66	UC

Boilers

New	9010
20/7/38	8975 from 5195
22/2/41	9027 from 5050
27/1/45	8971 from 5073
8/6/50	8947 from 5025
20/8/55	8960 from 45137
26/6/61	8655 from 45048 (domed)

Tenders

New	9174
19/3/55	9173

Mileage/(weekdays out of service)

1935	40,443 (40)
1936	46,551 (79)
1937	30,316 (113)
1938	37,643 (101)
1939	34,708 (81)
1940	25,207 (67)
1941	31,704 (57)
1942	36,213 (62)
1943	34,778 (63)
1944	33,409 (49)
1945	34,136 (63)
1946	22,031 (102)
1947	24,185 (80)
1948	21,783 (81)
1949	33,785 (38)
1950	34,537 (59)
1951	31,496 (46)
1952	33,277 (51)
1953	31,987 (69)
1954	34,692 (77)
1955	28,664 (104)
1956	35,959 (63)
1957	39,837

Mileage at 12/36: 86,994
Mileage at 31/12/50: 521,429

Sheds

Farnley Jct	23/3/35
Low Moor	17/8/35
Farnley Jct	14/11/36
Stourton	2/10/66
Holbeck	15/1/67

Stored
19/10/36-2/11/36
11/9/39-27/9/39

Withdrawn 30/9/67

Lots of clag from 45080 and the Jubilee behind it sometime in the late 1950s. It was allocated to Farnley Junction and has a 55C shedplate which was the depot code from September 1956. 45080 spent almost all of its time there apart from a brief spell at Low Moor in 1935/6 and its final year in service. The domeless boiler was replaced by a domed pattern in 1961, but the riveted tender lasted until withdrawal in September 1967. Photograph Millbrook House.

45081

Built as 5081 at Vulcan Foundry 16/3/35
Renumbered 45081 w.e. 10/4/48

Improvements and modifications

7/3/38	Removal of vacuum pump
25/9/43	BTH speed indicator
20/5/45	Steam sanding
?	Fitting BR ATC equipment

Repairs

13/11/35-21/11/35	LO
18/3/36-28/3/36	LS
4/3/37-26/3/37	LS
23/2/38-7/3/38	LS
12/9/38-4/10/38	HO
15/9/39-23/10/39	LS
23/7/40-10/8/40	HS
5/2/41-15/3/41	HO
9/10/41-14/10/41	LO
21/1/42-28/2/42	LS
15/12/42-22/1/43	LS
23/8/43-25/9/43	LS
7/2/44-14/2/44	LO
31/7/44-24/8/44	HG
24/1/45-15/2/45	LO
21/4/45-29/8/45	LS
3/6/46-5/4/46	LS
7/1/48-5/2/48	LS
11/3/48-10/4/48	LO
1/8/49-17/9/49	G
24/1/51-17/2/51	LI
7/3/51-9/3/51	NC(R)
22/3/51-23/3/51	NC(R)
9/9/52-11/10/52	HI
12/11/52-7/12/52	LC
9/2/53-6/3/53	LC
28/8/53-31/10/53	G
19/11/53-20/11/53	LC
8/3/54-20/3/54	LC(EO)
31/3/55-23/4/55	LI
6/5/55-11/5/55	NC(EO)
10/7/56-24/8/56	LI
15/4/57-24/4/57	LC(EO)
20/5/57-30/5/57	NC(EO)
15/7/57-17/8/57	HI
3/10/57	NC(EO)
13/3/58-26/3/58	LC(EO)
11/6/58-12/6/58	LC(EO)
29/1/59-21/2/59	HG
25/2/59-26/2/59	NC(EO)
4/5/60-14/5/60	LC(EO)
27/7/60-26/8/60	LI

Boilers

New	9011
4/10/38	9024 from 5094
15/3/41	8931 from 5176
17/9/49	8984 from 5096
31/10/53	8820 from 45083 (domed)
21/2/59	8957 (domed)

Tenders

New	9175
21/5/45	9103
29/8/45	9511 (welded)
3/6/46	9069
14/9/49	9062
11/10/52	9823 (welded)
6/3/53	9282 (welded)
30/10/53	10711 (part-welded)
17/11/53	9273 (welded)
21/4/55	10528 (welded)
23/12/62	9087
1/12/63	10590 (coal-weighing)
25/1/64	9087

Mileage/(weekdays out of service)

1935	45,637 (26)
1936	66,751 (44)
1937	58,130 (52)
1938	53,028 (88)
1939	54,859 (57)
1940	51,880 (49)
1941	53,298 (78)
1942	52,264 (62)
1943	53,065 (79)
1944	46,170 (73)
1945	47,863 (81)
1946	49,526 (79)
1947	50,590 (54)
1948	36,573 (124)
1949	42,501 (96)
1950	53,151 (32)
1951	44,695 (73)
1952	29,457 (98)
1953	37,068 (107)
1954	50,135 (66)
1955	43,432 (54)
1956	48,569 (71)
1957	34,832 (98)
1958	38,766 (66)
1959	47,765
1960	43,102

Mileage at 12/36: 112,388
Mileage at 31/12/50: 815,286

Sheds

Crewe	16/3/35
Bushbury	20/4/35
Crewe	4/5/35
Perth	16/11/35
St Rollox	22/7/39
Perth	30/3/40
St Rollox	20/4/40
Perth	20/8/41
Carlisle Kingmoor	18/11/44
Carlisle Upperby	10/2/62
Carlisle Kingmoor	22/6/63
Carlisle Upperby	27/6/64

Withdrawn w.e. 16/10/65

5081 at Aviemore while allocated to Perth sometime between November 1935 and July 1939. The vehicle behind is a Highland Railway postal van.

45082

Built as 5082 at Vulcan Foundry 16/3/35
Renumbered 45082 w.e 26/3/49

Improvements and modifications

12/5/38	Removal of vacuum pump
5/2/44	Steam sanding
3/7/54	Modernisation
28/12/56	Sloping throatplate boiler
?	Fitting BR ATC equipment

Repairs

14/10/35-28/10/35	LO
18/12/36-12/1/37	LS
26/4/37-20/5/37	LS
3/5/38-12/5/38	LS
21/4/39-2/6/39	HG
3/6/40-3/7/40	LS
29/3/41-19/4/41	LS
25/2/42-24/4/52	HG
18/12/42-9/1/43	LS
31/12/43-5/2/44	HG
21/2/44-7/3/44	LO
24/4/44-26/5/44	HS
11/1/45-22/2/45	LS
31/3/45-12/5/45	LO
8/10/46-9/11/46	LS
13/1/48-7/2/48	HG
25/2/49-26/3/49	HI
24/7/50-1/9/50	HI
19/3/51-18/4/51	LC
31/1/52-2/4/52	G
30/11/52-26/12/52	HI
11/8/53-29/9/53	LC
1/6/54-3/7/54	HI
19/7/54-25/8/54	LC(EO)
6/12/56-28/12/56	G
19/12/58-10/1/59	LI
12/12/60-21/1/61	HI
13/3/62-12/4/62	G
22/4/63-17/5/63	LC
5/8/64-14/8/64	LC(EO)

Boilers

New	9012
2/6/39	8954 from 5174
24/4/42	8973 from 5186
5/2/44	8820 from 5103 (domed)
7/2/48	8988 from 5173
2/4/52	9001 from 45159
28/12/56	14327 New (sloping throatplate)

Tenders

New	9176
19/8/41	9727 (welded)
26/8/41	9176
25/5/44	9015
20/2/45	9005
26/3/49	10556 (part-welded)
18/2/52	10585 (part-welded)
27/12/52	9283 (welded)
29/9/53	9117
6/12/56	10550 (part-welded)
28/12/56	10505 (welded)
9/7/66	9635 (welded)

Mileage/(weekdays out of service)

1935	46,354 (39)
1936	65,787 (57)
1937	57,196 (43)
1938	57,643 (64)
1939	48,951 (80)
1940	50,578 (59)
1941	48,958 (72)
1942	58,114 (77)
1943	63,633 (36)
1944	48,459 (91)
1945	44,953 (121)
1946	36,655 (104)
1947	41,511 (75)
1948	46,524 (89)
1949	43,890 (50)
1950	44,267 (71)
1951	29,570 (83)
1952	32,669 (127)
1953	45,269 (89)
1954	41,896 (88)
1955	46,567 (56)
1956	41,093 (72)
1957	49,643 (50)
1958	37,054 (68)
1959	47,497
1960	45,372

Mileage at 12/36: 112,141
Mileage at 31/12/50: 803,473

Sheds

Crewe	16/3/35
Bushbury	20/4/35
Crewe	4/5/35
Perth	@28/10/35
St Rollox	22/7/39
Perth	16/12/39
St Rollox	20/4/40
Perth	20/8/41
Carlisle Kingmoor	11/11/44
Carlisle Upperby	4/8/62
Carlisle Kingmoor	22/6/63

Withdrawn w.e. 9/7/66

5082 was one of the earliest with BR insignia following a Heavy General overhaul completed in February 1948. An 'M' prefix was applied above the LMS cab number, BRITISH RAILWAYS in full on the tender and the original LMS smokebox plate retained. It was renumbered as 45082 in March 1949 after a Heavy Intermediate overhaul. It carried every configuration of boiler and topfeed but is seen here domeless, albeit with St Rollox applied 'incorrect' topfeed cover, having carried a domed boiler from 1944 to 1948. Photograph R.K. Blencowe.

45083

Built as 5083 at Vulcan Foundry 23/3/35
Renumbered 45083 w.e. 20/3/48

Improvements and modifications

24/12/37	Removal of vacuum pump
20/5/45	Steam sanding

Repairs

14/10/35-29/10/35	LO
27/11/36-19/12/36	LS
24/4/37-3/5/39	LO
30/11/37-24/12/37	LO
10/10/38-2/11/38	LS
11/11/38-2/12/38	LO
26/10/39-1/12/39	HG
1/7/40-13/7/40	LS
3/5/41-4/6/41	LS
14/4/42-16/5/42	HG
27/11/42-30/12/42	LS
11/10/43-6/11/43	HS
28/11/43-30/11/43	LO
28/8/44-6/10/44	HS
30/8/45-27/9/45	LS
11/9/46-16/10/46	LS
23/2/48-20/3/48	HG
6/4/48-7/4/48	NC(R)
15/2/49-19/3/49	HI
28/9/50-28/10/50	HI
23/4/52-14/8/52	HI
18/5/53-20/6/53	HI
27/7/54-26/8/54	LI(EO)
16/11/54	LC(TO)
14/12/55-12/1/56	HI
19/9/56-13/10/56	LC
24/12/56-19/1/57	LI
26/2/57-16/3/57	LC(EO)
22/2/58-18/4/58	G
8/9/58-25/9/58	LC(EO)
4/7/59-8/8/59	LI
20/8/59	NC(EO)
6/6/61-1/7/61	LI
31/12/62-29/1/63	HG
29/5/64-12/6/64	LC
22/7/66-19/8/66	LC

Boilers

New	9013
1/12/39	8952 from 5172
16/5/42	9014 from 5171
6/10/44	8944 from 5176
20/3/48	8820 from 5082 (domed)
20/6/53	8945 from 45098
18/4/58	8659 (domed)

Tenders

New	9177
14/11/38	9280 (welded)
17/10/40	9265 (welded)
25/12/41	9597 (welded)
4/6/47	9487 (welded)
28/10/50	9836 (welded)
25/8/54	9713 (welded)
16/11/54	10505 (welded)
12/1/56	10694 (part-welded)
19/1/57	9261 (welded)
18/4/58	10713 (part-welded)

Mileage/(weekdays out of service)

1935	40,179 (57)
1936	65,706 (63)
1937	54,310 (65)
1938	47,211 (109)
1939	53,606 (66)
1940	65,008 (22)
1941	57,710 (62)
1942	51,385 (83)
1943	60,780 (49)
1944	54,078 (56)
1945	55,931 (54)
1946	40,360 (74)
1947	40,141 (100)
1948	46,029 (90)
1949	45,216 (60)
1950	30,088 (60)
1951	52,374 (42)
1952	31,159 (136)
1953	48,747 (77)
1954	45,061 (77)
1955	42,264 (74)
1956	45,448 (70)
1957	45,868 (71)
1958	40,191 (95)
1959	47,146
1960	49,676

Mileage at 12/36: 105,885
Mileage at 31/12/50: 807,738

Sheds

Crewe	23/3/35
Stoke	27/4/35
Crewe	4/5/35
Perth	29/10/35
Edinburgh	29/7/39
Perth	23/9/39
Inverness	28/9/40
Carlisle Kingmoor	17/5/47
Carlisle Upperby	4/8/62
Southport	18/5/63
Newton Heath	20/6/64

Withdrawn w.e. 16/12/67

45083 at Newton Heath on 22 September 1963 with no shedplate; it had been re-allocated to Southport the previous May. It has a domeless boiler, although the last recorded on its History Card was a domed pattern fitted in April 1958 when it also acquired the part-welded tender. Photograph www.rail-online.co.uk

45084

Built as 5084 at Vulcan Foundry 23/3/35
Renumbered 45084 w.e. 10/7/48

Improvements and modifications

28/10/38	Removal of vacuum pump
20/5/45	Steam sanding
?	Fitting BR ATC equipment

Repairs

23/9/36-14/10/36	LS
5/5/37-13/5/37	LO
26/10/37-17/11/37	LS
10/10/38-28/10/38	HS
14/11/38-28/11/38	LO
25/3/39-26/4/39	HG
12/1/40-3/2/40	LS
5/3/41-2/4/41	HS
13/1/42-18/2/42	LS
20/3/42-20/5/42	HG
11/1/43-6/2/43	LS
2/12/43-15/1/44	LS
22/2/44-1/4/44	LO
17/2/45-17/3/45	HS
6/5/46-5/6/46	HG
6/6/47-16/7/47	HS
21/6/48-10/7/48	LO
4/5/49-11/6/49	LI
19/6/50-12/8/50	HG
26/8/50-31/8/50	NC
11/9/51-6/10/51	LI
17/12/52-17/1/53	HI
2/5/53-16/5/53	LC(EO)
3/8/53-6/8/53	NC(EO)
12/8/53-22/8/53	LC(EO)
8/9/53-23/9/53	LC(EO)
12/10/53-24/10/53	LC(EO)
15/2/54-6/4/54	LC(EO)
4/9/54-10/11/54	G
17/3/55-24/3/55	LC
12/4/55-20/4/55	LC(EO)
7/9/55-16/9/55	LC(EO)
30/1/56-18/2/56	LC(EO)
21/5/56-4/7/56	LC
15/1/57-7/2/57	HI
26/3/58-3/4/58	LC
16/4/58-26/4/58	LC(EO)
20/8/58-12/9/58	HI
23/10/58-30/10/58	LC(EO)
30/4/59-9/5/59	LC(EO)
23/6/59-26/6/59	NC(EO)
25/9/59-3/10/59	NC(EO)
28/12/59-8/1/60	NC(EO)
8/3/60-17/3/60	LC(EO)
29/3/60-7/4/60	LC(EO)
19/4/60-13/5/60	LC(EO)
13/6/60-24/6/60	LC(EO)
4/7/60-26/8/60	G
28/8/61-5/9/61	LC(EO)
19/10/61-27/10/61	LC(EO)
2/5/62-10/5/62	LC(EO)
23/8/62-22/9/62	LI
19/6/63-4/7/63	LC
9/10/63-9/11/63	LC(EO)
11/11/64-25/12/64	LI
18/2/65	NC(TO)
19/1/66-5/2/66	LC(EO)

Boilers

New	9014
26/4/39	8956 from 5176
25/5/42	8953 from 5010
15/6/46	8956 from 5085
12/8/50	8648 from 5179 (domed)

Tenders

New	9178
13/10/38	9042
8/5/42	9005
16/8/42	9280 (welded)
5/2/43	9487 (welded)
4/6/47	9597 (welded)
1/7/48	9116
9/6/50	9668 (welded)
?	9015
3/11/54	9193
17/9/55	9717 (welded)
18/2/56	10695 (part- welded)
4/7/56	10718 (part- welded)
7/2/57	10719 (part- welded)
6/7/60	10547 (part- welded)
22/8/63	10679 (part- welded)
9/10/64	9620 (welded)

Mileage/(weekdays out of service)

1935	40,282 (23)
1936	52,548 (67)
1937	55,095 (45)
1938	53,710 (83)
1939	60,793 (59)
1940	61,982 (42)
1941	48,810 (47)
1942	48,941 (103)
1943	50,046 (61)
1944	44,283 (88)
1945	55,147 (56)
1946	47,841 (53)
1947	48,882 (73)
1948	34,634 (83)
1949	26,817 (85)
1950	37,125 (98)

Mileage at 12/36: 92,830
Mileage at 31/12/50: 766,936

Sheds

Crewe	23/3/35
Perth	26/10/35
Inverness	28/9/40
Carlisle	31/5/47
Stirling	30/3/52
Corkerhill	21/5/66
Carstairs	11/6/66 (PE)

Withdrawn 29/11/66

45084, with large close-spaced 10in cab numbers, at Stirling in the 1960s still has its Vulcan Foundry worksplate on the smokebox side. This was one of the ScR engines for which the post-1950 History Card did not survive – the AWS fitting date is therefore not known. The last recorded boiler fitted in 1950 was domed and it remained so at the date of this picture. 45084 was shedded at 65J Stirling from 1952 until Carstairs June 1966. Part welded tender from 1956 until October 1964. Note the domed covers from the firebox shoulders have gone missing and it has an odd set of coupled wheels with hollowed-out axles on the centre pair. Photograph www.rail-online.co.uk

45085

Built as 5085 at Vulcan Foundry 23/3/35
Renumbered 45085 w.e. 17/7/48

Improvements and modifications

12/1/39	Removal of vacuum pump
14/9/39	Steam sanding
2/10/54	Modernisation

Repairs

18/8/36-9/9/36	LS
19/5/37-26/5/37	LO
15/10/37-4/11/37	LS
21/12/38-12/1/39	LS
8/8/39-14/9/39	HG
20/5/40-5/6/40	HS
16/6/41-22/7/41	LS
1/6/42-14/7/42	HG
19/5/43-1/7/43	HG
7/2/44-21/3/44	LS
7/12/44-6/1/45	LS
8/2/46-7/3/46	HG
7/2/47-13/3/47	LS
16/10/47-28/11/47	LO
31/5/48-12/7/48	HS
16/8/48-18/8/48	NC(R)
3/5/49-11/6/49	LI
9/2/50-22/4/50	G
2/8/50-8/8/50	LC
23/12/50-3/2/51	LC(EO)
28/12/51-19/1/52	LI
1/2/52-13/2/52	LC(EO)
11/10/52-12/11/52	LC(EO)
25/4/53-23/5/53	HI
30/6/53-11/7/53	LC(EO)
16/8/54-2/10/54	G
26/12/55-7/1/56	LC(EO)
15/9/56-13/10/56	HI
31/10/56-2/11/56	NC
5/9/57-10/9/57	LC(EO)
14/10/57-29/11/57	HI
19/2/58-26/2/58	LC(EO)
5/3/58-15/3/58	LC(EO)
31/7/58-6/8/58	NC(EO)
16/2/59-20/3/59	G
2/6/60-8/6/60	NC(EO)
27/6/60-6/7/60	NC(TO)
17/4/61-6/5/61	LI
21/2/62-7/3/62	NC(EO)

Boilers

New	9015
14/9/39	8938 from 5158
14/7/42	8956 from 5084
7/3/46	8676 from 5005 (domed)
22/4/50	8826 from 5007
2/10/54	9022 from 45172
20/4/59	8937 from 45018

Tenders

New	9179
1/10/41	9211
12/7/48	9266 (welded)
14/4/50	9101
18/1/52	10684 (part-welded)
23/5/53	9595 (welded)
30/9/54	9672 (welded)
18/7/56	9719 (welded)
13/10/56	10547 (part-welded)
6/6/60	10719 (part-welded)
6/5/61	10546 (part-welded)

Mileage/(weekdays out of service)

1935	36,021 (26)
1936	67,821 (42)
1937	55,200 (68)
1938	58,191 (74)
1939	51,883 (91)
1940	66,123 (39)
1941	55,968 (63)
1942	50,710 (83)
1943	56,356 (63)
1944	43,263 (97)
1945	54,782 (47)
1946	56,498 (58)
1947	45,936 (155)
1948	39,174 (104)
1949	47,265 (76)
1950	33,667 (120)
1951	48,671 (62)
1952	28,273 (132)
1953	42,289 (71)
1954	34,924 (82)
1955	42,642 (49)
1956	32,533 (97)
1957	41,580 (87)
1958	42,042 (76)
1959	39,678
1960	42,687
1961	37,647
1962	31,485

Mileage at 12/36: 103,842
Mileage at 31/12/50: 818,858

Sheds

Crewe	23/3/35
Perth	26/10/35
St.Margarets	11/2/50 (PE)
Edinburgh	4/11/50
Polmadie	17/3/51
Motherwell	29/9/51

Stored
19/11/62-29/12/62

Withdrawn w.e. 29/12/62

45085 at Coatbridge Junction on 25 June 1953 with burnished fittings and motion for a Royal Train working as the second engine. The crew are receiving last-minute instructions from the man in the hat. 45085 was allocated to Polmadie and had a domeless boiler and newly acquired welded tender. The insignia on both the cab and tender are the large 10in version. Photograph www.transporttreasury.co.uk

45086

Built as 5086 at Vulcan Foundry 23/3/1935
Renumbered 45086 w.e. 26/6/48

Improvements and modifications

5/5/38	Removal of vacuum pump
2/2/44	Steam sanding
24/6/59	Fitting BR ATC equipment

Repairs

6/5/36-23/5/36	LS
25/5/37-11/6/37	LS
27/4/38-5/5/38	LS
11/4/39-15/5/39	HG
7/8/40-28/8/40	LS
13/10/41-15/11/41	LS
28/9/42-17/10/42	LS
30/1/43-27/2/43	HS
5/1/44-2/2/44	HG
30/1/45-14/3/45	LS
8/2/46-9/3/46	LS
3/4/47-24/5/47	HS
21/5/48-21/6/48	HG
12/7/48-13/7/48	TRO
30/10/48-3/11/48	NC
30/5/49-16/7/49	LI
27/10/49-3/12/49	LC
3/3/50-31/3/50	LC
27/9/50-3/11/50	LI
12/2/51-28/2/51	LC
22/11/51-15/12/51	HI
3/1/52-4/1/52	NC
6/8/52-6/11/52	G
7/4/54-7/5/54	G
17/11/55-14/12/55	HI
22/6/56-6/7/56	LC
16/3/57-13/4/57	HI
20/11/57-27/11/57	NC(EO)
7/5/58-29/5/58	LC(EO)
2/6/58-12/6/58	LC(EO)
21/1/59-13/2/59	G
16/6/59-24/6/59	NC(EO)
25/8/59-19/9/59	LC(EO)
6/10/59-13/10/59	LC(EO)
6/1/61-4/2/61	HI
8/3/62-20/3/62	LC(EO)

Boilers

New	9016
15/5/39	8951 from 5171
15/11/41	8964 from 5204
2/2/44	8989 from 5104
21/6/48	8658 from 5194 (domed)
6/11/52	8946 from 45154
7/5/54	9044 from 45167
13/2/59	8961

Tenders

New	9180
25/10/52	9064
4/5/54	9620 (welded)
12/8/55	10502 (welded)
14/12/55	9122
13/4/57	9829 (welded)
26/11/62	10678 (part-welded)

Mileage/(weekdays out of service)

1935	34,898 (38)
1936	63,380 (47)
1937	54,888 (69)
1938	54,458 (69)
1939	54,931 (76)
1940	60,742 (44)
1941	57,675 (62)
1942	66,126 (41)
1943	53,272 (51)
1944	61,824 (44)
1945	58,337 (59)
1946	49,976 (112)
1947	49,514 (83)
1948	44,852 (98)
1949	38,492 (103)
1950	42,307 (86)
1951	36,028 (91)
1952	44,989 (107)
1953	49,013 (30)
1954	48,930 (44)
1955	46,181 (47)
1956	45,496 (36)
1957	42,660 (55)
1958	26,468 (76)
1959	34,309
1960	44,222
1961	35,341
1952	19,011

Mileage at 12/36: 98,278
Mileage at 31/12/50: 845,672

Sheds

Crewe	23/3/35
Perth	26/10/35
Aberdeen	1/10/49
Perth	29/10/49
Carstairs	4/8/51
Dalry Road	29/9/51

Stored
19/11/62-29/12/62

Withdrawn w.e. 29/12/62

45086 in the late 1950s before AWS was fitted in June 1959. It was one of the early Scottish Region withdrawals from Dalry Road at the end of 1962, and had the highest mileage recorded to 31 December 1950 of 845,672. It has tablet exchange apparatus and was domeless apart from 1948 to 1952 and 1952 and acquired its third welded tender in April 1957. Photograph www.rail-online.co.uk

45087

Built as 5087 at Vulcan Foundry 30/3/35
Renumbered 45087 w.e. 10/4/48

Improvements and modifications

16/3/38	Removal of vacuum pump
20/5/45	Steam sanding
2/9/55	Sloping throatplate boiler
10/12/60	Fitting BR ATC equipment

Repairs

22/5/36-5/6/36	LS
8/3/37-2/4/37	LS
5/3/38-16/3/38	LS
25/1/39-18/2/39	HG
29/1/40-21/2/40	LS
13/12/40-16/1/41	LS
17/10/41-26/11/41	LS
11/6/42-30/7/42	HG
26/4/43-22/5/43	LS
28/10/43-7/12/43	HS
16/12/44-18/1/45	LS
5/3/46-6/4/46	HG
19/6/47-2/8/47	HS
29/3/48-10/4/48	LO
3/12/48-5/2/49	LI
14/2/49-15/2/49	NC(R)
12/3/49-26/3/49	NC
17/10/49-18/11/49	LI
22/6/50-13/7/50	LC
7/12/50-17/3/51	G
4/1/52-11/1/52	NC
8/1/53-31/1/53	HI
15/3/54-28/4/54	LI
26/7/55-2/9/55	G
23/10/56-17/11/56	LI
30/11/56-1/12/56	NC(EO)
11/6/57-28/6/57	LC(EO)
6/1/58-1/2/58	HI
8/9/58-13/9/58	LC(EO)
22/9/58-25/9/58	LC(EO)
1/11/58-13/11/58	LC(EO)
15/12/58-8/1/59	HI
16/2/59-14/3/59	LC(EO)
18/2/60-5/3/60	NC
29/10/60-10/12/60	G
26/4/61-6/5/61	LC
24/2/62-30/3/62	LI
19/4/62-21/4/62	NC

Boilers

New	9017
15/2/39	9028 from 5098
30/7/42	8666 from 5131 (domed)
6/4/46	8638 from 5032 (domed)
17/3/51	9011 from 5157
2/9/55	10372 (sloping throatplate)
10/12/60	13348 from 45462 (sloping throatplate)

Tenders

New	9181
15/3/38	9104
2/4/48	9060
9/4/48	9724 (welded)
14/7/50	9727 (welded)
31/1/53	10525 (welded)
2/9/55	10808 (part-welded)
1/2/58	10510 (welded)
31/3/59	10445 (welded)
1/3/62	10586 (part-welded)

Mileage/(weekdays out of service)

1935	42,794 (31)
1936	63,388 (60)
1937	55,767 (71)
1938	56,735 (65)
1939	60,417 (45)
1940	60,104 (56)
1941	52,195 (87)
1942	61,232 (57)
1943	54,136 (75)
1944	57,973 (53)
1945	46,622 (71)
1946	48,258 (63)
1947	47,202 (75)
1948	33,357 (120)
1949	40,573 (106)
1950	27,745 (90)
1951	33,860 (84)
1952	42,743 (44)
1953	41,406 (47)
1954	39,929 (86)
1955	42,151 (84)
1956	34,813 (79)
1957	48,581 (52)
1958	37,416 (122)
1959	38,808
1960	25,305
1961	35,448
1962	22,850

Mileage at 12/36: 106,182
Mileage at 31/12/50: 808,498

Sheds

Crewe	30/3/35
Perth	5/10/35
Inverness	25/6/49
Carstairs	22/10/49

Withdrawn w.e. 26/7/63

45087 at Kingmoor between 1951 when it received a domed boiler and September 1955 when it was converted to the sloping throatplate type. It was one of two engines to carry every configuration of boiler and topfeed. Here it is domeless with a St Rollox 'incorrect' topfeed cover, large 10in cab numbers and welded tender. 45087 was allocated to Carstairs from 1949 until withdrawn in 1963. Photograph P. Wilson.

45088

Built as 5088 at Vulcan Foundry 30/3/35
Renumbered 45088 w.e. 2/4/49

Improvements and modifications

23/2/38	Removal of vacuum pump
30/1/39	Steam sanding
18/10/60	Fitting Smith-Stone speedometer

Repairs

30/4/36-21/5/36	LS
10/4/37-26/4/37	LO
15/6/37-14/7/37	LO
11/10/37-2/11/37	LS
28/1/38-23/2/38	LO
4/1/39-30/1/39	HG
27/4/40-20/5/40	LS
31/8/41-2/10/41	LS
2/9/42-20/9/42	LO
23/2/43-16/3/43	HG
11/7/44-1/8/44	LS
3/5/46-25/5/46	LS
29/10/46-13/12/46	LO
1/8/47-9/10/47	HG
15/3/49-1/4/49	HI
24/1/51-22/2/51	HG
8/5/52-6/6/52	LI
1/9/53-23/9/53	LI
12/5/54-12/6/54	LC(EO)
25/4/55-10/6/55	HG
16/1/57-8/2/57	HI
24/5/58-17/6/58	LI
29/12/58-27/2/59	HG
10/8/59-16/9/59	HC(EO)
1/2/60-7/4/60	HC(EO)
12/9/60-18/10/60	LI
25/10/60-2/11/60	RC(Rect)EO
26/4/62-23/5/62	HI

Boilers

New	9018
30/1/39	8920 from 5140
16/3/43	8948 from 5159
9/10/47	8669 from 5078 (domed)
22/2/51	8928 from 5062
10/6/55	8642 from 45079 (domed)
27/2/59	8995 from 45205

Tenders

New	9182
13/9/60	10464 (welded)

Mileage/(weekdays out of service)

1935	45,801(51)
1936	41,885 (125)
1937	37,772 (127)
1938	51,108 (71)
1939	50,501 (64)
1940	32,874 (58)
1941	33,273 (60)
1942	36,709 (54)
1943	38,617 (52)
1944	30,992 (54)
1945	28,286 (109)
1946	27,466 (107)
1947	35,477 (40)
1948	40,729 (78)
1949	36,125 (55)
1950	38,018 (69)
1951	41,679 (56)
1952	42,623 (48)
1953	41,210 (56)
1954	38,728 (66)
1955	36,374 (76)
1956	36,119 (87)
1957	43,744 (49)
1958	39,446 (69)
1959	46,081
1960	37,213

Mileage at 12/36 87,686
Mileage at 31/12/50: 605,633

Sheds

Crewe	13/4/35
Sheffield	19/10/35
Millhouses	10/4/37
Sheffield	25/9/37
Toton	2/3/40
Derby	4/7/42
Southport	2/9/44 (loan)
Southport	30/9/44
Derby	9/12/44 (loan)
Derby	18/1/45
Longsight	14/2/48 (loan)
Derby	21/2/48
Millhouses	29/5/48
Sheffield	15/1/49
Leicester	12/11/49
Nottingham	28/11/53
Saltley	21/11/59
Leicester	3/8/63
Derby	30/11/63

Stored
14/10/63-18/11/63

Withdrawn w.e. 12/9/64

Nottingham's 45088 on 22 August 1959 waiting to begin a Heavy Casual repair which ended on 16 September. This was its second Heavy overhaul that year, suggesting something had gone badly awry. It had reverted to a domeless boiler at a Heavy General completed on 27 February after its second spell with a domed one. Other than its first six months in service and a brief loan spell at Southport during the war, 45088 spent its whole life on the Midland Division.

45089

Built as 5089 at Vulcan Foundry 6/4/35
Renumbered 45089 w.e. 6/10/48

Improvements and modifications

20/3/38	BTH speed indicator
26/6/39	Removal of vacuum pump
4/10/39	Steam sanding
19/11/57	Modernisation
22/4/60	Fitting BR ATC equipment

Repairs

8/10/35-4/11/35	LO
12/6/36-1/7/36	LS
30/3/37-16/4/37	HS
21/10/37-19/11/37	HG
29/10/38-23/12/38	LS
10/3/39-22/3/39	LO
29/8/39-4/10/39	HS
22/8/40-11/9/40	LS
3/3/41-1/4/41	LO
7/5/42-10/6/42	LO
4/7/42-13/8/42	LO
13/5/43-10/6/43	LS
10/10/45-3/11/45	HS
18/6/46-1/7/46	LO
5/11/46-7/12/46	LS
17/9/48-13/10/48	HG
18/7/49-16/8/49	LC
7/12/49-18/1/50	LI
27/8/51-15/9/51	LI
8/11/51-2/1/52	LC
17/6/52-12/8/52	LC(EO)
1/4/53-16/4/53	LC
12/6/53-29/7/53	HG
4/9/54-14/10/54	HI
6/6/56-20/7/56	LI
1/10/57-19/11/57	HG
26/11/58-10/12/58	LC(EO)
28/2/60-22/4/60	LI

Boilers

New	9019
3/11/37	8684 from 5067 (domed)
4/10/39	8926 from 5146
10/6/43	8665 from 5139 (domed)
13/10/48	9041 from 5181
29/7/53	8685 from 45000 (domed)
19/11/57	8676 from 45046 (domed)

Tenders

New	9183
29/12/51	9434
11/9/54	9884 (welded)

Mileage/(weekdays out of service)

1935	39,184 (64)
1936	62,025 (55)
1937	48,311 (90)
1938	54,673 (111)
1939	44,908 (108)
1940	43,905 (61)
1941	39,402 (66)
1942	33,485 (104)
1943	32,046 (54)
1944	22,762 (81)
1945	19,767 (53)
1946	34,210 (67)
1947	36,177 (49)
1948	29,315 (62)
1949	31,651 (76)
1950	33,683 (65)
1951	24,886 (92)
1952	40,287 (81)
1953	37,314 (90)
1954	41,522 (62)
1955	39,946 (54)
1956	35,025 (60)
1957	29,121 (72)
1958	46,313 (42)
1959	42,790
1960	38,007

Mileage at 12/36: 101,209
Mileage at 31/12/50: 605,504

Sheds

Crewe	13/4/35
Sheffield	19/10/35
Millhouses	25/9/37
York	26/3/38
Millhouses	30/9/39
Leeds	5/7/41
Patricroft	26/9/42 (loan)
Patricroft	17/10/42
Crewe North	27/3/43
Willesden	28/5/49
Bletchley	27/9/57
Holyhead	5/7/58
Bletchley	4/10/58
Bescot	14/3/64
Banbury	2/10/65
Chester	10/9/66
Crewe South	29/4/67

Withdrawn w.e. 26/8/67

45089 on 13 August 1966 at its home shed of Banbury with painted 2D code in place of the cast plate. It stayed there for a year from September 1965 before moving on to Chester. The History Cards record three periods with a domeless boiler but not this final fitting. 45089 had a welded tender from 1954 onwards and AWS from April 1960.

45090

Built as 5090 at Vulcan Foundry 6/4/35
Renumbered 45090 w.e. 3/7/48

Improvements and modifications

6/3/39	Removal of vacuum pump
1/3/41	BTH speed indicator
12/7/47	Steam sanding
?	Fitting BR ATC equipment

Repairs

6/6/36-26/6/36	LS
1/1/38-31/1/38	HG
6/2/39-6/3/39	LS
4/2/41-1/3/41	HG
18/2/42-23/3/42	LS
13/5/42-13/6/42	LS
13/4/43-13/5/43	LS
17/11/43-9/12/43	HS
16/11/44-15/12/44	HG
7/1/46-28/1/46	LS
24/10/46-30/11/46	LS
12/6/48-2/7/48	HG
8/7/48-10/7/48	TRO
3/2/49-4/2/49	TRO
26/9/49-11/11/49	LI
17/8/50-13/9/50	LC
26/10/50-15/12/50	HI
28/12/51-1/2/52	LI
7/3/53-18/4/53	G
30/10/53-6/11/53	LC(EO)
23/11/53-25/11/53	NC
19/12/53-21/1/54	NC(EO)
5/8/54-10/9/54	HI
7/12/54-8/12/54	NC(EO)
18/1/55-5/2/55	LC(EO)
11/3/55-18/3/55	NC(EO)
11/10/55-18/11/55	HI
27/12/55-29/12/55	NC(EO)
23/2/56-8/3/56	NC(EO)
25/12/56-23/1/57	HI
31/7/57-16/8/57	LC
6/9/57-12/9/57	NC(EO)
11/11/57-13/11/57	NC(EO)
19/12/57-24/12/57	NC(EO)
15/3/58-7/6/58	G
25/3/60-23/4/60	HI
17/7/61-1/9/61	LC(EO)
19/12/62-1/2/63	G
18/5/64-12/6/64	LC(EO)

Boilers

New	9020
17/1/38	8822 from 5005 (domed)
1/3/41	8656 from 5206 (domed)
15/12/44	8659 from 5171 (domed)
2/7/48	8924 from 5168

Tenders

New	9184
13/10/42	9058
12/12/44	9070
30/6/48	9821 (welded)
?	9261 (welded)
23/1/57	10694 (part-welded)
7/6/58	9824 (welded)
22/11/65	9277 (welded)

Mileage/(weekdays out of service)

1935	45,795 (60)
1936	48,949 (88)
1937	39,859 (88)
1938	54,095 (68)
1939	35,000 (116)
1940	31,507 (84)
1941	43,490 (47)
1942	53,185 (81)
1943	43,665 (84)
1944	43,719 (68)
1945	51,012 (37)
1946	41,904 (85)
1947	47,409 (32)
1948	47,231 (51)
1949	38,478 (82)
1950	32,290 (114)

Mileage at 12/36: 94,744
Mileage at 31/12/50: 697,588

Sheds

Crewe	13/4/35
Sheffield	19/10/35
York	8/2/36
Millhouses	21/11/36
Patricroft	2/1/37 (loan)
Patricroft	16/1/37
Blackpool	26/6/37
Aintree	2/11/40
Agecroft	22/3/41
Inverness	30/8/41
Perth	27/2/60
Hamilton	25/9/61
Polmadie	29/10/62
Carstairs	28/4/64

Stored
13/3/39-3/4/39
17/4/39-8/5/39

Withdrawn 6/12/65

45090 at Perth on 20 September 1952 was an Inverness engine from 1941 to 1960. It has the St Rollox domeless 'style' of topfeed cover which it received in 1948 having previously had three domed boilers. Note the tablet exchange apparatus causing the large 10in cab numbers to be squeezed upwards instead of in line with BRITISH RAILWAYS on the tender. Like many of the ScR engines, the bufferbeam has the holes drilled for fitting a small snowplough.

45091

Built as 5091 at Vulcan Foundry 6/4/35
Renumbered 45091 w.e. 3/7/48

Improvements and modifications

1/7/39	BTH speed indicator
1/7/39	Removal of vacuum pump
?	Steam sanding
16/5/59	Fitting BR ATC equipment

Repairs

5/5/36-19/5/36	LS
3/3/37-22/3/37	HS
4/1/38-31/1/38	HG
1/6/39-1/7/39	HS
3/9/40-24/9/40	HG
23/5/42-20/6/42	LS
14/5/43-10/6/43	LS
31/10/44-15/11/44	HG
7/1/46-22/1/46	LO
26/1/46-23/2/46	LO
7/2/47-15/3/47	LS
29/5/48-3/7/48	LO
6/8/48-30/8/48	NC
24/3/49-3/5/49	HG
2/8/49-23/8/49	LC
11/8/50-28/8/50	LI
25/5/51-22/6/51	LC
26/4/52-21/6/52	HG
31/10/53-19/11/53	LI
18/10/54-10/11/54	LI
22/11/55-15/12/55	HI
13/3/56-20/4/56	LC(EO)
28/5/56-26/7/56	HC(EO)
18/3/57-10/4/57	LI
24/2/58-20/3/58	HI
13/4/59-16/5/59	LI
8/8/60-17/9/60	HI
1/8/62-30/8/62	HG

Boilers

New	9021
17/1/38	8675 from 5058 (domed)
24/9/40	8660 from 5188 (domed)
15/11/44	8998 from 5201
3/5/49	8968 from 5093
21/6/52	8948 from 45104
26/7/56	8939 from 45148
8/62	9045 from 45132

Tenders

New	9185
23/2/46	9512 (welded)

Mileage/(weekdays out of service)

1935	42,963 (26)
1936	60,388 (47)
1937	52,817 (70)
1938	51,148 (84)
1939	55,058 (82)
1940	42,599 (56)
1941	30,843 (31)
1942	31,020 (55)
1943	33,659 (35)
1944	28,814 (50)
1945	35,182 (50)
1946	38,401 (60)
1947	37,965 (71)
1948	31,157 (113)
1949	32,643 (95)
1950	44,395 (46)
1951	42,250 (80)
1952	44,480 (74)
1953	36,406 (74)
1954	38,712 (49)
1955	39,115 (65)
1956	32,466 (135)
1957	39,261 (49)
1958	41,231 (48)
1959	39,771
1960	32,853

Mileage at 12/36: 103,351
Mileage at 31/12/50: 649,052

Sheds

Crewe	13/4/35
Willesden	2/5/36
Shrewsbury	25/9/37
Swansea	5/11/38
Crewe	27/4/40
Shrewsbury	15/6/40
Bescot	5/4/41
Bushbury	26/7/41
Crewe North	19/9/42
Carnforth	23/10/42
Mold Junction	20/2/43
Edge Hill	8/5/43
Preston	11/5/46
Northampton	5/11/49
Edge Hill	19/11/60
Llandudno Jct	2/3/63
Crewe South	8/5/65
Springs Branch	24/7/65

Withdrawn w.e. 10/9/66

Northampton allocated from 1949 to 1960 45091 is seen in the early 1950s with a typical train of mixed LMS coaches, most in carmine and cream. It had the domeless boiler and welded tender configuration from 1946 onwards. Photograph Colourrail.co.uk

45092

Built as 5092 at Vulcan Foundry 13/4/35
Renumbered 45092 w.e. 31/12/48

Improvements and modifications

26/6/39	Removal of vacuum pump
9/5/44	Steam sanding
23/10/59	Fitting BR ATC equipment

Repairs

11/10/35-28/10/35	LO
16/5/36-5/6/36	LS
15/9/36-29/9/36	LO
27/3/37-23/4/37	HS
14/3/38-19/5/38	HG
20/6/39-15/7/39	LS
31/8/40-21/9/40	HG
23/9/41-30/10/41	HS
18/11/42-19/12/42	LS
16/6/43-30/6/43	LO
15/4/44-9/5/44	HG
21/2/46-20/3/46	LS
11/11/46-21/12/46	LO
22/9/47-19/12/47	LS
22/11/48-28/12/48	HG
24/7/50-23/8/50	LI
31/12/51-1/2/52	HG
2/2/52-5/2/52	NC(Rect)
30/7/53-28/8/53	LI
10/6/55-1/7/55	HG
28/9/57-26/10/57	LI
28/10/57-15/11/57	NC(Rect)EO
18/9/59-23/10/59	LI
21/11/61-6/1/62	HG
18/12/63-18/1/64	HI

Boilers

New	9022
3/5/38	8653 from 5036 (domed)
21/9/40	8683 from 5066 (domed)
9/5/44	8671 from 5211 (domed)
28/12/48	8927 from 5045
1/2/52	9036 from 45181
1/7/55	8908 from 45069
6/1/62	9006

Tenders

New	9186

Mileage/(weekdays out of service)

1935	41,928 (47)
1936	52,262 (107)
1937	36,080 (132)
1938	52,572 (142)
1939	41,993 (94)
1940	47,707 (68)
1941	45,107 (90)
1942	47,296 (72)
1943	53,029 (35)
1944	39,300 (66)
1945	29,034 (85)
1946	41,316 (100)
1947	39,266 (98)
1948	38,887 (75)
1949	43,136 (52)
1950	37,629 (69)
1951	33,931 (40)
1952	50,880 (62)
1953	42,649 (75)
1954	34,755 (46)
1955	40,879 (65)
1956	42,522 (37)
1957	34,069 (63)
1958	39,939 (36)
1959	27,082
1960	36,964

Mileage at 12/36: 94,190
Mileage at 31/12/50: 686,542

Sheds

Crewe	13/4/35
Sheffield	19/10/35
York	21/11/36
Millhouses	25/9/37
Trafford Park	7/1/39
Leeds	2/12/39
Crewe North	1/1/48 (loan)
Crewe North	5/3/49
Rugby	29/4/50
Willesden	9/12/50
Carnforth	9/2/52
Holyhead	14/6/58
Springs Branch	27/9/58
Crewe South	2/4/60 (loan)
Springs Branch	25/6/60
Carlisle Upperby	16/6/62
Carnforth	22/6/63

Withdrawn w.e. 16/12/67

45092 pictured in August 1964 at Carnforth; it was allocated there from June 1963 until withdrawn at the end of 1967. It had a domeless boiler from 1948 onwards, AWS was fitted in October 1959 and the tender was its original riveted one from 1935. Photograph N.E. Preedy.

45093

Built as 5093 at Vulcan Foundry 13/4/35
Renumbered 45093 w.e. 29/1/49

Improvements and modifications

12/6/38	BTH speed indicator
25/8/39	Removal of vacuum pump
16/2/44	Steam sanding
25/2/59	Fitting BR ATC equipment

Repairs

20/11/35-4/12/35	LO
26/10/36-12/11/36	LS
13/4/37-27/4/37	LO
16/11/37-15/12/37	HG
22/1/38-16/2/38	HO
11/8/39-25/8/39	LS
3/5/40-10/6/40	LO
6/1/41-15/2/41	HG
14/1/42-21/2/42	HS
8/1/43-13/2/43	LS
3/12/43-22/12/43	LO
18/1/44-16/2/44	HG
27/11/44-21/12/44	LO
4/7/45-31/8/45	LS
29/3/47-23/4/47	LS
8/1/49-25/1/49	HG
2/1/50-1/2/50	HO
9/8/50-7/9/50	HI
25/7/52-23/8/52	LI
21/12/53-27/1/54	HG
2/1/56-25/1/56	HI
19/11/57-18/11/57	HI
23/8/58-26/9/58	LC(EO)
19/2/59-25/2/59	NC(EO)
17/3/59-1/5/59	LC(EO)
19/5/59-25/5/59	LC
4/6/59-18/6/59	NC(Rect)EO
2/5/60-10/6/60	HG
1/2/62-27/2/62	LI
19/2/63-15/3/63	HC
27/8/63-21/9/63	LI

Boilers

New	9023
29/11/37	8655 from 5038 (domed)
10/2/38	8922 from 5142
15/2/41	8675 from 5091 (domed)
16/2/44	8968 from 5146
25/1/49	8983 from 5038
1/2/50	8995 from 5005
27/1/54	9056 from 45219
10/6/60	8955 from 45041

Tenders

New	9187
13/2/43	9251 (welded)
2/9/63	10569 (welded)

Mileage/(weekdays out of service)

1935	39,565 (39)
1936	55,225 (47)
1937	31,423 (144)
1938	54,288 (113)
1939	45,471 (111)
1940	42,464 (85)
1941	49,601 (50)
1942	52,264 (64)
1943	40,117 (85)
1944	36,416 (106)
1945	37,912 (97)
1946	32,223 (90)
1947	36,018 (57)
1948	27,479 (49)
1949	36,519 (46)
1950	37,061 (75)
1951	39,254 (39)
1952	35,400 (62)
1953	39,912 (51)
1954	43,556 (46)
1955	38,986 (53)
1956	40,044 (49)
1957	36,362 (66)
1958	41,544 (54)
1959	35,698
1960	39,124

Mileage at 12/36: 94,790
Mileage at 31/12/50: 654,046

Sheds

Crewe	13/4/35
Bangor	6/7/35
Gloucester	19/10/35
Trafford Park	11/9/37
Leeds	3/9/38
Crewe North	7/6/47 (loan)
Crewe North	28/6/47
Willesden	26/7/47
Crewe North	2/8/47
Crewe South	11/10/47
Holyhead	12/6/54
Crewe South	30/10/54
Stoke	14/6/58
Crewe North	20/9/58
Crewe South	14/9/63

Withdrawn w.e. 6/11/65

45093 climbing Shap on 3 April 1956 with a relatively short freight which hardly warrants the banking assistance. It was shedded at Crewe South from 1954 to 1958, was domeless from 1941 onwards and the welded tender was fitted in 1943.

45094

Built as 5094 at Vulcan Foundry 13/4/35
Renumbered 45094 w.e. 2/7/49

Improvements and modifications

2/9/39	BTH speed indicator
2/9/39	Removal of vacuum pump
31/5/45	Steam sanding
28/7/56	Modernisation
16/7/60	Fitting BR ATC equipment

Repairs

12/8/36-7/9/36	LS
27/4/37-10/5/37	LO
11/10/37-22/11/37	HG
14/8/39-2/9/39	LS
5/7/41-25/7/41	HG
30/10/43-13/11/43	HS
16/5/45-31/5/45	HG
15/4/46-4/5/46	LO
29/11/47-8/1/48	LS
14/5/49-2/7/49	HG
12/8/50-20/9/50	HI
20/4/52-15/5/52	HI
22/10/52-2/12/52	HG
11/9/53-30/9/53	LC(EO)
21/3/55-14/4/55	HI
2/6/56-28/7/56	HG
3/12/57-1/1/58	HI
15/6/60-28/6/60	NC(EO)
2/11/60-3/12/60	HI

Boilers

New	9024
5/11/37	8638 from 5021 (domed)
25/7/41	9038 from 5138
31/5/45	8830 from 5072
2/7/49	9018 from 5042
2/12/52	8927 from 45092
28/7/56	8909 from 45141

Tenders

New	9188

Mileage/(weekdays out of service)

1935	44,807 (34)
1936	56,165 (110)
1937	35,187 (78)
1938	41,661 (36)
1939	36,754 (37)
1940	31,303 (36)
1941	27,746 (61)
1942	29,220 (28)
1943	33,114 (56)
1944	40,536 (32)
1945	24,040 (66)
1946	41,013 (52)
1947	23,840 (56)
1948	36,528 (47)
1949	32,823 (63)
1950	32,037 (62)
1951	37,408 (34)
1952	34,052 (89)
1953	35,596 (36)
1954	42,799 (28)
1955	38,761 (64)
1956	39,798 (75)
1957	39,862 (54)
1958	42,000 (33)
1959	38,458
1960	27,013

Mileage at 12/36: 100,972
Mileage at 31/12/50: 566,774

Sheds

Crewe	13/4/35
Bangor	6/7/35
Bristol	19/10/35
Preston	2/1/37 (loan)
Preston	16/1/37
Springs Branch	19/6/37
Crewe	13/4/40
Carlisle W	8/4/44
Bank Hall	19/9/44 (loan)
Bank Hall	30/9/44
Carlisle W	9/12/44 (loan)
Carlisle W	13/1/45
Edge Hill	15/9/45
Longsight	22/9/45
Edge Hill	5/1/46 (loan)
Crewe South	8/5/48
Aston	3/6/48
Edge Hill	21/10/61

Withdrawn w.e. 25/2/67

With a train full of Midlands holidaymakers 45094 passes through Holywell Junction on 4 September 1954. Note the LNWR seat with name on back and LMS 'hawkeye' station sign and the ever-present Palethorpes advert. 45094 was at 3D Aston from 1948 to 1961, carried domeless boilers from 1941 and still had its original riveted tender. Photograph Colourrail.co.uk

45095

Built as 5095 at Vulcan Foundry 13/4/35
Renumbered 45095 w.e. 31/7/48

Improvements and modifications

25/5/38	Removal of vacuum pump
26/8/42	Steam sanding
17/4/59	Fitting BR ATC equipment

Repairs

16/4/35-16/5/35	LO
28/9/35-18/10/35	LO
23/6/36-20/7/36	LS
7/4/37-28/5/37	HS
17/3/38-25/5/38	HG
5/10/39-4/11/39	LS
3/3/41-20/3/41	HS
23/7/42-26/8/42	HG
22/5/44-7/6/44	LS
11/3/46-3/4/46	HS
10/1/47-29/1/47	LO
5/3/48-2/4/48	LS
11/6/48-29/7/48	LO
16/2/49-23/3/49	HC
6/2/50-23/3/50	HG
28/8/51-29/9/51	HI
22/9/52-23/10/53	HG
16/4/54-21/5/54	HI
1/10/54-13/10/54	LC(EO)
8/6/56-29/6/56	HG
17/3/59-17/4/59	HI
9/6/59-25/6/59	LC(EO)
30/11/59-30/1/60	LI(EO)
11/2/61-28/3/61	LC

Boilers

New	9025
11/5/38	8646 from 5039 (domed)
26/8/42	9046 from 5008
3/4/46	8672 from 5013 (domed)
23/3/50	8910 from 5218
23/10/52	8967 from 45110
29/6/56	8963 from 45128

Tenders

New	9189

Mileage/(weekdays out of service)

1935	36,176 (78)
1936	53,964 (118)
1937	32,245 (138)
1938	37,223 (82)
1939	34,075 (80)
1940	35,692 (28)
1941	32,311 (42)
1942	25,423 (71)
1943	34,615 (27)
1944	25,600 (67)
1945	25,080 (61)
1946	28,838 (54)
1947	25,364 (79)
1948	32,579 (91)
1949	30,549 (58)
1950	41,048 (66)
1951	36,022 (79)
1952	33,516 (108)
1953	36,120 (47)
1954	34,796 (66)
1955	33,777 (45)
1956	33,049 (48)
1957	35,286 (26)
1958	28,657 (40)
1959	31,205
1960	35,642

Mileage at 12/36: 90,140
Mileage at 31/12/50: 530,782

Sheds

Bristol	13/4/35
Springs Branch	7/8/37
Warrington	13/11/37
Llandudno Jct	28/5/49
Chester	26/8/50 (loan)
Chester	18/11/50
Holyhead	7/7/51
Chester	15/9/51
Mold Jct	24/5/52
Willesden	8/11/52 (loan)
Mold Jct	29/11/52
Patricroft	27/6/53
Polmadie	16/3/63
Patricroft	22/6/63
Agecroft	9/11/63
Carnforth	9/5/64

Withdrawn w.e. 3/8/68

Central Division 45095 seen here in the early 1950s was always domeless and paired with the original riveted tender. It moved to Carnforth from Agecroft in May 1964 and was withdrawn from there at the end of BR steam in August 1968. Photograph www.rail-online.co.uk

45096

Built as 5096 at Vulcan Foundry 20/4/35
Renumbered 45096 w.e. 3/4/48

Improvements and modifications

3/5/38	Removal of vacuum pump
?	Steam sanding
2/5/59	Fitting BR ATC equipment

Repairs

23/4/35-21/5/35	Cost borne by contractors
28/1/36-13/2/36	LS
24/2/37-12/3/37	HS
1/3/38-3/5/38	HG
27/10/39-14/11/39	LS
5/8/40-27/8/40	LO
19/1/42-21/2/42	HG
14/12/42-7/1/43	LO
9/9/43-1/10/43	LS
22/4/44-25/5/44	LS
7/2/45-24/2/45	LO
26/3/45-21/4/45	LO
28/3/46-18/4/46	HG
23/4/47-27/5/47	LS
27/2/48-1/4/48	HS
24/11/48-24/12/48	LO
1/4/49-10/5/49	HG
9/12/50-26/1/51	LI
5/6/51-2/8/51	LC
5/11/51-18/12/51	LC(EO)
24/10/52-21/11/52	HG
16/3/54-6/4/54	HI
16/7/55-13/8/55	HI
29/8/56-29/9/56	HG
2/11/56-21/11/56	NC(EO)
26/4/57-17/5/57	LC(EO)
29/5/58-26/6/58	LI
20/4/59-2/5/59	NC(EO)
19/5/59-3/6/59	LC
16/9/60-14/10/60	LI

Boilers

New	9023
14/4/38	9057 from 5073
21/2/42	8947 from 5753
18/4/46	8984 from 5184
10/5/49	8919 from 5017
21/11/52	8832 from 45132
29/9/56	8927 from 45094

Tenders

New	9190
8/2/45	9027
26/5/47	9579 (welded)

Mileage/(weekdays out of service)

1935	42,481 (67)
1936	62,877 (62)
1937	47,768 (73)
1938	38,524 (136)
1939	40,845 (88)
1940	35,237 (78)
1941	38,161 (65)
1942	38,830 (56)
1943	54,030 (55)
1944	53,454 (57)
1945	38,644 (98)
1946	48,718 (76)
1947	53,469 (64)
1948	36,568 (120)
1949	43,131 (64)
1950	33,611 (78)
1951	33,918 (133)
1952	42,262 (76)
1953	52,329 (53)
1954	42,966 (55)
1955	36,079 (84)
1956	35,877 (90)
1957	46,656 (64)
1958	46,651 (55)
1959	36,536
1960	24,784

Mileage at 12/36: 105,358
Mileage at 31/12/50: 706,348

Sheds

Bristol	20/4/35
Patricroft	2/1/37
Blackpool	26/6/37
Carlisle N	31/10/42 (loan)
Carlisle N	28/11/42
Crewe North	28/5/49 (loan)
Crewe North	25/6/49
Carlisle Canal	1/10/49
Preston	2/6/51
Patricroft	18/4/59
Agecroft	26/10/63
Trafford Park	22/10/66
Rose Grove	9/3/68

Stored
31/10/38-20/1/39
19/9/66-26/2/68

Withdrawn w.e. 3/8/68

45096 from Patricroft at Carlisle on 18 October 1960. It was always domeless, had a welded tender from 1947 and was fitted with AWS in May 1959. Photograph D. Forsyth, Colourrail.co.uk

45097

Built as 5097 at Vulcan Foundry 27/4/35
Renumbered 45097 w.e. 11/12/48

Improvements and modifications

8/3/37	Sloping throatplate boiler
?	Removal of vacuum pump
7/9/40	BTH speed indicator
?	Steam sanding
14/3/55	Modification
26/3/59	Fitting BR ATC equipment

Repairs

13/11/35-18/2/35	LO
15/4/36-15/5/36	LS
8/2/37- 23/3/37	HG
19/11/38 14/12/38	LS
20/9/39-2/10/39	LO
17/10/40-8/11/40	HG
11/3/42-16/4/42	HS
15/7/43-7/8/43	HS
11/5/44-26/5/44	LO
28/4/45-18/5/45	LS
31/12/46-24/1/47	HG
18/11/48-10/12/48	LS
14/8/50-1/9/50	HI
23/11/51-4/1/52	HG
2/10/53-31/10/53	LI
4/2/55-14/3/55	HG
8/3/57-27/3/57	LI
19/2/59-26/3/59	HG

Boilers

New	9027
8/3/37	9741 New (sloping throatplate)
8/11/40	9514 from 5394 (sloping throatplate)
7/8/43	9492 from 5384 (sloping throatplate)
24/1/47	9379 from 5272 (sloping throatplate)
4/1/52	9517 from 45279 (sloping throatplate)
14/3/55	11922 from 45300 (sloping throatplate)
26/3/59	9397 from 45398 (sloping throatplate)

Tenders

New	9191
8/10/46	9506 (welded)

Mileage/(weekdays out of service)

1935	40,790 (61)
1936	55,487 (83)
1937	35,069 (65)
1938	32,388 (78)
1939	36,915 (37)
1940	29,839 (53)
1941	28,686 (59)
1942	27,508 (61)
1943	34,024 (44)
1944	38,969 (47)
1945	33,440 (46)
1946	30,351 (41)
1947	31,534 (65)
1948	32,403 (67)
1949	39,088 (52)
1950	29,413 (55)
1951	30,496 (60)
1952	48,196 (29)
1953	33,911 (45)
1954	40,817 (52)
1955	41,210 (77)
1956	56,922 (42)
1957	45,565 (50)
1958	37,414 (44)
1959	41,558
1960	42,140

Mileage at 12/36: 96,277
Mileage at 31.12.50: 555,827

Sheds

Bristol	27/4/35
Crewe North	20/12/36
Carlisle W	8/4/44
Edge Hill	15/9/45
Crewe South	29/9/45
Northampton	10/1/48 (loan)
Crewe South	6/3/48
Willesden	18/12/48
Carnforth	22/10/55
Crewe South	2/4/60
Carnforth	25/6/60
Carlisle Kingmoor	10/11/62

Withdrawn w.e. 18/6/66

The fireman is on the top of the tender preparing the coal for the journey home, watched by his driver. 45097 pictured at Brighton in the early 1950s had been converted to sloping throatplate boiler in March 1937. The class was frequently seen on the south coast in the 1950s with excursion trains from the north. 45097 was allocated to 1A Willesden from 1948 until late-1955, and was paired with a welded tender from 1946. Photograph www.rail-online.co.uk

45098

Built as 5098 at Vulcan Foundry 25/4/35
Renumbered 45098 w.e. 21/8/48

Improvements and modifications

12/12/38	Steam sanding
12/12/38	Removal of vacuum pump
21/1/61	Fitting BR ATC equipment

Repairs

9/6/36-2/7/36	LS
6/9/37-7/10/37	LS
29/3/38-6/4/38	LO
2/11/38-12/12/38	HG
22/4/40-10/5/40	HS
26/11/41-26/12/41	LS
28/10/42-1/12/42	LS
4/9/43-2/10/43	HG
5/7/44-8/9/44	LO
4/5/45-7/5/45	LO
10/8/45-20/9/45	LS
30/7/46-24/8/46	HS
23/8/47-9/10/47	HG
7/2/48-19/2/48	LO
27/7/48-20/8/48	LO
29/1/49-3/3/49	LI
12/12/49-1/2/50	HI
25/10/50-14/11/50	LC
30/4/51-2/6/51	LI
13/11/51-16/11/51	LC(EO)
8/4/52-9/5/52	NC(EO)
8/11/52-10/1/53	HG
5/2/53-10/2/53	SD
9/1/54-13/2/54	LI
26/2/55-8/4/55	HI
23/4/56-29/5/56	HI
22/11/56-23/11/56	NC(EO)
15/2/57-20/3/57	LC(EO)
5/9/57-5/10/57	G
4/8/58-21/8/58	LI
15/9/59-21/10/59	LI
30/10/59-2/11/59	NC(EO)
5/1/60-8/1/60	NC(EO)
19/12/60-21/1/61	LI

Boilers

New	9028
12/12/38	8679 from 5062 (domed)
2/10/43	9003 from 5017
1/11/47	8945 from 5119
10/1/53	9053 from 45112
5/10/57	8824 from 45152

Tenders

New	9192
25/5/43	9218
6/2/45	9063
20/9/45	9298 (welded)
10/8/48	9823 (welded)
24/8/48	9298 (welded)
6/1/53	10682 (part-welded)
18/10/62	10698 (part-welded)

Mileage/(weekdays out of service)

1935	36,721 (37)
1936	41,883 (88)
1937	38,561 (104)
1938	45,155 (95)
1939	46,412 (68)
1940	35,402 (55)
1941	32,418 (82)
1942	60,597 (55)
1943	66,518 (39)
1944	46,523 (94)
1945	53,985 (71)
1946	56,680 (49)
1947	46,401 (65)
1948	53,025 (67)
1949	49,576 (77)
1950	32,086 (114)
1951	41,773 (65)
1952	32,172 (105)
1953	47,879 (43)
1954	41,881 (58)
1955	36,199 (75)
1956	35,988 (80)
1957	25,107 (101)
1958	45,558 (40)
1959	37,807
1960	38,464
1961	30,449
1962	17,334

Mileage at 12/36: 78,604
Mileage at 31/12/50: 741.943

Sheds

Newton Heath	27/4/35
Agecroft	29/8/36
Inverness	30/8/41
Polmadie	8/3/60

Stored
24/4/36-22/5/36
1/10/62-29/12/62

Withdrawn w.e. 29/12/62

45098 was shedded at Inverness from 1941 to 1960 and is seen there in June 1959. It has a St Rollox cast 1946 style smokebox numberplate and has the supports for a snowplough still in place below the bufferbeam - perhaps they were expecting snow early in Scotland that year! 45098 has a part-welded tender and domeless boiler with blanking plates on the firebox showing it was one of the three original 21 element boilers which did not have the domed covers.

45099

Built as 5099 at Vulcan Foundry 26/4/35
Renumbered 45099 w.e. 4/2/50

Improvements and modifications

26/10/38	Steam sanding
26/10/38	Removal of vacuum pump
9/4/60	Fitting BR ATC equipment

Repairs

10/9/36-8/10/36	LS
25/9/37-27/10/37	LS
27/8/38-26/10/38	HG
1/3/40-15/3/40	LS
11/2/41-14/3/41	HS
8/8/42-22/8/42	HG
7/2/44-25/2/44	LS
6/5/45-16/6/45	LS
18/6/46-6/7/46	HS
13/1/48-8/3/48	HG
6/1/50-4/2/50	LI
11/5/50-7/6/50	HC
4/5/51-2/6/51	HI
15/10/51-18/10/51	NC
1/5/52-6/5/52	NC
13/2/53-26/3/53	HI
22/9/54-29/10/54	G
17/11/54-25/11/54	LC(BO)
7/6/56-4/7/56	HI
24/7/56-2/8/56	NC(EO)
15/9/58-3/10/58	HI
20/2/60-9/4/60	G
26/10/60-25/11/60	HC(EO)
4/11/61-16/12/61	HI

Boilers

New	9029
26/10/38	8651 from 5034 (domed)
22/8/42	9008 from 5199
8/3/48	9013 from 5222
7/6/50	8923 from 5224
29/10/54	8991 from 45179
9/4/60	8648 from 45007 (domed)

Tenders

New	9193
27/10/54	9845 (welded)
4/7/56	10811 (part-welded)

Mileage/(weekdays out of service)

1935	35,266 (31)
1936	44,614 (76)
1937	38,378 (100)
1938	36,184 (125)
1939	49,312 (63)
1940	33,653 (67)
1941	28,816 (61)
1942	30,883 (44)
1943	39,331 (20)
1944	38,351 (46)
1945	46,981 (47)
1946	43,643 (52)
1947	22,966 (55)
1948	29,771 (83)
1949	28,904 (42)
1950	25,332 (68)
1951	38,148 (54)
1952	48,761 (74)
1953	43,684 (72)
1954	35,656 (78)
1955	49,770 (40)
1956	41,315 (91)
1957	50,071 (47)
1958	40,260 (87)
1959	43,556
1960	32,842
1961	28,499
1962	37,567

Mileage at 12/36: 79,880
Mileage at 31/12/50: 572,385

Sheds

Newton Heath	27/4/35
Agecroft	23/5/36
Newton Heath	27/5/44
Accrington	21/4/45
Southport	14/12/45 (loan)
Accrington	2/2/46
Newton Heath	6/7/46
Low Moor	12/10/46
Huddersfield	26/10/46
Fleetwood	15/5/48
Perth	8/9/51 (loan)
Motherwell	10/11/51

Withdrawn w.e. 16/9/63

45099 at Motherwell on 28 June 1952. It was allocated there from 1951 to withdrawal in September 1963, having previously been a Central Division engine for almost 20 years. It has a 21 element domeless boiler and its original riveted tender which it kept until 1954.

45100

Built as 5100 at Vulcan Foundry 1/5/35
Renumbered 45100 w.e. 29/5/48

Improvements and modifications

18/5/38	Removal of vacuum pump
12/7/47	Steam sanding

Repairs

25/3/36-16/4/36	LS
1/4/38-18/5/38	HG
6/9/39-9/10/39	LS
30/7/40-29/8/40	HG
22/4/42-6/6/42	HS
5/10/43-30/10/43	LS
6/12/44-5/1/45	HG
7/9/45-6/10/45	LS
19/9/46-18/10/46	HS
29/4/48-29/5/48	LS
24/5/49-2/7/49	G
10/3/50-14/4/50	LC
16/11/50-12/12/50	LI
8/9/52-25/10/52	HI
4/2/53-28/2/53	LC
13/3/54-24/4/54	G
17/5/54-21/5/54	LC(BO)
31/12/55-27/1/56	HI
18/5/56-30/6/56	LC(EO)
31/12/56-11/1/57	LC(EO)
13/3/57-6/4/57	HI
10/2/58-14/3/58	G
10/6/58-27/6/58	LC(EO)
6/9/58	LC(EO)
8/8/59-4/9/59	HI
15/5/60-3/6/60	LC(EO)
7/11/60-9/12/60	HI

Boilers

New	9030
26/4/38	9026 from 5096
7/9/40	9000 from 5220
5/1/45	8982 from 5125
2/7/49	8936 from 45011
24/4/54	8984 from 45081
10/2/58	8658 from 45174 (domed)

Tenders

New	9194
27/4/44	9720 (welded)
28/12/44	9164
8/10/45	9530 (welded)
2/4/47	9261 (welded)
13/2/48	9077
9/3/48	9261 (welded)
13/12/50	9511 (welded)
27/1/56	9097
14/3/58	9185

Mileage/(weekdays out of service)

1935	34,598 (38)
1936	48,238 (70)
1937	39,655 (87)
1938	44,295 (104)
1939	40,446 (83)
1940	33,874 (69)
1941	31,980 (44)
1942	35,651 (62)
1943	51,948 (40)
1944	53,184 (51)
1945	49,232 (79)
1946	49,053 (75)
1947	52,136 (50)
1948	33,375 (71)
1949	39,235 (75)
1950	37,526 (105)
1951	60,864 (33)
1952	43,194 (90)
1953	47,653 (65)
1954	46,938 (82)
1955	39,199 (67)
1956	43,399 (90)
1957	49,823 (72)
1958	40,812 (83)
1959	42,777
1960	32,777

Mileage at 12/36: 82,836
Mileage at 31/12/50: 674,426

Sheds

Farnley Jct	4/5/35
Newton Heath	17/8/35
Agecroft	23/5/36
Newton Heath	21/3/42
Carlisle Kingmoor	22/11/42
Carlisle Canal	18/8/62
Carlisle Kingmoor	3/11/62

Withdrawn w.e. 28/9/63

5100 on 29 August 1935 at Symington with a Glasgow-Manchester train – note the Caledonian Railway pattern route indicator. It had been transferred to Newton Heath from Farnley Junction two weeks before.

45101

Built as 5101 at Vulcan Foundry 3/5/35
Renumbered 45101 w.e. 18/3/50

Improvements and modifications

?	Steam sanding
?	Removal of vacuum pump
18/1/58	Modification
14/12/61	Fitting BR ATC equipment

Repairs

15/9/36-7/10/36	LS
17/3/37-23/4/37	LO
19/10/37-26/10/37	LO
18/12/37-7/1/38	LS
26/11/38-23/12/38	HG
18/5/40-6/6/40	LS
2/7/42-31/7/42	HG
28/4/44-27/5/44	LS
17/10/45-17/11/45	LS
3/12/47-5/2/48	HG
18/2/50-15/3/50	HI
13/10/50-30/10/50	NC
12/5/52-4/7/52	HG
5/4/54-1/5/54	LI
14/12/55-19/1/56	LI
25/11/57-18/1/58	HG
21/5/58-25/6/58	NC(EO)
13/11/59-2/1/60	LC(EO)
27/1/61-13/3/61	LI
23/11/61-14/12/61	NC
8/12/64-9/1/65	HI

Boilers

New	9030
23/12/38	9029 from 5099
31/7/42	8943 from 5161
5/2/48	8649 from 5104 (domed)
4/7/52	8989 from 5017
18/1/58	9023 from 5015
9/1/65	8925

Tenders

New	9195

Mileage/(weekdays out of service)

1935	35,473 (24)
1936	44,599 (57)
1937	42,232 (86)
1938	44,016 (93)
1939	44,392 (37)
1940	31,731 (40)
1941	25,158 (76)
1942	30,541 (73)
1943	33,741 (18)
1944	24,795 (74)
1945	19,707 (53)
1946	29,172 (43)
1947	21,188 (70)
1948	39,149 (63)
1949	29,904 (71)
1950	30,482 (69)
1951	27,859 (47)
1952	31,571 (89)
1953	29,118 (65)
1954	26,831 (77)
1955	26,022 (77)
1956	43,463 (45)
1957	26,656 (96)
1958	31,919 (66)
1959	29,552
1960	40,405

Mileage at 12/36: 80,072
Mileage at 31/12/50: 526,280

Sheds

Farnley Jct	4/5/35
Newton Heath	17/8/35
Agecroft	29/6/40
Newton Heath	21/3/42
Wakefield	6/3/43
Carlisle Kingmoor	12/5/45 (loan)
Accrington	19/5/45
Wakefield	8/10/49
Fleetwood	4/2/56
Wakefield	16/6/56
Newton Heath	8/9/56

Withdrawn w.e. 16/3/68

45101, under the electric wires at Sheffield Victoria, was shedded at 25A Wakefield from October 1949 until February 1956. It received the domeless boiler in July 1952, and retained its original riveted tender until withdrawn in 1968. Photograph www.rail-online.co.uk

45102

Built as 5102 at Vulcan Foundry 10/5/35
Renumbered 45102 w.e. 8/5/48

Improvements and modifications

?	Steam sanding
?	Removal of vacuum pump
?	Fitting BR ATC equipment

Repairs

28/3/36-5/5/36	LS
5/3/37-19/3/37	LO
23/6/37-15/7/37	LS
17/10/38-29/11/38	HG
4/5/40-17/5/40	LS
6/11/41-22/11/41	HS
17/11/42-12/12/42	HG
15/5/44-27/5/44	LS
26/1/45-10/2/45	LO
14/6/45-13/7/45	LS
23/9/46-9/11/46	HS
23/7/47-15/8/47	LO
24/3/48-3/5/48	HG
5/12/49-4/1/50	LI
19/3/51-14/4/51	LC
7/1/52-8/2/52	LI
17/12/52-24/1/53	HG
26/3/53-18/4/53	LC(EO)
5/4/55-17/5/55	HI
9/8/56-1/9/56	LI
16/5/58-25/6/58	HG
8/2/60-13/4/60	HI
25/9/61-30/10/61	LI
4/12/62-2/1/63	HI
21/2/63-8/3/63	LC

Boilers

New	9032
29/11/38	8979 from 5199
12/12/42	8834 from 5154
3/5/48	8825 from 5077
24/1/53	8644 from 5033 (domed)
25/6/58	9035 from 5037

Tenders

New	9196

Mileage/(weekdays out of service)

1935	36,661 (16)
1936	42,725 (90)
1937	31,992 (82)
1938	33,682 (95)
1939	43,447 (57)
1940	34,382 (38)
1941	25,289 (79)
1942	31,962 (54)
1943	40,829 (22)
1944	37,241 (33)
1945	28,606 (83)
1946	19,312 (108)
1947	34,463 (46)
1948	38,870 (53)
1949	34,339 (61)
1950	32,334 (47)
1951	32,081 (52)
1952	31,508 (72)
1953	38,271 (64)
1954	33,070 (54)
1955	32,352 (73)
1956	36,995 (67)
1957	36,780 (32)
1958	33,880 (76)
1959	38,170
1960	34,942

Mileage at 12/36: 79,386
Mileage at 31/12/50: 546,134

Sheds

Low Moor	11/5/35
Newton Heath	17/8/35
Agecroft	29/6/40
Newton Heath	21/3/42
Blackpool	2/7/60
Burton	25/5/63

Stored
17/4/39-4/5/39

Withdrawn w.e. 30/1/65

45102 from Newton Heath at Shrewsbury in the late-1950s. It was domeless until January 1953 and from June 1958 and has its original riveted tender.

45103

Built as 5103 at Vulcan Foundry 9/5/35
Renumbered 45103 w.e. 12/2/49

Improvements and modifications

1/8/38	Removal of vacuum pump
20/4/39	Steam sanding
27/9/61	Fitting BR ATC equipment

Repairs

11/11/36-1/12/36	LS
12/3/37-2/4/37	LO
17/9/37-24/9/37	LO
22/10/37-11/11/37	LS
6/7/38-1/8/38	LO
9/3/39-20/4/39	HG
9/4/41-30/4/41	LS
7/11/42-19/12/42	HS
5/4/43-17/4/43	LO
13/12/43-3/1/44	HG
20/12/44-27/1/45	LS
22/1/46-2/2/46	LO
17/9/46-10/10/46	LS
16/9/47-29/10/47	HS
16/12/47-1/1/48	TRO
3/1/49-11/2/49	HG
1/12/50-4/1/51	LI
19/6/52-12/7/52	LI
24/4/53-23/5/53	HI
11/2/55-23/3/55	HG
4/5/57-6/6/57	HI
28/10/58-29/11/58	LI
31/3/60-14/5/60	HG
12/9/61-27/9/61	NC(EO)

Boilers

New	9033
20/4/39	8820 from 5008 (domed)
3/1/44	9040 from 5068
11/2/49	8663 from 5196 (domed)
23/3/55	8983 from 5223
14/5/60	8949 from 5202

Tenders

New	9197

Mileage/(weekdays out of service)

1935	33,230 (30)
1936	46,081 (68)
1937	44,138 (78)
1938	41,826 (91)
1939	37,495 (87)
1940	32,834 (47)
1941	35,473 (47)
1942	29,536 (79)
1943	36,700 (39)
1944	43,037 (31)
1945	32,470 (70)
1946	28,241 (89)
1947	30,060 (84)
1948	35,665 (43)
1949	32,932 (59)
1950	24,971 (69)
1951	33,257 (43)
1952	31,083 (55)
1953	34,418 (62)
1954	37,922 (43)
1955	35,341 (67)
1956	36,087 (72)
1957	39,035 (47)
1958	35,506 (64)
1959	35,340
1960	32,758

Mileage at 12/36: 79,311
Mileage at 31/12/50: 564,689

Sheds

Low Moor	11/5/35
Newton Heath	17/8/35
Agecroft	29/6/40
Newton Heath	17/5/41
Patricroft	2/7/60
Agecroft	12/11/60
Carlisle Canal	19/1/63
Carlisle Kingmoor	22/6/63
Newton Heath	13/7/63
Speke Jcn	5/10/63
Edge Hill	11/1/64

Stored

24/4/36-22/5/36
11/9/39-18/9/39

Withdrawn w.e. 10/10/64

45103 appears to have just been renumbered in this picture at Newton Heath. It was given its BR number during w.e. 12/2/49 when it was also newly fitted with a domed boiler. The riveted tender still has LMS insignia on it. 45103 was allocated to Newton Heath from 1941 to 1960 and was withdrawn in October 1964. Photograph Eric Blakey, www.transporttreasury.co.uk

45104

Built as 5104 at Vulcan Foundry 11/5/35
Renumbered 45104 w.e. 11/11/50

Improvements and modifications

29/6/39	BTH speed indicator
29/6/39	Steam sanding
?	Removal of vacuum pump
29/3/62	Fitting BR ATC equipment

Repairs

5/10/36-4/11/36	LS
12/3/37-24/3/37	LO
17/1/38-21/1/38	TRO
2/2/38-5/3/38	HS
7/9/38-10/9/38	LO
6/6/39-29/6/39	HG
29/3/41-12/4/41	LS
17/8/42-9/9/42	HS
7/1/43-23/1/43	LO
12/6/43-19/6/43	LO
2/10/43-30/10/43	HG
16/11/44-2/12/44	LS
29/7/46-6/9/46	HS
29/10/47-13/12/47	HG
3/1/49-28/1/49	LI
13/10/50-10/11/50	LI
12/2/52-26/3/52	HG
6/11/53-2/12/53	LI
2/9/55-24/9/55	HI
16/2/57-23/3/57	HG
17/12/58-22/1/59	HI
29/4/60-11/6/60	HI
15/6/61-16/8/61	LC(EO)
9/3/62-29/3/62	NC
19/12/62-21/1/63	HG
20/8/65-6/10/65	LI

Boilers

New	9034
29/6/39	8989 from 5209
30/10/43	8649 from 5078 (domed)
13/12/47	8948 from 5088
26/3/52	9031 from 5191
23/3/57	8970 from 5209
?	8985

Tenders

New	9198
6/9/46	9072

Mileage/(weekdays out of service)

1935	31,418 (27)
1936	46,198 (61)
1937	46,909 (55)
1938	39,023 (85)
1939	32,280 (54)
1940	35,771 (39)
1941	31,118 (65)
1942	36,297 (46)
1943	33,419 (75)
1944	37,953 (34)
1945	40,542 (23)
1946	28,278 (67)
1947	25,276 (90)
1948	45,320 (31)
1949	33,275 (74)
1950	31,399 (85)
1951	33,978 (45)
1952	35,459 (62)
1953	33,639 (55)
1954	39,488 (44)
1955	27,909 (59)
1956	43,435 (43)
1957	33,891 (60)
1958	36,359 (67)
1959	39,945
1960	33,260

Mileage at 12/36: 77,616
Mileage at 31/12/50: 574,476

Sheds

Newton Heath	11/5/35
Agecroft	29/6/40
Newton Heath	19/4/41
Low Moor	26/1/46 (loan)
Newton Heath	20/7/46
Agecroft	26/10/46
Newton Heath	10/6/50
Aintree	11/1/64
Newton Heath	27/6/64
Bury	14/11/64
Bolton	10/4/65

Stored
19/9/66-13/5/67

Withdrawn w.e. 29/6/68

45104 at Blackburn around 1967 has both a 9K shedplate and its depot name BOLTON painted on the bufferbeam - this was its final shed from April 1965 until withdrawn in June 1968. It was one of the last fitted with AWS, in April 1962. 45104 always had a riveted tender and was domeless from 1947 onwards. Photograph www.rail-online.co.uk

45105

Built as 5105 at Vulcan Foundry 15/5/35
Renumbered 45105 2/7/49

Improvements and modifications

?	Steam sanding
?	Removal of vacuum pump
1/11/40	BTH speed indicator
1/11/61	Fitting BR ATC equipment

Repairs

5/11/36-7/12/36	LS
13/3/37-7/4/37	LO
4/10/37-26/10/37	LS
21/1/39-13/2/39	HG
15/10/40-1/11/40	LS
10/1/42-7/2/42	LS
16/6/43-14/7/43	HG
20/12/44-12/1/45	LS
31/8/45-22/9/45	LO
11/9/46-1/11/46	LS
29/10/47-18/12/47	HG
13/6/49-29/6/49	HI
12/5/51-14/6/51	HG
19/2/52-21/3/52	LC(EO)
21/5/53-17/6/53	LI
3/5/54-21/5/54	HC(EO)
20/1/55-26/2/55	HG
14/3/57-15/3/57	Special Exam
15/3/57-6/4/57	HI
15/5/57-11/6/57	NC(EO)
21/10/58-19/11/58	HI
27/11/58-16/12/58	LC(EO)
30/10/59-12/12/59	LI
30/9/60-9/12/60	LC(EO)
26/9/61-1/11/61	HG

Boilers

New	9035
13/2/39	8919 from 5139
14/7/43	9035 from 5189
18/12/47	8908 from 5202
14/6/51	9006 from 45130
26/2/55	8931 from 45025
1/11/61	9055 from 45021

Tenders

New	9199

Mileage/(weekdays out of service)

1935	34,017 (32)
1936	41,333 (76)
1937	44,491 (83)
1938	44,502 (69)
1939	41,057 (65)
1940	35,240 (53)
1941	33,300 (57)
1942	31,009 (76)
1943	33,180 (65)
1944	36,890 (44)
1945	37,760 (39)
1946	28,828 (80)
1947	31,147 (78)
1948	32,503 (49)
1949	35,473 (61)
1950	35,845 (67)
1951	30,289 (71)
1952	29,138 (87)
1953	35,606 (61)
1954	37,187 (47)
1955	37,457 (80)
1956	36,565 (47)
1957	30,643 (82)
1958	27,826 (64)
1959	37,253
1960	32,168

Mileage at 12/36: 75,350
Mileage at 31/12/50: 576,575

Sheds

Newton Heath	18/5/35
Southport	28/1/61
Carlisle Canal	26/1/63
Carlisle Kingmoor	22/6/63

Withdrawn w.e. 29/10/66

5105 in typical post-war grime with high positioned 12in cab numbers on 14 September 1947 at Aintree. It was a Newton Heath engine from new until transferred to Southport in January 1961. It was always domeless and kept its original riveted tender throughout. Photograph T.C. Cole, www.transporttreasury.co.uk

45106

Built as 5106 at Vulcan Foundry 16/5/35
Renumbered 45106 w.e. 19/2/49

Improvements and modifications

3/1/39	Steam sanding
3/1/39	Removal of vacuum pump
16/11/56	Modification
7/6/60	Fitting BR ATC equipment

Repairs

2/10/36-27/10/36	LS
15/3/37-14/4/37	LO
23/6/37-24/7/37	LS
13/10/38-14/10/38	LO
3/12/38-3/1/39	HG
11/9/40-26/9/40	LS
30/3/42-6/5/42	HS
13/9/43-2/10/43	HG
29/12/43-17/1/44	LO
19/9/45-15/10/45	LS
26/2/47-27/3/47	LO
15/11/47-15/1/48	HG
25/1/49-14/2/49	HI
25/10/49-21/11/49	LC
21/3/50-18/4/50	LC
2/11/50-15/12/50	LI
15/4/52-13/6/52	HG
7/6/53-27/6/53	LC
15/8/54-29/9/54	LI
21/8/55-13/9/55	HI
24/9/56-16/11/56	HG
13/11/57-12/12/57	LO
4/2/58-8/3/58	LI
5/8/59-27/8/59	LC/EO
25/5/60-7/6/60	NC(EO)
6/2/61-20/3/61	HG

Boilers

New	9036
3/1/39	9042 from 5112
2/10/43	8681 from 5222 (domed)
15/1/48	8835 from 5203
13/6/52	8651 from 45199 (domed)
16/11/56	8913 from 45130
20/3/61	8661 from 45221 (domed)

Tenders

New	9200
18/12/57	9656 (welded)

Mileage/(weekdays out of service)

1935	35,500 (33)
1936	48,824 (47)
1937	38,683 (99)
1938	39,360 (97)
1939	45,531 (39)
1940	36,464 (43)
1941	35,878 (38)
1942	29,591 (99)
1943	26,620 (44)
1944	28,453 (86)
1945	33,337 (77)
1946	38,789 (42)
1947	16,643 (97)
1948	43,453 (56)
1949	41,023 (67)
1950	38,972 (79)
1951	44,502 (35)
1952	45,669 (70)
1953	42,758 (72)
1954	42,682 (76)
1955	39,664 (47)
1956	41,982 (76)
1957	42,478 (45)
1958	38,638 (72)
1959	42,560
1960	35,702

Mileage at 12/36: 84,324
Mileage at 31/12/50: 577,121

Sheds

Newton Heath	18/5/35
Carlisle W	9/10/43 (Loan)
Carlisle W	20/11/43
Aston	25/6/55
Carlisle Upperby	9/7/55
Patricroft	22/6/57
Carlisle Upperby	21/9/57
Carlisle Kingmoor	22/6/63
Carlisle Upperby	11/7/64
Carlisle Kingmoor	7/11/64

Stored

11/9/39-18/9/39

Withdrawn w.e. 14/1/67

45106 in the early 1950s pilots a Jubilee up Shap. It was domed from June 1952 to November 1956 and still had its first riveted tender. 45106 was allocated to Carlisle West, aka Upperby, from 1943 to September 1957, after which it alternated between there and Kingmoor until withdrawn in 1967. Photograph R. Sellar, www.transporttreasury.co.uk

45107

Built as 5107 at Vulcan Foundry 18/5/35
Renumbered 45107 w.e. 29/10/49

Improvements and modifications

6/4/38	Removal of vacuum pump
?	Steam sanding
4/12/61	Fitting BR ATC equipment

Repairs

6/8/36-21/8/36	LO
18/1/37-1/2/37	LS
5/3/37-19/3/37	LO
8/5/38-6/4/38	HG
2/3/40-15/3/40	LS
22/9/41-11/10/41	HS
28/12/42-23/1/43	HS
31/8/43-30/9/43	LO
19/4/44-20/5/44	LS
17/4/45-5/5/45	HG
13/5/46-6/6/46	LS
24/2/48-8/4/48	HS
12/9/49-27/10/49	HG
27/8/51-29/9/51	LI
16/12/52-22/1/53	LC(EO)
14/9/53-3/10/53	LI
17/12/55-26/1/56	HG
20/10/58-19/11/58	HI
4/8/59-10/9/59	LC(EO)
31/5/61-4/7/61	HG
22/11/61-4/12/61	NC
22/4/63-28/5/63	INT
15/11/65-11/12/65	LI

Boilers

New	9037
14/3/38	8655 from 5137 (domed)
11/10/43	9039 from 5141
5/5/45	9020 from 5205
27/10/49	9025 from 5212
26/1/56	8669 from 45216 (domed)
4/7/61	8954

Tenders

New	9201

Mileage/(weekdays out of service)

1935	28,547 (58)
1936	39,706 (99)
1937	45,175 (79)
1938	39,903 (113)
1939	26,494 (133)
1940	35,337 (47)
1941	27,366 (68)
1942	39,421 (23)
1943	36,458 (68)
1944	37,565 (50)
1945	34,876 (65)
1946	38,399 (43)
1947	27,411 (75)
1948	26,566 (73)
1949	24,463 (89)
1950	33,535 (31)
1951	26,732 (57)
1952	32,317 (44)
1953	29,259 (74)
1954	27,913 (71)
1955	27,629 (78)
1956	26,407 (81)
1957	31,928 (55)
1958	27,023 (91)
1959	30,974
1960	30,638

Mileage at 12/36: 68,253
Mileage at 31/12/50: 541,622

Sheds

Newton Heath	18/5/35
Low Moor	12/10/46
Fleetwood	29/11/47
Blackpool	10/6/50
Fleetwood	14/10/50
Lostock Hall	19/2/66

Stored

25/11/35-18/12/35
1/1/36-16/3/36
17/10/38-22/12/38
2/1/39-6/3/39
13/3/39-3/4/39
17/4/39-17/5/39

Withdrawn w.e. 16/9/67

Fleetwood allocated 45107 on 19 August 1961 at Skew Bridge near Chorley. It had only recently completed a Heavy General repair on 4 July when it reverted to a domeless boiler. It kept its original riveted tender throughout and was fitted with AWS at the end of the year. Photograph A.W. Battson, www.transporttreasury.co.uk

45108

Built as 5108 at Vulcan Foundry 22/5/35
Renumbered 45108 w.e. 8/1/49

Improvements and modifications

24/8/38	Removal of vacuum pump
20/6/45	Sloping throatplate boiler
20/6/45	Steam sanding
17/5/56	Modification
5/3/59	Fitting BR ATC equipment

Repairs

2/12/36-16/12/36	LS
1/6/37-14/6/37	LO
24/9/37-14/10/37	LS
16/7/35-24/8/38	HG
30/3/40-13/4/40	HS
30/10/41-15/11/41	HG
11/8/43-26/8/43	LS
23/5/45-20/6/45	HG
12/6/47-2/8/47	HS
11/12/48-6/1/49	LI
8/5/50-8/6/50	HG
10/5/51-12/6/51	LC
9/4/52-30/4/52	LI
25/11/52-13/12/52	LC(EO)
20/7/54-1/9/54	HG
26/3/56-17/5/56	HG
13/2/58-8/3/58	LC(EO)
29/10/58-6/12/58	HG
26/2/59-5/3/59	NC(EO)
18/9/61-17/10/61	LI

Boilers

New	9039
24/8/38	9051 from 5121
15/11/41	8655 from 5107 (domed)
20/6/45	9517 from 5254 (sloping throatplate)
8/6/50	9452 from 5312 (sloping throatplate)
1/9/54	9417 from 44842 (sloping throatplate)
17/5/56	9479 from 45026 (sloping throatplate)
6/12/58	9422 from 45419 (sloping throatplate)

Tenders

New	9202

Mileage/(weekdays out of service)

1935	30,546 (23)
1936	47,987 (52)
1937	47,139 (53)
1938	48,969 (56)
1939	52,472 (38)
1940	44,771 (35)
1941	37,881 (45)
1942	34,912 (18)
1943	31,391 (40)
1944	26,881 (37)
1945	31,465 (75)
1946	33,037 (32)
1947	28,883 (95)
1948	27,670 (82)
1949	39,113 (39)
1950	36,676 (69)
1951	36,638 (54)
1952	33,909 (58)
1953	41,763 (36)
1954	36,937 (60)
1955	39,640 (51)
1956	36,684 (61)
1957	42,878 (37)
1958	35,957 (80)
1959	42,645
1960	33,134

Mileage at 12/36: 78,533
Mileage at 31/12/50: 599,793

Sheds

Crewe	25/5/35
Holyhead	8/6/35
Stoke	12/6/37
Crewe North	24/9/38
Carlisle W	16/9/39
Longsight	26/10/40
Rugby	17/5/41
Willesden	21/3/42
Springs Branch	2/5/42
Crewe North	9/12/44
Crewe South	24/2/45
Longsight	20/6/59
Springs Branch	12/9/59

Withdrawn w.e. 11/12/65

Watched by some very young trainspotters standing in front of Harrow No2 Box, 45108 was a wartime conversion to a sloping throatplate boiler and has the later pattern of top feed cover. Still with its first riveted tender, it received AWS in March 1959. 45108 was shedded at Crewe South until transferred to Wigan Springs Branch the month after this picture was taken on 15 August 1959. Photograph www.rail-online.co.uk

45109

Built as 5109 at Vulcan Foundry 25/5/35
Renumbered 45109 w.e. 8/5/48

Improvements and modifications

?	Removal of vacuum pump
24/6/46	Steam sanding
7/5/48	Sloping throatplate boiler
17/5/58	Modification
22/5/59	Fitting BR ATC equipment

Repairs

25/9/36-15/10/36	LS
28/6/37-19/7/37	LO
28/1/38-28/2/38	HG
15/1/40-30/1/40	LS
21/8/41-6/9/41	HG
25/6/43-10/6/43	HS
29/10/43-13/11/43	LO
11/9/45-31/10/45	LS
31/5/46-24/6/46	HG
13/4/48-7/5/48	HS
27/2/50-28/3/50	HI
9/7/51-11/8/51	LC
26/10/51-23/11/51	HI
23/2/53-27/3/53	HG
21/7/53-13/8/53	LC (EO)
30/8/54-29/9/54	LI
9/12/55-5/1/56	LI
8/10/56-17/11/56	LC
1/3/58-17/5/58	HG
12/5/59-22/5/59	NC (EO)
19/5/61-20/6/61	LI
8/1/64-18/2/64	HG

Boilers

New	9039
15/2/38	8913 from 5133
6/9/41	8907 from 5065
24/6/46	8666 from 5087 (domed)
7/5/48	11899 from 4839 (sloping throatplate)
27/3/53	11921 from 45394 (sloping throatplate)
17/5/58	9496 from 44866 (sloping throatplate)
18/2/64	9364 (sloping throatplate)

Tenders

New	9203
22/2/64	9165

Mileage/(weekdays out of service)

1935	32,074 (20)
1936	50,998 (47)
1937	47,843 (49)
1938	51,231 (67)
1939	51,736 (60)
1940	39,480 (55)
1941	34,422 (56)
1942	37,640 (22)
1943	24,773 (75)
1944	29,652 (43)
1945	23,874 (63)
1946	28,464 (53)
1947	26,961 (67)
1948	40,905 (50)
1949	31,925 (71)
1950	38,850 (47)
1951	24,540 (101)
1952	43,101 (38)
1953	44,857 (71)
1954	46,695 (41)
1955	39,733 (63)
1956	42,439 (79)
1957	39,474 (30)
1958	37,072 (77)
1959	41,682
1960	33,770

Mileage at 12/36: 83,072
Mileage at 31/12/50: 590,828

Sheds

Crewe	1/6/35
Holyhead	8/6/35
Longsight	5/6/37
Chester	9/7/38
Edge Hill	14/12/40
Warrington	5/9/42
Longsight	5/7/52
Springs Branch	12/9/59
Newton Heath	27/7/63
Southport	24/8/63
Bank Hall	12/10/63
Warrington	21/11/64

Withdrawn w.e. 1/4/67

45109 pictured on 6 September 1954 at Willesden was a post-war sloping throatplate boiler conversion, in May 1948. It was shedded at Longsight from 1952 until 1959.

45110

Built as 5110 at Vulcan Foundry 29/5/35
Renumbered 45110 w.e. 9/4/49

Improvements and modifications

16/6/38	Removal of vacuum pump
14/9/39	BTH speed indicator
14/9/39	Steam sanding
31/1/57	Modification
6/5/59	Fitting BR ATC equipment

Repairs

8/10/36-23/10/36	LS
12/3/37-5/4/37	LO
2/6/38-16/6/38	LS
10/8/39-14/9/39	HG
21/4/41-3/5/41	LS
23/2/42-7/3/42	LS
19/7/43-31/7/43	HG
12/3/45-13/4/45	LS
4/8/46-22/8/46	HG
1/5/48-4/6/48	LS
5/3/49-5/4/49	LC
22/6/50-17/8/50	HG
7/8/51-1/9/51	LI
30/4/52-23/5/52	LI
10/7/52-16/9/52	HG
29/9/53-23/10/53	LI
11/11/54-27/11/54	LI
10/12/55-16/1/56	LC(EO)
5/12/56-31/1/57	HG
16/5/58-10/6/58	HI
22/4/59-6/5/59	NC(EO)
12/5/59-26/5/59	LC(EO)
27/6/60-10/8/60	HI
22/2/62-29/3/62	HG
2/5/66-25/6/66	LI

Boilers

New	9040
14/9/39	8910 from 5130
31/7/43	9037 from 5120
28/8/46	8646 from 5039 (domed)
17/8/50	8967 from 5186
16/9/52	9008 from 5004
31/1/57	8675 from 5200 (domed)
?	8963

Tenders

New	9204
31/1/57	9572 (welded)

Mileage/(weekdays out of service)

1935	30,064 (24)
1936	51,094 (44)
1937	48,862 (52)
1938	40,999 (60)
1939	39,688 (68)
1940	46,308 (59)
1941	45,338 (37)
1942	52,302 (31)
1943	42,102 (35)
1944	49,858 (23)
1945	46,262 (44)
1946	41,998 (48)
1947	39,477 (38)
1948	30,261 (63)
1949	28,904 (99)
1950	36,636 (89)
1951	47,038 (64)
1952	43,842 (98)
1953	50,723 (48)
1954	48,142 (40)
1955	40,193 (46)
1956	39,037 (75)
1957	46,844 (62)
1958	40,166 (54)
1959	45,106
1960	31,618

Mileage at 12/36: 81,158
Mileage at 31/12/50: 670,158

Sheds

Crewe	1/6/35
Holyhead	8/6/35
Stafford	7/3/64
Bolton	24/7/65
Lostock Hall	6/7/68

Stored
25/7/66-28/10/67

Withdrawn w.e. 17/8/68

45110 was in store from July 1966 until October 1967, hence the crude hand painted smokebox number. It was then reinstated and had a starring role on the '15 Guinea' final BR steam special in August 1968 before entering preservation on the Severn Valley Railway. It was shedded at Bolton, where it is being polished in this photograph, from July 1965 until its final move to Carnforth in June 1968. 45110 had a welded tender from January 1957 and was fitted with AWS in May 1959. Photograph www.rail-online.co.uk

45111

Built as 5111 at Vulcan Foundry 30/5/35
Renumbered 45111 w.e. 27/11/48

Improvements and modifications

15/6/38	Removal of vacuum pump
5/2/44	Steam sanding
2/8/57	Modification
5/9/59	Fitting BR ATC equipment

Repairs

22/10/36-5/11/36	LS
4/8/37-18/8/37	LO
24/4/38-15/6/38	HG
1/2/39-14/3/39	HO
28/10/39-10/11/39	LS
4/11/41-22/11/41	LS
29/9/42-28/10/42	HS
19/1/44-5/2/44	HG
24/1/46-15/2/46	LS
9/7/47-29/8/47	LS
21/10/48-25/11/48	HG
15/4/50-3/5/50	HI
17/2/51-8/3/51	HI
18/12/51-11/1/52	LC
11/6/53-3/7/53	HG
28/8/54-1/10/54	LI
20/4/56-25/5/56	HI
24/5/57-2/8/57	HG
23/7/59-5/9/59	HI
30/6/60-?	INT
12/10/64-7/11/64	LI

Boilers

New	9041
31/5/38	8650 from 5033 (domed)
14/3/39	8905 from 5125
5/2/44	9007 from 5076
25/11/48	9016 from 5073
3/7/53	8821 from 45074 (domed)
2/8/57	9016 from 45149
5/9/59	8642 from 45088 (domed)

Tenders

New	9205
14/2/39	9687 (welded)
14/10/42	9637 (welded)
17/1/44	9682 (welded)

Mileage/(weekdays out of service)

1935	29,764 (23)
1936	49,839 (46)
1937	41,612 (67)
1938	45,281 (92)
1939	44,725 (77)
1940	37,432 (31)
1941	30,609 (48)
1942	38,446 (39)
1943	40,621 (11)
1944	32,533 (34)
1945	44,596 (24)
1946	41,700 (45)
1947	38,679 (72)
1948	29,066 (84)
1949	46,472 (42)
1950	43,060 (53)
1951	37,943 (49)
1952	34,870 (50)
1953	40,003 (45)
1954	35,268 (57)
1955	37,518 (50)
1956	38,896 (56)
1957	31,785 (93)
1958	48,786 (29)
1959	41,903
1960	41,362

Mileage at 12/36: 79,603
Mileage at 31/12/50: 634,435

Sheds

Crewe	1/6/35
Edge Hill	15/6/35
Holyhead	6/7/35
Carnforth	5/6/37
Patricroft	15/7/39
Holyhead	3/8/46
Crewe South	15/9/51
Edge Hill	26/1/52
Crewe South	30/10/54
Crewe North	23/11/57
Longsight	14/6/58
Monument Lane	30/4/60
Longsight	29/10/60
Carlisle Upperby	19/11/60 (loan)
Willesden	31/3/62
Chester	27/4/63
Mold Jct	2/10/65
Llandudno Jct	27/11/65
Mold Jct	4/12/65
Holyhead	23/4/66
Rose Grove	20/8/66

Withdrawn w.e. 28/10/67

Crewe North's 45111 under the footbridge from the station to the shed, being based there from November 1957 until June 1958. It was domed for a short spell of two years from August 1957 until September 1959, and had been paired with a welded tender since 1939. Photograph www.rail-online.co.uk

45112

Built as 5112 at Vulcan Foundry 1/6/35
Renumbered 45112 w.e. 29/7/50

Improvements and modifications

12/11/38	Steam sanding
12/11/38	Removal of vacuum pump
5/10/56	Modification

Repairs

29/12/36-12/1/37	LS
2/9/37-17/9/37	LO
21/10/38-12/11/38	HG
28/3/40-12/4/40	LS
11/2/42-24/2/42	HS
15/9/43-1/10/43	HG
4/11/44-18/11/44	HS
26/6/46-27/7/46	LS
26/11/47-6/2/48	HG
22/4/49-27/5/49	HI
24/6/50-27/7/50	HI
29/3/51-14/4/51	LI
14/4/52-6/5/52	LC
3/7/52-13/9/52	G
1/10/52	NC
21/9/53-24/10/53	HI
10/9/54-15/10/54	HI
19/3/55-2/4/55	LC(EO)
5/12/55-17/12/55	LC(EO)
21/8/56-5/10/56	G
13/8/58-29/8/58	HI
14/1/59-30/1/59	LC(EO)
24/11/60-31/12/60	HG

Boilers

New	9042
26/11/38	8677 from 5060 (domed)
2/10/43	8910 from 5110
18/11/44	9034 from 5038
21/2/48	9053 from 5050
13/9/52	8958 from 45168
5/10/56	8652 from 45163 (domed)
31/12/60	9024

Tenders

New	9206
8/8/52	10533 (welded)
24/10/53	10677 (part-welded)
5/10/56	9027
30/8/58	10718 (part-welded)

45112 at Eastfield in the 1950s with the front footplate cover open. It had a riveted tender up to August 1952 and a domeless boiler until 1956. The absence of a shedplate suggests it may have been in the process of moving to Carlisle Kingmoor in May 1952 when this photograph was taken. Photograph www.rail-online.co.uk

Mileage/(weekdays out of service)

1935	26,774 (20)
1936	51,115 (41)
1937	45,601 (58)
1938	42,028 (59)
1939	64,340 (24)
1940	41,582 (44)
1941	45,022 (38)
1942	44,562 (34)
1943	42,162 (38)
1944	41,311 (42)
1945	44,164 (26)
1946	31,092 (72)
1947	31,718 (79)
1948	43,579 (68)
1949	40,773 (70)
1950	41,469 (60)
1951	43,274 (38)
1952	26,353 (139)
1953	47,496 (56)
1954	46,626 (67)
1955	46,294 (59)
1956	42,473 (74)
1957	54,029 (40)
1958	34,930 (69)
1959	47,555
1960	25,330

Mileage at 12/36: 77,889
Mileage at 31/12/50: 677,292

Sheds

Crewe	8/6/35
Edge Hill	15/6/35
Holyhead	6/7/35
Llandudno Jct	28/6/47
Shrewsbury	21/2/48
Eastfield	8/12/51
Carlisle Kingmoor	7/5/52
Carlisle Upperby	14/2/59
Carlisle Kingmoor	20/6/59
Aintree	18/5/63
Carlisle Kingmoor	23/11/63

Withdrawn w.e. 15/10/66

45113

Built as 5113 at Vulcan Foundry 5/6/35
Renumbered 45113 w.e. 8/5/48

Improvements and modifications

7/6/38	Removal of vacuum pump
?	Steam sanding
14/12/40	BTH speed indicator
12/3/59	Fitting BR ATC equipment

Repairs

5/1/37-26/1/37	LS
2/9/37-20/9/37	LO
24/3/38-7/6/38	HG
28/10/39-10/11/39	LS
26/11/40-14/12/40	LS
13/1/42-31/1/42	HG
25/2/43-13/3/43	HS
1/8/44-17/8/44	LS
25/10/44-25/11/44	LO
24/7/45-23/8/45	LS
3/9/46-20/9/46	HG
5/4/48-7/5/48	HS
10/6/49-27/7/49	HG
3/10/50-1/11/50	LI
6/3/52-4/4/52	LI
18/7/53-26/8/53	HG
21/4/55-14/5/55	LI
13/12/55-26/1/56	LC(EO)
12/8/56-29/9/56	HG
20/8/58-18/9/58	LI
3/3/59-12/3/59	NC(EO)
11/2/60-16/3/60	LI
9/2/61-18/3/61	LC(EO)

Boilers

New	9043
20/5/38	8670 from 5053 (domed)
31/1/42	8644 from 5059 (domed)
20/9/46	9047 from 5025
27/7/49	9017 from 5078
26/8/53	8683 from 45046 (domed)
29/9/56	8906 from 45048

Tenders

New	9207

Mileage/(weekdays out of service)

1935	27,591 (24)
1936	48,174 (45)
1937	44,639 (62)
1938	38,721 (90)
1939	46,324 (50)
1940	40,202 (41)
1941	36,398 (26)
1942	41,794 (55)
1943	40,970 (39)
1944	33,306 (67)
1945	45,398 (54)
1946	42,828 (46)
1947	47,314 (62)
1948	40,101 (89)
1949	35,226 (81)
1950	43,039 (48)
1951	45,027 (27)
1952	41,716 (44)
1953	39,610 (56)
1954	40,082 (47)
1955	37,983 (93)
1956	39,030 (78)
1957	43,871 (47)
1958	30,780 (46)
1959	43,146
1960	37,062

Mileage at 12/36: 75,765
Mileage at 31/12/50: 652,025

Sheds

Crewe	8/6/35
Edge Hill	15/6/35
Holyhead	6/7/35
Edge Hill	4/11/50
Longsight	10/3/56
Rugby	21/4/56
Longsight	2/6/56
Carlisle Upperby	13/10/56
Crewe North	20/10/56
Walsall	3/8/57
Crewe North	17/8/57
Monument Lane	20/6/59
Rugby	17/9/60
Crewe South	19/9/64
Rugby	28/11/64
Northampton	9/1/65
Rugby	27/2/65
Nuneaton	29/5/65

Withdrawn w.e. 3/7/65

45113 at Rugby on 31 July 1963 during the third of four spells allocated there, from September 1960 to September 1964. The final domed boiler is not recorded on the Engine History Card unlike the AWS, fitted in March 1959. Photograph www.rail-online.co.uk

45114

Built as 5114 at Vulcan Foundry 6/6/35
Renumbered 45114 w.e. 14/1/50

Improvements and modifications

11/8/38	Removal of vacuum pump
?	Steam sanding
8/2/58	Modification
14/5/59	Fitting BR ATC equipment

Repairs

28/11/36-17/12/36	LS
19/8/37-3/9/37	LO
29/6/38-11/8/38	HG
10/1/40-31/1/40	LS
5/9/40-21/9/40	LO
15/1/41-29/1/41	LO
29/11/41-30/12/41	LS
3/9/42-19/9/42	LO
31/3/43-23/4/43	HG
13/6/44-26/6/44	LS
26/6/45-11/8/45	LO
11/3/46-30/3/46	LS
27/1/48-8/3/48	HG
10/12/49-9/1/50	HI
10/6/51-29/6/51	LI
12/1/53-6/2/53	HG
6/3/54-8/4/54	LI
19/3/55-19/4/55	LI
4/5/56-4/6/56	HI
7/1/58-8/2/58	HG
27/4/59-14/5/59	NC(EO)
28/3/60-7/5/60	LI

Boilers

New	9044
1/8/38	8669 from 5052 (domed)
23/4/43	8650 from 5202 (domed)
8/3/48	8681 from 5106 (domed)
6/2/53	9018 from 45094
8/2/58	8998 from 45006

Tenders

New	9208
11/8/45	9651 (welded)

Mileage/(weekdays out of service)

1935	30,827 (19)
1936	49,387 (60)
1937	50,079 (50)
1938	44,278 (72)
1939	40,263 (55)
1940	36,193 (88)
1941	34,683 (73)
1942	43,512 (50)
1943	45,669 (56)
1944	35,732 (66)
1945	12,735 (90)
1946	28,447 (49)
1947	33,940 (25)
1948	29,310 (64)
1949	32,448 (55)
1950	39,696 (37)
1951	32,801 (41)
1952	35,519 (29)
1953	39,694 (53)
1954	40,117 (56)
1955	37,268 (66)
1956	36,617 (67)
1957	34,311 (40)
1958	35,426 (60)
1959	37,652
1960	31,967

Mileage at 12/36: 80,214
Mileage at 31/12/50: 587,199

Sheds

Crewe	8/6/35
Holyhead	6/7/35
Edge Hill	1/10/38
Longsight	29/4/39
Chester	10/2/40
Bletchley	3/5/41
Rugby	24/5/41
Willesden	28/10/44
Stoke	3/5/47
Carnforth	22/3/52
Aston	12/4/52
Carlisle Upperby	13/10/56
Aston	20/10/56
Bescot	9/3/57
Aston	20/6/59
Crewe North	22/8/59
Aston	5/9/59
Banbury	2/10/65
Colwick	19/2/66
Heaton Mersey	28/5/66

Stored
16/1/67-14/8/67

Withdrawn w.e. 13/1/68

45114, pictured at Saltley in the 1960s, had been a Birmingham engine since 1952, apart from a loan spell at Carlisle in 1956 and stayed at Aston until December 1965. It is in final condition with lowered top lamp iron and AWS received in May 1959. It had carried domeless boilers since 1953 having had three domed boilers prior to that, and a welded tender since 1945.

45115

Built as 5115 at Vulcan Foundry 10/6/35
Renumbered 45115 w.e. 15/5/48

Improvements and modifications

6/1/39	Removal of vacuum pump
6/10/39	Steam sanding
?	Fitting BR ATC equipment

Repairs

19/1/37-18/2/37	LS
1/4/37-14/4/37	LO
6/12/37-30/12/37	HS
5/12/38-6/1/39	LS
3/2/39-22/2/39	LO
21/8/39-6/10/39	HG
12/8/40-30/8/40	LS
21/3/41-25/4/41	HS
2/7/42-2/9/42	LS
3/7/43-14/8/43	HG
25/7/44-24/8/44	LS
26/11/45-19/12/45	LS
31/1/46-20/2/46	LO
15/3/47-5/5/47	HG
2/10/47-17/10/47	LO
25/3/48-15/5/48	HS
7/3/49-9/4/49	LC
4/7/49-27/8/49	HI
15/2/50-3/3/50	LC
5/9/50-17/10/50	HI
28/2/52-19/4/52	G
19/8/52-4/9/52	LC(EO)
10/2/53-14/3/53	LC(EO)
14/9/53-3/10/53	HI
30/9/54-1/10/54	NC(EO)
7/1/55-28/1/55	HI
3/2/55-5/2/55	NC(EO)
19/3/56-29/3/56	LC(EO)
18/4/56-11/5/56	LI
28/5/56-2/6/56	NC(EO)
28/5/56-2/6/56	NC(EO)
28/9/56	NC(EO)
7/5/57-11/5/57	NC(EO)
14/9/57-19/10/57	G
9/10/58-25/10/58	LC
5/5/59-8/5/59	NC(EO)
23/2/60-19/3/60	HI
15/12/60-23/12/60	LC(EO)
13/3/61-1/4/61	LC(EO)
25/9/61-4/10/61	LC(EO)
17/11/61-24/11/61	LC(TO)
28/12/61	LC(TO)
2/4/62-19/5/62	G
16/10/63-23/10/63	LC
21/4/65-15/5/65	LC

Boilers

New	9045
6/10/39	8955 from 5175
14/8/43	9052 from 5123
5/5/47	8645 from 5049 (domed)

Tenders

New	9209
11/2/46	9264 (welded)
11/5/48	9278 (welded)
8/7/49	10621 (part-welded)
27/8/49	9060
7/4/52	10523 (welded)
5/10/53	9570 (welded)
28/1/55	9269 (welded)
11/5/56	9255 (welded)
16/3/61	9287 (welded)
10/3/64	9064
4/11/65	9198

Mileage/(weekdays out of service)

1935	35,450 (10)
1936	68,807 (33)
1937	50,782 (88)
1938	51,713 (85)
1939	49,355 (77)
1940	49,983 (35)
1941	50,690 (62)
1942	39,715 (99)
1943	44,696 (67)
1944	51,688 (51)
1945	43,613 (53)
1946	44,527 (52)
1947	35,786 (86)
1948	31,122 (121)
1949	29,844 (135)
1950	34,361 (109)

Mileage at 12/36: 104,257
Mileage at 31/12/50: 712,132

Sheds

Crewe	15/6/35
Edge Hill	6/7/35
Carlisle M	2/11/35
Perth	4/7/36
Carlisle N	10/10/36
St Rollox	22/11/41
Dumfries	18/1/65
Hurlford	11/6/66 (PE)

Withdrawn 29/11/66

45115 in 1964 at Eastfield is carrying a 65B St Rollox shedplate, with polished rim, and was shedded there from 1941 until December 1965. There is no surviving post-1950 History Card so the dates of the domeless boiler and AWS fitting are unknown, although the riveted tender is recorded from March 1964.

45116

Built as 5116 at Vulcan Foundry 12/6/35
Renumbered 45116 w.e. 17/4/48

Improvements and modifications

5/4/38	Removal of vacuum pump
26/2/44	Steam sanding
25/5/56	Modernisation
24/3/61	Fitting Smith-Stone speedometer

Repairs

4/3/37-8/4/37	LS
23/7/37-13/8/37	LO
23/3/38-5/4/38	LS
20/1/39-30/1/39	LO
24/3/39-29/4/39	HG
28/5/40-12/6/40	LO
19/11/40-7/12/40	HS
15/3/41-28/4/41	Tender Only
14/1/42-14/2/42	HG
20/12/42-23/1/43	LS
3/2/43-2/3/43	LO
27/1/44-26/2/44	LS
7/11/44-24/11/44	HS
8/8/45-15/9/45	LS
12/9/46-15/11/46	HG
21/11/46-29/11/46	LO
23/12/47-22/1/48	LS
12/3/48-16/4/48	LO
24/11/48-5/1/49	LC
15/3/50-20/4/50	LI
25/12/50-26/1/51	LC
2/8/51-27/10/51	G
25/2/53-28/3/53	LI
19/1/54-23/1/54	LC(EO)
11/5/54-12/6/54	HI
22/8/55-17/9/55	HI
3/1/56-10/1/56	NC(EO)
10/4/56-25/5/56	G
10/4/58-8/5/58	HI
13/5/58-29/5/58	NC(Rect)
14/2/61-24/3/61	HI

Boilers

New	9046
29/4/39	8831 from 5014
14/4/42	8939 from 5016
15/11/46	8962 from 5144
27/10/51	8934 from 45124
25/5/56	8647 from 45214 (domed)
4/62	8681 from 45188 (domed)

Tenders

New	9210
8/4/37	9271 (welded)
25/11/40	9258 (welded)
22/2/41	9061
10/3/43	9724 (welded)
16/4/48	9060
13/5/48	9599 (welded)
22/3/50	9120
19/4/50	9175
19/10/51	9826 (welded)
20/2/53	10678 (part-welded)
25/3/53	10697 (part-welded)
11/6/54	9298 (welded)
17/9/55	9266 (welded)
25/5/56	10448 (welded)

Mileage/(weekdays out of service)

1935	34,062 (14)
1936	73,212 (36)
1937	51,802 (77)
1938	59,166 (61)
1939	48,757 (61)
1940	42,853 (72)
1941	42,812 (91)
1942	56,134 (38)
1943	41,043 (60)
1944	34,884 (87)
1945	43,464 (47)
1946	41,803 (94)
1947	53,002 (36)
1948	34,819 (112)
1949	33,494 (89)
1950	36,051 (78)
1951	27,682 (136)
1952	44,867 (59)
1953	45,088 (84)
1954	40,607 (73)
1955	41,298 (64)
1956	38,716
1957	34,207 (39)
1958	32,495 (80)
1959	31,478
1960	27,123

Mileage at 12/36: 107,274
Mileage at 31/12/50: 727,358

Sheds

Crewe	15/6/35
Edge Hill	6/7/35
Durran Hill	2/11/35
Perth	4/7/36
Carlisle N	10/10/36
St Rollox	22/11/41
Agecroft	2/3/57
Leicester Cen	10/10/59 (loan)
Leicester Cen	7/11/59
Annesley	9/1/60
Cricklewood	26/1/63
Woodford Halse	18/5/63
Llandudno Jct	2/11/63
Mold Jct	8/5/65
Holyhead	23/4/66
Chester	10/12/66
Springs Branch	20/5/67 (loan)
Springs Branch	27/5/67

Withdrawn w.e. 29/7/67

An immaculate 45116 at its home, Balornock shed, on 27 October 1951 after completion of a General repair in St Rollox Works during which it acquired a welded tender. Note the former private owner wagon on the coal ramp still clearly displaying the legend 'The Great Grimsby Salt and Canning Co. Ltd'. Photograph AG Ellis

45117

Built as 5117 at Vulcan Foundry 14/6/35
Renumbered 45117 w.e. 16/10/48

Improvements and modifications

10/3/38	Removal of vacuum pump
19/5/45	Steam sanding
?	Fitting BR ATC equipment

Repairs

4/2/37-13/3/37	LS
5/11/37-26/11/37	LO
11/12/37-12/1/35	LO
1/3/38-10/3/38	LS
1/9/38-10/9/38	LO
2/1/39-20/1/39	LS
2/6/39-12/8/39	HO
16/5/40-8/6/40	LS
30/8/41-27/9/41	HS
2/2/42-2/4/42	HG
4/11/42-12/12/42	LS
21/8/43-11/9/43	LS
8/6/44-22/6/44	HS
27/3/45-19/5/45	LS
10/10/46-30/11/46	HG
7/2/48-26/2/48	HS
30/9/48-15/10/48	LO
2/11/48-1/12/48	LO
11/11/49-17/12/49	HI
27/2/50-17/3/50	NC
4/6/51-8/9/51	G
10/10/52-22/11/52	INT
10/1/53-18/2/53	C(EO)
27/8/53-25/9/53	HI
26/3/54-17/4/54	LC
28/9/54-16/10/54	LI
29/6/55-15/7/55	LC(EO)
29/9/55-24/11/55	G
14/5/56-9/6/56	LC(EO)
18/2/57-27/3/57	HI
20/4/57-27/4/57	NC(EO)
26/11/57	NC(EO)
24/3/58-1/4/58	NC(EO)
27/10/58-31/10/58	NC(EO)
4/12/58-23/1/59	LI
17/3/59-4/4/59	LC(EO)
7/7/59-16/7/59	NC(EO)
8/1/60-27/1/60	NC(EO)
26/9/60-29/10/60	G
12//863-13/9/63	LI
19/10/64-31/10/64	LC(EO)

Boilers

New	9047
12/8/39	8950 from 5170
2/4/42	8932 from 5170
30/11/46	9005 from 5163

Tenders

New	9211
8/4/37	9210
2/4/46	9179
17/12/49	10550 (part-welded)
?	9593
7/10/52	10550 (part-welded)
25/3/54	10594 (part-welded)
15/10/54	9101
24/11/55	9209
27/3/57	9250 (welded)
4/6/54	9481 (welded)

Mileage/(weekdays out of service)

1935	28,212 (26)
1936	67,849 (29)
1937	43,234 (110)
1938	55,764 (58)
1939	41,917 (91)
1940	47,054 (54)
1941	48,387 (61)
1942	38,380 (105)
1943	56,020 (47)
1944	27,698 (51)
1945	35,981 (74)
1946	33,533 (82)
1947	47,982 (41)
1948	37,219 (83)
1949	38,169 (71)
1950	36,582 (58)

Mileage at 12/36: 96,061
Mileage at 31/12/50: 683,981

Sheds

Crewe	15/6/35
Edge Hill	6/7/35
Carlisle N	9/11/35
Perth	4/7/36
Carlisle N	3/10/36
St Rollox	10/5/42
Carstairs	22/10/49
Polmadie	9/12/50
St Margarets	27/1/51 (PE)
Polmadie	24/3/51 (PE)
St Margarets	6/10/51 (PE)
Perth S	23/3/52
Inverness	21/10/57
Corkerhill	10/4/62
Hurlford	17/4/62

Withdrawn 22/10/65

45117 on 26 August 1959 at Strathcarron on the 9.10am Inverness-Kyle. It has the usual features of an Inverness Black 5, a tablet catcher and two vertical lines of holes in the front bufferbeam where a snowplough has been attached. It has a domeless boiler and a welded tender which it acquired in March 1957. 45117 moved briefly to Corkerhill in April 1962 before going to Hurlford from where it was withdrawn in October 1965. Photograph WAC Smith, www.transporttreasury.co.uk

45118

Built as 5118 at Vulcan Foundry 20/6/35
Renumbered 45118 w.e. 7/5/49

Improvements and modifications

27/8/38	Removal of vacuum pump
25/5/45	Steam sanding
14/11/57	Modification

Repairs

8/12/36-9/1/37	LS
10/4/37-21/4/37	LO
9/10/37-5/11/37	LS
18/7/38-27/8/38	HG
1/4/40-23/4/40	HS
7/5/41-28/5/41	LS
4/5/42-5/6/42	HG
25/11/42-19/12/42	LS
22/2/44-11/3/44	LS
17/8/45-21/9/45	HG
18/2/47-29/3/47	LS
30/3/49-5/5/49	LI
1/9/50-28/10/50	G
27/3/51-6/4/51	LC
19/10/51-10/11/51	HI
27/6/52-11/7/52	LC
21/7/52-25/8/52	LC
2/2/53-20/3/53	G
30/8/54-18/9/54	LI
22/9/54-23/9/54	LC(EO)
30/1/56-24/2/56	HI
19/10/57-14/11/57	G
17/1/58-12/2/58	LC
4/12/59-8/1/60	LI
18/2/60-4/3/60	LC(EO)
9/5/60-21/5/60	LC(EO)
8/6/61-13/7/61	HI
27/9/61-17/11/61	LC(EO)

Boilers

New	9048
27/8/38	9010 from 5080
5/6/42	8952 from 5082
21/9/45	8977 from 5024
28/10/50	8676 from 5085 (domed)
20/3/53	8682 from 45148 (domed)
14/11/57	8952

Tenders

New	9212
8/8/39	9257 (welded)
20/11/42	9077
9/9/44	9028
19/2/45	9257 (welded)
26/6/47	10526 (welded)
18/10/51	9211
16/9/54	10580 (part-welded)
24/2/56	9818 (welded)
14/11/57	9282 (welded)

Mileage/(weekdays out of service)

1935	34,312 (7)
1936	69,302 (41)
1937	48,296 (80)
1938	54,864 (78)
1939	62,960 (19)
1940	50,686 (53)
1941	50,465 (58)
1942	46,263 (99)
1943	57,874 (20)
1944	51,732 (52)
1945	37,307 (104)
1946	46,485 (66)
1947	45,224 (76)
1948	41,111 (92)
1949	45,573 (83)
1950	36,170 (101)
1951	50,833 (52)
1952	34,012 (119)
1953	49,364 (91)
1954	52,381 (54)
1955	51,182 (50)
1956	54,713 (50)
1957	43,273 (78)
1958	47,960 (80)
1959	39,626
1960	43,662

Mileage at 12/36: 103,614
Mileage at 31/12/50: 778,624

Sheds

Crewe	22/6/35
Edge Hill	6/7/35
Carlisle N	28/9/35
Perth	4/7/36
Carlisle N	10/10/36
Perth	8/7/50
Carlisle Kingmoor	22/12/51
Aintree	18/5/63
Newton Heath	22/6/63
Carlisle Kingmoor	5/10/63

Withdrawn w.e. 8/10/66

Kingmoor shedded 45118 waits with a freight at Stockport on 19 March 1960. The close spaced large cab numbers show its Scottish roots. 45118 had been domeless since 1957 having had two domed boilers previously. Photograph D. Forsyth, Colourrail.co.uk

45119

Built as 5119 at Vulcan Foundry 21/6/35
Renumbered 45119 w.e. 24/4/48

Improvements and modifications

7/4/38	Removal of vacuum pump
?	Steam sanding
29/4/59	Fitting BR ATC equipment
1960	Fitting Stone-Smith speedometer

Repairs

19/4/37-14/5/37	LS
28/3/38-7/4/38	LS
18/11/38-9/12/38	LS
23/3/39-4/4/39	LO
4/5/39-22/6/39	HG
11/7/40-26/7/40	HS
28/1/41-15/2/41	LS
7/1/42-14/2/42	HS
26/9/42-31/10/42	HG
14/12/42-7/2/43	HO
12/8/43-3/9/43	LO
3/11/43-24/11/43	LO
15/2/44-8/3/44	LO
23/3/44-20/4/44	LO
28/10/44-10/11/44	LS
5/4/46-24/4/46	LS
15/7/47-6/9/47	HG
15/4/48-24/4/48	LO
18/8/49-6/10/49	LI
15/12/50-9/2/51	LI
20/9/51-24/9/51	LC(TO)
18/2/52-17/5/52	G
2/12/53-8/1/54	HI
2/6/54-15/6/54	LC
3/2/55	NC(EO)
19/4/55-30/4/55	LC(EO)
8/8/55-3/9/55	HI
24/11/55-10/12/55	LC(EO)
22/2/56-1/3/56	LC(EO)
26/1/57-14/2/57	G
7/12/57-28/12/57	HI
23/5/58-14/6/58	LC(EO)
20/1/0/58-23/10/58	NC(EO)
5/12/58-20/12/58	HI
5/1/59-6/1/59	NC(EO)
23/4/59-29/4/59	NC(EO)
26/5/60-2/7/60	HI
8/7/60-9/7/60	NC(EO)
15/11/60-16/11/60	NC(EO)

Boilers

New	9049
22/6/39	8946 from 5166
31/10/42	8645 from 5039
5/2/43	8945 from 5160 (domed)
6/9/47	8824 from 5125
17/5/52	8929 from 45192
14/2/57	8958 from 45120

Tenders

New	9213
29/11/46	9365
3/11/50	10585 (part-welded)
6/5/52	9665 (welded)
4/6/54	9603 (welded)
30/4/55	10719 (part-welded)
14/2/57	10533 (welded)
28/12/57	9842 (welded)

Mileage/(weekdays out of service)

1935	32,512 (5)
1936	61,666 (63)
1937	50,258 (86)
1938	55,124 (62)
1939	44,975 (88)
1940	44,907 (60)
1941	48,777 (57)
1942	41,320 (106)
1943	38,053 (108)
1944	30,887 (139)
1945	40,466 (68)
1946	33,644 (127)
1947	37,707 (111)
1948	44,196 (67)
1949	33,329 (89)
1950	35,658 (66)
1951	41,520 (60)
1952	29,928 (95)
1953	41,473 (56)
1954	37,228 (70)
1955	25,778 (106)
1956	37,087 (45)
1957	36,538 (54)
1958	35,549 (60)
1959	46,372
1960	33,367
1961	33,620
1962	4,476

Mileage at 12/36: 94,178
Mileage at 31/12/50: 673,479

Sheds

Crewe	22/6/35
Edge Hill	6/7/35
Carlisle N	16/11/35
Perth	4/7/36
Carlisle N	3/10/36
Perth	8/7/50
Corkerhill	28/7/51
Grangemouth	29/9/51
Eastfield	29/5/54
St Rollox	29/11/54
Stirling	19/9/55
St Rollox	29/10/56

Stored
4/6/62-29/12/62

Withdrawn w.e. 29/12/62

5119 was built at Vulcan Foundry in June 1935 and was one of several Class Fives to go, after running in at Crewe, to Edge Hill and then to the Northern Division at Carlisle in November 1935. It differs from the earlier Vulcan engines because it has the Crewe 60in spacing of LMS on the tender and the works plate on the frames. Photograph J.T. Rutherford, www.transporttreasury.co.uk

45120

Built as 5120 at Vulcan Foundry 22/6/35
Renumbered 45120 w.e. 19/2/49

Improvements and modifications

27/5/38	Removal of vacuum pump
12/6/43	Steam sanding

Repairs

5/10/36-22/10/36	LS
29/7/37-23/8/37	HS
23/3/38-27/5/38	HG
11/4/40-24/4/40	LS
7/5/41-24/5/41	LS
22/7/42-22/8/42	HS
6/5/43-12/6/43	HG
25/3/44-22/4/44	LS
7/4/45-2/6/45	LS
12/6/45-25/8/45	LO
11/5/46-19/6/46	LS
4/8/47-1/10/47	HG
29/12/48-16/2/49	LI
23/6/49-1/7/49	LC
12/8/49-18/8/49	LC
5/9/49-23/9/49	LC
12/6/50-27/7/50	HI
11/6/51-11/8/51	LI
3/12/51-13/12/51	LC
30/1/52-29/2/52	HC
17/3/52-27/3/52	NC
1/9/52-16/10/52	LI
27/10/52-12/12/52	LC
25/5/53-29/5/53	NC(EO)
4/5/54-3/6/54	HI
26/5/55-25/6/55	HI
3/10/55-7/10/55	NC(EO)
16/11/56-8/12/56	G
21/6/57-29/6/57	LC(EO)
7/4/58-3/5/58	HI
6/5/60-4/6/60	LI
9/11/61-25/11/61	NC
20/9/62-25/10/62	HG
12/5/65-27/5/65	INT

Boilers

New	9050
13/5/38	9037 from 5107
12/6/43	8920 from 5083
1/10/47	9052 from 5115
29/2/52	8953 from 45121
8/12/56	8822 (domed)

Tenders

New	9214
9/5/42	9556 (welded)
9/11/44	9067
15/2/49	10528 (welded)
12/12/52	10599 (part-welded)
25/6/55	10670 (part-welded)
3/5/58	10507 (welded)

Mileage/(weekdays out of service)

1935	32,478 (7)
1936	45,014 (40)
1937	43,667 (51)
1938	43,081 (71)
1939	45,365 (37)
1940	38,006 (40)
1941	42,755 (51)
1942	54,050 (47)
1943	51,532 (74)
1944	48,563 (78)
1945	33,081 (138)
1946	37,722 (76)
1947	27,387 (109)
1948	42,815 (60)
1949	31,580 (131)
1950	38,686 (72)
1951	38,233 (95)
1952	28,518 (129)
1953	45,749 (69)
1954	51,372 (49)
1955	40,848 (82)
1956	32,481 (67)
1957	54,481 (52)
1958	44,179 (61)
1959	20,438
1960	31,367

Mileage at 12/36: 77,492
Mileage at 31/12/50: 655,782

Sheds

Crewe	29/6/35
Edge Hill	6/7/35
Inverness	20/9/41
Motherwell	27/10/45
Inverness	10/12/49
Carlisle Kingmoor	20/12/52
Aintree	18/5/63
Carlisle Kingmoor	23/11/63

Withdrawn w.e. 1/7/67

45120 pauses at Carlisle on 3 July 1960 with a parcels train headed up by an LMS Stove R and then a SR bogie utility van. It was shedded at Carlisle Kingmoor from December 1952 until 1963 and had its first domed boiler from December 1956. It reverted to a welded tender in 1958, having previously been paired with two part-welded examples. There is a holder for a train staff above the cab number. Photograph D. Forsyth, Colourrail.co.uk

45121

Built as 5121 at Vulcan Foundry 27/6/35
Renumbered 45121 w.e. 28/8/48

Improvements and modifications

8/3/38	Removal of vacuum pump
20/5/39	Steam sanding
11/3/61	Fitting BR ATC equipment

Repairs

26/10/36-9/11/36	LS
2/37	?
31/1/38-8/3/38	LS
14/4/39-20/5/39	HG
31/1/41-13/2/41	LS
16/1/42-13/2/42	HS
31/8/42-10/10/42	HG
17/4/43-13/5/43	LS
23/10/43-8/11/43	LO
1/5/44-23/5/44	LS
14/6/45-25/7/45	LS
27/6/46-17/8/46	HS
24/8/46-5/9/46	LO
9/4/47-1/5/47	LO
23/6/47-9/8/47	LO
12/7/48-27/8/48	LS
18/2/49-11/3/49	LC
4/4/49-6/4/49	NC
14/5/49-2/6/49	LC
25/4/50-1/6/50	HI
20/10/50-31/10/50	NC
28/6/51-3/11/51	G
22/11/51-23/11/51	NC
8/9/52-24/9/52	HC
14/4/53-8/5/53	HI
15/9/53-26/9/53	LC
6/11/53-18/11/53	LC
13/9/54-25/9/54	LC(EO)
18/10/54-3/11/54	LC(EO)
12/3/55-16/4/55	G
29/12/56-25/1/57	HI
8/9/58-3/10/58	HI
20/3/59-23/9/59	LC(EO)
9/6/60-30/6/60	LC(EO)
1/2/61-11/3/61	G
23/6/62-11/8/62	HI
25/9/62-12/10/62	LC

Boilers

New	9051
2/37	8637
20/5/39	8969 from 5189
10/10/42	9054 from 5197
17/8/46	8953 from 5084
3/11/51	8977 from 45119
16/4/55	8982 from 45008
11/3/61	8940

Tenders

New	9215
5/9/46	9826 (welded)
29/10/51	9502 (welded)
17/6/52	10507 (welded)
6/5/53	9257 (welded)
14/4/55	10710 (part-welded)
6/2/61	10810 (part-welded)
8/5/63	10712 (part-welded)

Mileage/(weekdays out of service)

1935	29,948 (5)
1936	46,808 (37)
1937	47,812 (50)
1938	53,124 (54)
1939	47,203 (53)
1940	39,279 (48)
1941	49,370 (32)
1942	46,161 (105)
1943	51,327 (79)
1944	48,281 (75)
1945	52,460 (58)
1946	30,012 (96)
1947	35,781 (105)
1948	33,566 (83)
1949	34,227 (109)
1950	34,512 (80)
1951	16,802 (155)
1952	46,981 (63)
1953	38,647 (78)
1954	45,198 (48)
1955	35,719 (77)
1956	44,265 (58)
1957	45,965 (63)
1958	36,954 (89)
1959	44,263
1960	39,109
1961	40,724
1962	26,248

Mileage at 12/36: 76,756
Mileage at 31/12/50: 679,871

Sheds

Crewe	29/6/35
Edge Hill	6/7/35
Crewe North	25/6/38
Carlisle W	16/9/39
Springs Branch	16/8/41
Inverness	20/9/41
Motherwell	27/10/45

Withdrawn 18/6/64

45121 in 1961 at Carlisle before fitting with AWS in March has a St Rollox 1946 style numberplate and close-spaced large cab numbers. It always had a domeless boiler and was paired with a part-welded tender from 1955 onwards. It was allocated to Motherwell from 1945 until withdrawn in 1964. Photograph D. Forsyth, Colourrail.co.uk

45122

Built as 5122 at Vulcan Foundry 29/6/35
Renumbered 45122 w.e. 10/4/48

Improvements and modifications

2/7/38	Removal of vacuum pump
?	Steam sanding

Repairs

26/10/36-10/11/36	LS
10/5/38-2/7/38	HG
30/11/39-23/12/39	LS
8/3/41-9/4/41	HG
24/9/42-10/10/42	HS
11/3/43-10/4/43	HG
31/12/43-12/2/44	LS
8/6/44-13/7/44	LO
15/7/44-11/8/44	LO
26/3/45-27/4/45	LS
4/2/46-15/3/46	HG
10/5/47-7/6/47	LS
29/11/47-23/12/47	LO
5/3/48-10/4/48	LS
7/7/48-9/7/48	NC
28/7/48-14/9/48	LO
30/4/49-18/6/49	HI
3/12/49-17/12/49	LC
20/12/49-22/12/49	LC
24/5/50-8/7/50	HG
26/2/51-27/2/51	NC
28/5/51-30/6/51	LI
16/1/52-17/1/52	LC
16/8/52-10/10/52	LI
27/11/52-16/12/52	NC
23/7/53-15/8/53	LC
13/1/54-10/2/54	HI
14/5/54-29/5/54	LC(EO)
4/7/55-26/8/55	G
25/3/57-25/4/57	LI
14/4/58-17/5/58	HI
30/9/58-3/10/58	LC(EO)
21/1/60-27/2/60	HG
27/9/60-8/10/60	LC(EO)

Boilers

New	9052
14/6/38	8977 from 5197
19/4/41	8975 from 5080
9/10/42	8818 from 5198
10/4/43	9044 from 5183
15/3/46	9024 from 5177
8/7/50	8940 from 5155
26/8/55	8977 from 45121
5/1/60	8828 from 45010

Tenders

New	9216
10/1/47	9265 (welded)
17/12/49	9192
28/6/50	9721 (welded)
26/8/55	9263 (welded)
25/4/57	9192
17/5/58	9229 (welded)

Mileage/(weekdays out of service)

1935	27,917 (15)
1936	51,216 (31)
1937	48,246 (43)
1938	44,001 (68)
1939	48,464 (50)
1940	43,184 (49)
1941	45,327 (46)
1942	58,448 (53)
1943	60,484 (45)
1944	39,434 (107)
1945	29,451 (161)
1946	50,193 (63)
1947	43,853 (69)
1948	35,348 (116)
1949	44,258 (86)
1950	44,220 (83)
1951	44,821 (76)
1952	34,227 (98)
1953	41,172 (77)
1954	46,537 (91)
1955	34,823 (94)
1956	55,543 (40)
1957	45,699 (62)
1958	45,804 (67)
1959	28,991
1960	39,249

Mileage at 12/36: 79,133
Mileage at 31/12/50: 714,044

Sheds

Crewe	6/7/35
Edge Hill	13/7/35
Crewe North	3/7/37
Edge Hill	14/8/37
Carlisle W	29/4/39
Springs Branch	26/7/41
Inverness	20/9/41
Carlisle Kingmoor	25/10/52

Withdrawn w.e. 11/4/64

5122 was at Edge Hill from November 1935 until transferred to Carlisle in April 1939. It is in 1936 livery and was to remain domeless until withdrawn. Photograph www.transporttreasury.co.uk

45123

Built as 5123 at Vulcan Foundry 3/7/35
Renumbered 45123 w.e. 1/5/48

Improvements and modifications

2/8/38	Removal of vacuum pump
28/5/43	Steam sanding
19/9/58	Modernisation
21/8/59	Fitting BR ATC equipment

Repairs

16/11/36-11/12/36	LS
16/6/38-2/8/38	HG
30/11/39-23/12/39	LS
12/2/41-27/2/41	LS
1/5/42-6/6/42	HS
22/4/43-28/5/43	HG
25/2/44-16/3/44	LS
23/2/45-24/3/45	LS
28/1/46-23/2/46	LS
12/10/46-23/11/46	HS
29/11/47-31/12/47	HG
9/4/48-1/5/48	LO
1/1/49-4/2/49	LI
30/3/49-8/4/49	NC
19/4/49-11/5/49	NC
21/9/49-2/11/49	LC
5/12/49-29/12/49	LC
19/9/50-20/10/50	HI
7/1/51-9/1/51	NC
21/5/51-6/6/51	LC
19/7/51-11/9/51	LC
6/3/52-26/4/52	LI
13/7/53-29/8/53	G
18/9/54-3/11/54	HI
5/11/55-16/12/55	LI
28/9/56-17/10/56	HC(EO)
15/2/57-19/3/57	LI
11/9/57-25/9/57	NC(EO)
25/12/57-28/12/57	LC
11/2/58-28/2/58	NC(EO)
9/8/58-19/9/58	G
18/5/59-5/6/59	HC
8/10/60-5/11/60	LI
1/12/60-21/12/60	LC(EO)
21/12/62-27/12/62	NC

Boilers

New	9053
18/7/38	9052 from 5122
28/5/43	9004 from 5029
31/12/47	8667 from 5164 (domed)
29/8/53	8924 from 45090
19/9/58	8932

Tenders

New	9217
17/10/46	9192
28/12/49	9146
28/8/53	9830 (welded)

Mileage/(weekdays out of service)

1935	25,217 (29)
1936	48,932 (41)
1937	43,655 (58)
1938	42,607 (59)
1939	44,565 (59)
1940	37,998 (26)
1941	44,649 (39)
1942	53,990 (60)
1943	57,715 (46)
1944	52,375 (65)
1945	55,247 (68)
1946	40,612 (109)
1947	50,173 (56)
1948	55,101 (57)
1949	21,521 (180)
1950	45,299 (71)
1951	36,297 (90)
1952	41,034 (75)
1953	38,972 (85)
1954	38,747 (74)
1955	39,734 (73)
1956	43,090 (45)
1957	39,209 (80)
1958	34,188 (122)
1959	51,366
1960	28,318
1961	22,759
1962	10,561

Mileage at 12/36: 74,149
Mileage at 31/12/50: 719,656

Sheds

Edge Hill	6/7/35
Inverness	20/9/41
Corkerhill	10/4/62
Hurlford	17/4/62

Withdrawn w.e. 16/9/63

45123 at Wick in a lovely early 1950s scene. It was allocated to 60A Inverness from 1941 until transferred to Corkerhill in 1962 and was domed from December 1947 until August 1953. Its early BR cab numbers are in the high position and it has BRITISH RAILWAYS on the riveted tender. Photograph R.K. Blencowe.

45124

Built as 5124 at Vulcan Foundry 6/7/35
Renumbered 45124 w.e. 1/5/48

Improvements and modifications

1/7/38	Removal of vacuum pump
25/7/42	Steam sanding
6/51	Sloping throatplate boiler
?	Fitting BR ATC equipment

Repairs

19/5/38-1/7/38	HG
4/3/40-19/3/40	LS
25/4/41-13/5/41	LS
11/6/42-25/7/42	HG
17/5/43-17/6/43	LS
1/5/44-24/5/44	LS
14/4/45-16/6/45	LS
25/1/46-7/3/46	HS
31/5/46-26/6/46	LO
7/9/46-26/9/46	LO
21/2/47-17/4/47	HG
27/3/48-30/4/48	LS
20/11/48-17/12/48	LO
2/5/49-5/5/49	NC
6/10/49-3/11/49	HI
5/6/50-30/6/50	LC
24/3/51-2/6/51	G
22/9/51-5/10/51	LC(EO)
23/5/52-3/7/52	HI
14/5/53-18/6/53	LI
20/1/54-25/1/54	HI
14/6/54-17/6/54	NC(EO)
28/10/54-25/11/54	LC(EO)
19/3/55-30/3/55	LC(EO)
14/5/55-25/6/55	G
1/7/55	LC(TO)
28/12/56-29/12/56	LC(EO)
12/6/57-9/8/57	HI
11/12/57-21/12/57	NC(EO)
8/9/58	LC
9/1/59-22/1/59	LC(EO)
14/10/59-4/12/59	LC
10/2/61-24/3/61	G
24/11/61-6/12/61	LC(EO)
11/10/62-24/10/62	LC(EO)
27/2/63-19/4/63	G
24/11/65-25/11/65	NC

Boilers

New	9054
13/6/38	8652 from 5035 (domed)
25/7/42	8952 from 5083
17/4/47	8934 from 5166
2/6/51	Sloping throatplate
25/6/55	?

Tenders

New	9218
25/5/43	9192
1/5/45	9214
?	9717 (welded)
25/6/55	10713 (part-welded)
1/7/55	10599 (part-welded)
28/2/63	9261 (welded)
17/4/63	10445 (welded)
13/2/65	10599 (part-welded)

Mileage/(weekdays out of service)

1935	29,249 (9)
1936	47,989 (48)
1937	48,611 (58)
1938	47,137 (54)
1939	46,352 (35)
1940	37,723 (38)
1941	44,351 (37)
1942	59,997 (52)
1943	54,933 (42)
1944	50,585 (58)
1945	51,837 (84)
1946	36,609 (105)
1947	44,243 (71)
1948	45,079 (77)
1949	42,183 (76)
1950	49,196 (59)

Mileage at 12/36: 77,238
Mileage at 31/12/50: 736,074

Sheds

Edge Hill	6/7/35
Inverness	20/9/41
Corkerhill	31/5/60
Hurlford	13/6/60
Corkerhill	31/12/66 (PE)
Motherwell	4/2/67 (PE)

Polmadie 8/4/67 (PE)

Withdrawn 1/5/67

The last of the Vulcan Foundry built engines, 45124 at Wick in April 1952. Allocated to Inverness since 1941, this picture was taken during its period with a sloping throatplate boiler between 1951 and 1955, when it reverted to a domeless boiler. It has tablet exchange apparatus partly obscuring the large cab numbers and brackets below the bufferbeam to attach a snowplough. Photograph H Brighty, www.transporttreasury.co.uk

45125

Built as 5125 at Armstrong Whitworth 29/4/35
Renumbered 45125 w.e. 10/7/48

Improvements and modifications

23/12/38	Steam sanding
23/12/38	Removal of vacuum pump
29/1/60	Fitting BR ATC equipment

Repairs

8/5/35-22/5/35	LO
9/7/36-4/8/36	LS
20/11/36-29/12/36	LO
18/8/37-7/9/37	HS
15/11/38-23/12/38	HG
15/5/40-30/5/40	LS
28/7/41-12/8/41	LS
17/3/42-1/5/42	HS
3/2/43-20/2/43	HG
3/12/43-7/1/44	LS
14/1/44-26/2/44	LO
24/4/44-26/5/44	HO
7/11/44-25/11/44	LO
14/5/45-16/6/45	LS
27/3/46-18/4/46	HS
16/5/47-24/6/47	HS
23/12/47-31/12/47	NC
10/6/48-8/7/48	HS
16/8/48	TRO
12/5/49-23/6/49	LI
15/8/49-17/9/49	LC
3/6/50-1/7/50	HI
5/7/50-6/7/50	NC(R)
24/7/50-11/8/50	LC
28/12/50-31/1/51	LC
5/6/51-16/6/51	LC
14/11/51-21/12/51	G
4/1/52-8/1/52	NC(TO)
13/3/53-18/4/53	LI
19/6/54-10/7/54	LI
7/12/54-30/12/54	HC(EO)
20/6/55-20/8/55	G
5/9/55-10/9/55	LC(EO)
20/9/55-22/9/55	NC(EO)
27/9/55-29/9/55	NC(EO)
28/10/55-4/11/55	NC(EO)
9/11/55-9/12/55	LC(EO)
5/9/56-12/10/56	LI
24/1/57-31/1/57	NC(EO)
11/11/57-6/12/57	HI
12/5/58-29/5/58	LC(EO)
29/7/59-19/9/59	G
21/1/60-29/1/60	NC(EO)
13/5/61-16/6/61	LI
22/8/61-30/9/61	LC(EO)
23/11/61-7/12/61	LC(EO)

Boilers

New	8905
24/12/38	8928 from 5148
20/2/43	8982 from 5067
26/5/44	8824 from 5164
12/7/47	9043 from 5161
21/12/51	9005 from 45117
20/8/55	8951 from 45013
19/9/59	8923 from 45013

Tenders

New	9229
21/6/49	9843
20/12/51	9625
20/8/55	9061 (riveted)
9/12/55	10526
19/9/59	10527

Mileage/(weekdays out of service)

1935	30,870 (35)
1936	48,179 (94)
1937	49,308 (60)
1938	44,053 (77)
1939	46,151 (38)
1940	40,147 (55)
1941	38,611 (39)
1942	61,839 (50)
1943	59,636 (56)
1944	39,899 (136)
1945	64,039 (73)
1946	60,096 (61)
1947	49,764 (92)
1948	52,550 (71)
1949	51,065 (83)
1950	40,753 (87)
1951	40,874 (101)
1952	53,916 (43)
1953	57,217 (49)
1954	52,027 (63)
1955	29,284 (159)
1956	40,851 (96)
1957	47,474 (83)
1958	44,012 (69)
1959	24,152
1960	49,532
1961	22,217
1962	29,885

Mileage at 12/36: 79,049
Mileage at 31/12/50: 776,960

Sheds

Crewe	4/5/35
Holyhead	22/5/35
Shrewsbury	2/11/35
Crewe North	3/7/37
Edge Hill	13/11/37
Crewe North	25/6/38
Carlisle W	16/9/39
Perth	27/12/41
Stirling	23/10/58
Stranraer	29/11/58
St.Rollox	13/7/59
Grangemouth	23/3/61

Withdrawn w.e. 13/5/63

First of the Armstrong Whitworth Class 5s 5125 in the late-1930s. It has been repainted in 1936 livery and has an 8A Edge Hill shedplate, where it was based from November 1937 until 1939. Photograph www.rail-online.co.uk

45126

Built as 5126 at Armstrong Whitworth 29/4/35
Renumbered 45126 w.e. 26/6/48

Improvements and modifications

1/5/39	Steam sanding
1/5/39	Removal of vacuum pump
19/6/54	Modernisation
?	Fitting BR ATC equipment

Repairs

2/1/36-27/1/36	HS
28/5/36-28/7/36	LO
21/8/37-20/9/37	HS
5/4/39-1/5/39	HG
11/10/40-26/10/40	LS
6/2/42-1/5/42	HS
3/11/42-2/12/42	LS
28/8/43-24/9/43	HG
26/10/44-25/11/44	LS
11/3/46-13/4/46	LS
14/2/47-3/4/47	HO
16/5/47-12/6/47	LO
28/5/48-25/6/48	HG
10/3/49-5/3/49	LC
18/10/49-1/12/49	LI
2/11/50-30/11/50	LI
8/6/51-21/6/51	LC
12/7/51-10/8/51	LC
30/8/51-11/9/51	LC
12/8/52-4/10/52	G
23/3/54-21/4/54	LI
16/4/56-12/5/56	LI(EO)
21/11/56-8/12/56	LC(EO)
20/5/58-20/6/58	G
14/9/59-15/10/59	HI
6/2/61-16/2/61	LC(EO)
4/5/61-24/6/61	LI
31/7/61-15/8/61	NC(EO)
6/9/61	NC(EO)
23/2/62	NC(EO)
19/3/63-18/4/63	LI
26/1/65-1/3/65	LI

Boilers

New	8906
20/5/39	8817 from 5000 (domed)
24/9/43	8994 from 5172
25/6/48	8944 from 5083
4/10/52	8965
20/6/58	8682 (domed)

Tenders

New	9230
27/1/36	9116 (riveted)
16/1/42	9271
24/9/43	9679
15/5/44	9364 (riveted)
13/4/46	9473
19/2/47	9720
18/2/49	10556 (part-welded)
4/3/49	9263
30/11/50	10502
18/7/51	9192 (riveted)
24/9/52	9255
12/5/56	9031 (riveted)
21/6/58	9365 (riveted)

Mileage/(weekdays out of service)

1935	30,699 (28)
1936	34,821 (101)
1937	39,609 (60)
1938	40,020 (40)
1939	38,017 (42)
1940	31,191 (61)
1941	38,099 (32)
1942	38,841 (126)
1943	54,583 (48)
1944	45,083 (93)
1945	47,889 (66)
1946	35,936 (81)
1947	37,454 (99)
1948	39,649 (74)
1949	25,008 (117)
1950	40,936 (58)
1951	43,808 (86)
1952	45,529 (87)
1953	52,136 (40)
1954	50,537 (51)
1955	53,355 (38)
1956	40,526 (81)
1957	51,716 (41)
1958	50,802 (65)
1959	47,502
1960	54,205

Mileage at 12/36: 65,520
Mileage at 31/12/50: 617,835

Sheds

Crewe	4/5/35
Holyhead	25/5/35
Springs Branch	5/10/35
Patricroft	14/6/41
Aberdeen	27/12/41
Carlisle Kingmoor	17/1/42

Withdrawn w.e. 20/5/67

A 1940s shot of 5126 carrying a 12A Carlisle Kingmoor plate which it had from January 1942 until withdrawn in 1967. It is domeless with a St Rollox style 'incorrect' top feed cover which dates the picture post September 1943 and probably 1946/7, when it reverted back to a welded tender after having a riveted tender between May 1944 and April 1946. The crosshead vacuum pump has long gone and there is a tablet staff holder above the cab number. Photograph R.K. Blencowe.

45127

Built as 5127 at Armstrong Whitworth 29/4/35
Renumbered 45127 w.e. 2/4/49

Improvements and modifications

11/6/38	Removal of vacuum pump
25/2/39	Steam sanding
?	Fitting BR ATC equipment

Repairs

4/5/35-17/5/35	LO
23/4/38-26/5/38	LO
17/1/39-16/2/39	HG
3/9/40-14/9/40	LS
27/10/41-17/11/41	LS
5/3/42-11/4/42	LS
4/11/42-8/12/42	HG
18/2/44-4/3/44	LS
27/6/45-18/8/45	LS
28/5/46-3/7/46	LS
4/1/47-21/1/47	LO
16/1/48-13/2/48	HG
26/2/48-28/2/48	NC(R)
28/2/49-29/3/49	LI
19/12/49-22/12/49	LC
23/3/50-3/5/50	LI
3/7/52-30/8/52	G
3/10/52-17/10/52	LC(EO)
13/3/53-11/4/53	LC(EO)
12/1/54-30/1/54	HI
5/10/54-13/10/54	LC(EO)
19/10/55-21/12/55	HI
8/5/57-7/6/57	G
20/10/58-13/11/58	HI
10/6/59-17/6/59	NC(EO)
19/10/60-18/11/60	HI
21/2/63-29/3/63	G
14/10/63-8/11/63	LC
15/4/65-26/4/65	LC
17/2/66-9/4/66	LC

Boilers

New	8907
25/2/39	9031 from 5101
8/12/42	8958 from 5167
3/2/48	8656 from 5036 (domed)

Tenders

New	9231
7/9/38	9530
9/12/41	9266
16/1/48	9713
?	9127 (riveted)
?	9070 (riveted)
5/4/55	9210 (riveted)
7/6/57	10549 (part-welded)
16/7/64	9097 (riveted)
?	9298
26/3/66	9226 (riveted)

Mileage/(weekdays out of service)

1935	29,892 (36)
1936	45,513 (35)
1937	41,065 (64)
1938	35,331 (73)
1939	29,647 (52)
1940	28,498 (57)
1941	36,119 (52)
1942	49,188 (80)
1943	58,113 (30)
1944	51,014 (57)
1945	43,444 (91)
1946	49,190 (74)
1947	45,329 (87)
1948	48,176 (71)
1949	41,560 (75)
1950	41,326 (62)

Mileage at 12/36: 75,405
Mileage at 31/12/50: 673,405

Sheds

Crewe	4/5/35
Holyhead	25/5/35
Springs Branch	5/10/35
Crewe	13/4/40
Springs Branch	26/7/41
Aberdeen	27/12/41
Carlisle Kingmoor	17/1/42
Aberdeen	1/10/49
Perth	29/10/49
Dalry Road	16/8/51
St Margarets	4/10/65
Dundee (Tay Bridge)	10/9/66 (PE)

Withdrawn 19/11/66

45127 was allocated to 62B Dundee (Tay Bridge) for the final two months until it was withdrawn in November 1966. It has AWS and a domeless boiler, but the dates for these are not recorded on the Engine History Card. It spent its early years on the Western Division, mainly at Springs Branch before moving to the Northern Division at the end of 1941, where it stayed until withdrawal. Photograph www.Rail-online.co.uk

45128

Built as 5128 at Armstrong Whitworth 16/5/35
Renumbered 45128 w.e. 28/5/49

Improvements and modifications

29/7/38	Removal of vacuum pump
?	Steam sanding
30/5/59	Fitting BR ATC equipment

Repairs

4/9/36-1/10/36	LS
12/7/37-27/7/37	HS
6/6/38-29/7/38	HG
19/2/40-2/3/40	LS
2/5/42-13/6/42	HG
22/3/43-17/4/43	LO
23/12/43-4/1/44	LO
7/6/44-21/6/44	LS
24/9/45-27/10/45	HS
9/4/47-9/5/47	HG
19/7/47-16/8/47	LO
10/5/49-27/5/49	HI
6/12/50-11/1/51	HI
24/2/52-27/3/52	HG
29/7/52-18/8/52	LC(EO)
10/6/54-28/6/54	LI
6/5/56-4/6/56	HG
19/4/58-14/5/58	HI
20/5/59-30/5/59	NC(EO)
8/6/59-18/6/59	LC(EO)
14/3/60-14/4/60	HI

Boilers

New	8908
1/7/38	8970 from 5190
13/6/42	8997 from 5129
9/5/47	8670 from 5033 (domed)
27/3/52	8963 from 45207
4/6/56	8942 from 45207
30/5/62	8649 from 45207 (domed)

Tenders

New	9232

Mileage/(weekdays out of service)

1935	34,829 (18)
1936	45,281 (46)
1937	51,816 (27)
1938	38,851 (86)
1939	49,197 (29)
1940	36,662 (29)
1941	31,696 (54)
1942	31,013 (62)
1943	34,029 (46)
1944	33,134 (43)
1945	30,017 (55)
1946	36,951 (51)
1947	30,879 (78)
1948	32,488 (45)
1949	34,302 (47)
1950	32,540 (48)
1951	39,311 (34)
1952	38,672 (62)
1953	43,282 (39)
1954	41,185 (45)
1955	39,176 (57)
1956	39,538 (48)
1957	35,929 (50)
1958	38,686 (52)
1959	33,222
1960	33,729

Mileage at 12/36: 80,110
Mileage at 31/12/50: 583,685

Sheds

Crewe	18/5/35
Holyhead	25/5/35
Llandudno Jct	6/7/35
Springs Branch	5/10/35
Edge Hill	7/3/36
Longsight	2/1/43 (loan)
Edge Hill	10/4/43
Crewe North	9/3/46 (loan)
Crewe North	4/5/46
Stafford	14/9/46
Crewe North	8/2/47
Preston	21/6/47
Crewe South	11/10/47
Bristol	8/7/50 (loan)
Sheffield	5/8/50 (loan)
Kentish Town	7/10/50 (loan)
Sheffield	21/10/50 (loan)
Crewe South	30/12/50
Crewe North	5/4/52
Edge Hill	31/5/52
Crewe North	5/7/52
Crewe South	18/4/53
Springs Branch	24/7/65

Withdrawn w.e. 10/9/66

45128 at Crewe North in May 1949 following completion of a Heavy Intermediate overhaul when it received plain black livery with no tender insignia and its BR number. It was allocated to one or other of the Crewe sheds for most of its life but went on loan several times. The domeless boiler was carried from May 1947 until early 1952 and the welded tender was the original. Photograph www.rail-online.co.uk

45129

Built as 5129 at Armstrong Whitworth 21/5/35
Renumbered 45129 w.e. 19/2/49

Improvements and modifications

?	Steam sanding
?	Removal of vacuum pump
16/11/40	BTH speed indicator
7/12/54	Modernisation
10/10/59	Fitting BR ATC equipment

Repairs

4/6/36-18/6/36	LS
14/6/37-28/6/37	HS
25/3/39-2/5/39	HG
4/11/40-16/11/40	LS
16/5/41-29/1/41	LO
3/4/42-1/5/42	HS
24/5/43-5/6/43	LS
26/5/45-23/6/45	LS
3/7/47-30/8/47	HG
13/1/49-15/2/49	HI
12/6/50-24/7/50	HG
26/7/51-30/8/51	LI
4/5/52-12/6/52	LI
7/6/53-26/6/53	LC
13/9/53-5/10/53	LC(EO)
28/10/54-7/12/54	HG
14/5/57-8/6/57	LI
5/9/59-10/10/59	HG
23/1/61-24/2/61	LC(EO)

Boilers

New	8909
2/5/39	8997 from 5217
1/5/42	8935 from 5017
30/8/47	9042 from 5057
24/7/50	9055 from 5190
7/12/54	8830 from 45205
10/10/59	9015 from 45032

Tenders

New	9233
23/6/45	9244
7/1/49	9301
12/11/55	9286

Mileage/(weekdays out of service)

1935	37,450 (31)
1936	61,813 (55)
1937	43,989 (52)
1938	41,485 (65)
1939	44,829 (58)
1940	36,566 (40)
1941	31,807 (59)
1942	28,820 (65)
1943	31,155 (40)
1944	25,953 (37)
1945	30,349 (60)
1946	28,424 (43)
1947	25,876 (86)
1948	31,917 (29)
1949	39,965 (65)
1950	40,894 (64)
1951	40,550 (62)
1952	41,300 (76)
1953	39,109 (78)
1954	37,073 (67)
1955	45,336 (45)
1956	32,526 (30)
1957	36,108 (38)
1958	36,730 (37)
1959	32,481
1960	38,646

Mileage at 12/36: 99,263
Mileage at 31/12/60: 582,292

Sheds

Crewe	25/5/35
Llandudno Jct	1/6/35
Edge Hill	16/9/39
Warrington	20/4/40
Crewe North	30/11/40
Patricroft	9/8/41
Springs Branch	23/8/41
Carlisle Upperby	22/11/47 (loan)
Springs Branch	7/2/48
Carlisle Upperby	23/10/48
Patricroft	12/6/54
Bank Hall	19/10/63
Warrington	21/11/64

Withdrawn w.e. 17/9/66

45129 between November 1964 and withdrawal in September 1966 when it was shedded at 8B Warrington. It was always both domeless and with a welded tender and has the usual late additions of overhead line warning flashes and lower top lamp iron, plus AWS fitted in October 1959. Photograph R.K. Blencowe, www.transporttreasury.co.uk

45130

Built as 5130 at Armstrong Whitworth 21/5/35
Renumbered 45130 w.e. 15/5/48

Improvements and modifications

22/4/39	Removal of vacuum pump
13/5/39	Steam sanding
20/1/59	Fitting BR ATC equipment

Repairs

9/7/36-27/7/36	LS
5/10/37-21/10/37	HS
20/4/39-13/5/39	HG
6/6/40-20/6/40	LS
10/5/42-24/6/42	LS
16/12/42-6/1/43	LO
2/2/44-19/2/44	HG
1/5/45-19/5/45	HS
17/2/47-12/3/47	HG
15/4/48-13/5/48	LO
6/11/48-26/11/48	HS
22/11/49-14/11/49	HI
13/10/50-25/11/50	HG
30/3/53-5/5/53	HG
15/1/55-14/2/55	LI
12/9/56-24/10/56	HG
31/10/56-9/11/56	NC(Rect)
19/9/58-9/10/58	HI
22/10/58-10/11/58	NC(Rect)(EO)
12/1/59-20/1/59	NC(EO)
19/9/60-15/10/60	HI
7/3/61-20/4/61	HC(EO)
29/8/62-5/10/62	HG
30/10/64-9/12/64	LI
2/2/66-21/3/66	Coll.Damage

Boilers

New	8910
18/5/39	8974 from 5194
19/2/44	8963 from 5140
12/3/47	9006 from 5197
25/11/50	9012 from 5015
5/5/53	8913 from 45060
24/10/56	8987 from 45107

Tenders

New	9234
11/8/67	9528

Mileage/(weekdays out of service)

1935	39,015 (35)
1936	61,431 (51)
1937	45,193 (71)
1938	46,770 (56)
1939	40,957 (81)
1940	30,770 (69)
1941	33,192 (47)
1942	25,957 (73)
1943	32,456 (60)
1944	36,358 (43)
1945	39,282 (64)
1946	44,636 (35)
1947	44,110 (63)
1948	31,177 (69)
1949	34,947 (55)
1950	34,809 (65)
1951	38,364 (47)
1952	34,301 (53)
1953	34,233 (52)
1954	41,942 (37)
1955	34,771 (61)
1956	34,416 (83)
1957	40,570 (29)
1958	37,172 (72)
1959	40,634
1960	38,629

Mileage at 12/36: 100,446
Mileage at 31/12/50: 621,060

Sheds

Crewe	25/5/35
Llandudno Jct	1/6/35
Chester	10/4/37(loan)
Llandudno Jct	17/4/37
Edge Hill	16/9/39
Crewe North	9/3/46 (loan)
Crewe North	4/5/46
Bletchley	14/9/46
Chester	20/10/51
Mold Jn	9/2/52
Southern Region	23/5/53 (loan)
Mold Jct	27/6/53
Aston	3/8/57 (loan)
Mold Jct	17/8/57
Crewe South	7/11/59
Willesden	10/6/61
Rugby	9/9/61
Chester	22/6/63
Croes Newydd	2/10/65
Birkenhead	10/5/67

Withdrawn w.e. 11/11/67

45130 slog s through Ashton with an up West Coast main line freight on 13 July 1961. It was allocated briefly to Willesden in the previous month but moved on to Rugby in September. 45130 was always domeless with a welded tender. It received AWS in January 1959. Photograph www.rail-online.co.uk

45131

Built as 5131 at Armstrong Whitworth 21/5/35
Renumbered 45131 w.e. 29/10/49

Improvements and modifications

9/8/38	Removal of vacuum pump
12/6/42	Steam sanding
13/12/55	Modernisation
27/2/60	Fitting BR ATC equipment

Repairs

8/10/36-23/10/36	LS
14/7/37-30/7/37	HS
15/6/38-9/8/38	HG
31/1/40-10/2/40	LS
12/5/42-12/6/42	HG
1/11/43-17/11/43	HS
2/8/44-19/8/44	HO
11/6/45-18/7/45	LS
4/8/47-2/10/47	HG
10/10/49-27/10/49	LI
29/5/50-22/6/50	HI
31/5/51-18/6/51	HG
11/6/52-8/7/52	LC
21/1/54-11/2/54	LI
18/11/55-13/12/55	HG
27/12/57-20/1/58	HI
25/1/60-27/2/60	LI
18/9/61-21/10/61	HG
24/3/65-17/4/65	INT
9/9/66-25/10/66	HC

Boilers

New	8911
9/8/38	8666 from 5049 (domed)
12/6/42	8986 from 5190
19/8/44	8682 from 5031 (domed)
2/10/47	8997 from 5128
18/6/51	8662 from 45220 (domed)
13/12/55	9037 from 45202
21/10/61	9013 from 45139

Tenders

New	9235
18/7/45	9259
?	9918
?	9259

Mileage/(weekdays out of service)

1935	27,811 (47)
1936	49,573 (49)
1937	41,914 (62)
1938	36,005 (82)
1939	38,630 (31)
1940	30,633 (42)
1941	32,280 (41)
1942	31,232 (43)
1943	38,592 (48)
1944	36,952 (51)
1945	35,148 (55)
1946	21,516 (55)
1947	22,192 (94)
1948	30,174 (64)
1949	28,723 (56)
1950	35,367 (50)
1951	35,211 (41)
1952	40,139 (55)
1953	39,196 (38)
1954	38,823 (52)
1955	36,051 (58)
1956	44,049 (23)
1957	38,763 (36)
1958	40,323 (51)
1959	37,004
1960	38,524

Mileage at 12/36: 77,384
Mileage at 31/12/50: 536,742

Sheds

Crewe	25/5/35
Patricroft	1/6/35
Bangor	20/7/35
Chester	5/10/35
Crewe	8/2/36
Monument Lane	7/3/36
Crewe South	15/10/38
Crewe North	20/3/43
Crewe South	4/3/44
Carlisle W	8/4/44
Crewe North	14/7/45
Crewe South	17/11/45
Holyhead	10/6/61
Edge Hill	28/10/61
Holyhead	23/6/62
Speke Junction	13/10/62

Withdrawn w.e. 20/4/68

5131 pictured at Crewe North had just completed a Heavy General repair in August 1938. It emerged in 1936 livery with a domed boiler and had lost its crosshead vacuum pump. It was shedded at Monument Lane from March 1936 until October 1938 when it went to Crewe South. Photograph E.R. Morten.

45132

Built as 5132 at Armstrong Whitworth 21/5/35
Renumbered 45132 w.e. 23/4/49

Improvements and modifications

23/3/39	Removal of vacuum pump
?	Steam sanding
27/4/56	Modification
30/5/59	Fitting BR ATC equipment

Repairs

9/6/36-24/6/36	LS
30/4/37-18/5/37	HS
19/11/37-6/12/37	LS
23/5/38-3/6/38	LO
7/2/39-23/3/39	HG
18/3/40-22/4/40	LS
20/3/41-5/4/41	HS
26/11/41-13/12/41	LO
7/11/42-12/12/42	LS
7/3/44-23/3/44	HG
12/1/46-31/1/46	LS
14/2/47-26/3/47	LO
17/1/48-12/2/48	LS
26/3/49-19/4/49	HG
9/9/50-5/10/50	HI
7/8/52-20/9/52	HG
19/3/53-28/4/53	LC
12/10/53-14/11/53	LI
26/2/55-24/3/55	LI
10/3/56-27/4/56	HG
14/3/58-10/4/58	HI
20/5/59-30/5/59	NC(EO)
5/6/59-10/7/59	LC
28/11/60-11/1/61	HI
9/5/62-8/6/62	HG
20/8/62-8/9/62	LC
1/4/64-12/5/64	INT
14/3/66-5/4/66	INT

Boilers

New	8912
23/3/39	8686 from 5069 (domed)
23/3/44	8973 from 5082
19/4/49	8832 from 5070
20/9/52	8835 from 45106
27/4/56	9045 from 45218

Tenders

New	9236
7/4/53	9098 (riveted)
24/3/57	9592

Mileage/(weekdays out of service)

1935	35,298 (8)
1936	58,263 (49)
1937	42,343 (52)
1938	55,089 (48)
1939	47,260 (64)
1940	38,121 (61)
1941	23,032 (102)
1942	31,836 (61)
1943	39,861 (22)
1944	34,861 (52)
1945	26,795 (28)
1946	43,457 (48)
1947	34,822 (61)
1948	36,178 (50)
1949	33,989 (40)
1950	32,424 (55)
1951	34,051 (49)
1952	35,171 (74)
1953	39,563 (110)
1954	40,456 (64)
1955	41,170 (52)
1956	37,233 (65)
1957	41,880 (44)
1958	40,140 (54)
1959	36,151
1960	32,144

Mileage at 12/36: 93,561
Mileage at 31/12/50: 613,629

Sheds

Crewe	25/5/35
Patricroft	1/6/35
Carlisle W	25/9/37
Crewe	21/3/42
Mold Junction	4/4/42
Aston	14/8/43
Mold Jct	24/4/48
Chester	11/10/52
Trafford Park	18/9/54
Aston	6/11/54
Crewe North	5/9/59
Stoke	14/9/63
Holyhead	20/6/64
Shrewsbury	2/10/65

Withdrawn w.e. 4/3/67

Crewe North allocated 45132 at Berkhamstead on 11 May 1963 with what looks like ECS, possibly heading to Wolverton Works. It had received AWS in May 1959, had carried a domeless boiler since 1944 and been paired with a welded tender since 1957.

45133

Built as 5133 at Armstrong Whitworth 21/5/35
Renumbered 45133 w.e. 2/10/48

Improvements and modifications

10/10/39	Removal of vacuum pump
20/10/45	Steam sanding
25/2/59	Fitting BR ATC equipment

Repairs

8/9/36-28/9/36	LS
20/5/37-23/6/37	HS
31/12/37-31/1/38	HG
14/9/39-10/10/39	LS
24/3/41-16/4/41	HG
13/3/42-28/3/42	LS
22/4/43-11/5/43	LS
23/2/44-9/3/44	LO
2/10/44-14/10/44	LS
1/10/45 20/10/45	HG
20/5/46-5/6/46	LO
24/3/47-29/4/47	HS
3/9/48-30/9/48	LS
5/3/50-5/4/50	HG
14/8/50-11/9/50	LC
22/12/51-28/1/52	LI
4/8/52-27/8/52	LC(EO)
11/8/53-14/9/53	HI
29/1/55-3/3/55	HG
28/3/55-7/4/55	NC(Rect)EO
18/4/55-26/4/55	NC(Rect)EO
17/8/56-15/9/56	LI
4/9/58-10/10/58	LI
19/2/59-25/2/59	NC(EO)
30/6/59-8/7/59	LC(EO)
12/4/60-25/5/60	HG
4/10/62-7/11/62	HI
21/7/65-20/8/65	LI

Boilers

New	8913
10/1/38	8672 from 5055 (domed)
16/4/41	8922 from 5093
20/10/45	8990 from 5079
5/4/50	8836 from 5063
3/3/55	8829 from 45006

Tenders

New	9237
14/10/44	9514

Mileage/(weekdays out of service)

1935	34,713 (10)
1936	51,276 (48)
1937	41,092 (62)
1938	47,661 (78)
1939	47,165 (71)
1940	44,912 (37)
1941	38,740 (53)
1942	23,772 (50)
1943	34,333 (51)
1944	33,001 (61)
1945	36,562 (66)
1946	37,016 (44)
1947	33,582 (65)
1948	38,574 (59)
1949	41,146 (49)
1950	31,746 (83)
1951	38,706 (47)
1952	43,487 (64)
1953	40,598 (70)
1954	43,845 (40)
1955	35,697 (71)
1956	39,643 (74)
1957	38,343 (40)
1958	25,000 (55)
1959	37,147
1960	34,185

Mileage at 12/36: 85,989
Mileage at 31/12/50: 615,291

Sheds

Crewe	25/5/35
Patricroft	1/6/35
Carlisle W	25/9/37
Carnforth	4/11/50
Holyhead	25/6/55
Llandudno Jct	19/11/55
Patricroft	22/6/57
Agecroft	9/11/63
Newton Heath	19/6/65
Warrington	6/8/66
Edge Hill	7/10/67

Stored
3/12/62-11/3/63

Withdrawn w.e. 3/2/68

45133 at Manchester Exchange in the early 1960s. The domed boiler was fitted in May 1960 and the AWS in February 1959. It was allocated to Patricroft from June 1957 until transferred to Agecroft in November 1963. Photograph Colourrail.co.uk

45134

Built as 5134 at Armstrong Whitworth 22/5/35
Renumbered 45134 w.e. 11/9/48

Improvements and modifications

3/9/38	Removal of vacuum pump
2/9/44	Steam sanding
27/3/57	Modification
30/10/59	Fitting BR ATC equipment

Repairs

31/8/36-14/9/36	**LS**
13/11/36-27/11/36	**LS**
28/4/37-18/5/37	**LO**
2/11/37-18/11/37	**LS**
5/8/38-31/8/38	**HG**
8/2/40-22/2/40	**LS**
22/4/41-10/5/41	**HG**
27/1/42-29/1/42	**TRO**
3/10/42-21/11/42	**HS**
30/9/43-28/10/43	**LO**
9/1/44-12/2/44	**LO**
4/7/44-5/8/44	**HS**
14/8/46-11/9/46	**LS**
12/6/47-5/7/47	**LO**
16/8/48-10/9/48	**HG**
26/6/50-28/7/50	**HI**
24/3/52-22/4/52	**HG**
26/1/53-28/2/53	**LC(EO)**
15/6/53-23/7/53	**LI**
29/1/55-24/2/55	**HI**
8/2/56-1/3/56	**LC(EO)**
16/2/57-27/3/57	**HG**
19/9/59-30/10/59	**HI**
3/4/62-2/5/62	**HG**
20/9/65-28/10/65	**LI**
10/8/66-17/10/66	**HC**

Boilers

New	8914
31/8/38	5994 from 5214
10/5/41	8985 from 5050
5/8/44	8685 from 5219 (domed)
10/9/48	9032 from 5146
22/4/52	8680 from 45050 (domed)
27/3/57	8959 from 45075

Tenders

New	9238
27/3/57	9325
?	10497

Mileage/(weekdays out of service)

1935	35,861(9)
1936	53,736(42)
1937	46,955(62)
1938	47,384(64)
1939	51,790(44)
1940	43,272(38)
1941	35,354(55)
1942	25,447(83)
1943	29,875(51)
1944	28,952(76)
1945	30,865(45)
1946	27,941(92)
1947	32,723(66)
1948	28,093(61)
1949	36,625(41)
1950	36,951(54)
1951	38,809(38)
1952	41,505(51)
1953	35,752(78)
1954	45,203(25)
1955	36,668(62)
1956	34,848(64)
1957	38,774(58)
1958	43,132(35)
1959	34,457
1960	39,645

Mileage at 12/36: 89,597
Mileage at 31/12/50: 591,824

Sheds

Crewe	25/5/35
Patricroft	1/6/35
Carlisle W	25/9/37
Crewe South	7/2/42
Crewe North	5/7/52
Carlisle Upperby	4/10/52 (loan)
Crewe North	25/10/52
Crewe South	18/4/53
Monument Lane	18/6/60
Bescot	17/9/60
Lancaster	14/10/61
Northampton	13/1/62
Tyseley	2/10/65
Shrewsbury	17/9/66
Carnforth	10/12/66

Withdrawn w.e. 3/8/68

45134 at Stafford on the down slow with an excursion had been domeless since March 1957 and received AWS in October 1959. The photo was taken between January 1962 and October 1965 while it was at 2E Northampton. Photograph www.rail-online.co.uk

45135

Built as 5135 at Armstrong Whitworth 22/5/35
Renumbered 45135 w.e. 7/8/48

Improvements and modifications

21/3/39	Removal of vacuum pump
24/4/46	Steam sanding
29/4/60	Fitting BR ATC equipment

Repairs

16/11/36-2/12/36	LS
29/4/37-17/5/37	LO
30/8/37-1/10/37	HG
23/2/39-21/3/39	LS
21/1/41-14/2/41	HG
15/10/41-1/11/41	HO
8/7/42-21/7/42	TRO
4/3/43-29/3/43	LS
18/2/44-23/3/44	LO
17/7/45-23/8/45	LS
3/4/46-24/4/46	HG
16/1/48-4/3/48	HS
21/7/48-6/8/48	LO
5/12/49-29/12/49	HI
23/7/51-31/8/51	HG
5/5/53-3/6/53	LI
12/6/55-2/7/55	HG
6/4/56-14/5/56	LC(EO)
16/5/56-17/5/56	NC(Rect)
5/3/58-27/3/58	HI
27/6/59-8/7/59	LC(EO)
20/4/60-29/4/60	NC(EO)
23/9/60-29/10/60	HG
12/12/62-7/1/63	HI
21/1/63-6/2/63	LC
8/3/66-29/3/66	HI

Boilers

New	8915
16/9/37	8661 from 5044 (domed)
14/2/41	8647 from 5042 (domed)
24/4/46	8966 from 5028
31/8/51	8997 from 45131
2/7/55	9042 from 45021
29/10/60	8640 from 45195 (domed)

Tenders

New	9239
17/12/43	9680
8/3/66	9173 (riveted)

Mileage/(weekdays out of service)

1935	34,574 (12)
1936	50,367 (43)
1937	46,807 (79)
1938	52,875 (38)
1939	42,812 (55)
1940	36,675 (57)
1941	28,802 (107)
1942	37,250 (24)
1943	36,324 (30)
1944	34,888 (45)
1945	35,813 (54)
1946	43,838 (38)
1947	38,408 (45)
1948	29,969 (93)
1949	24,851 (49)
1950	39,017 (34)
1951	31,734 (60)
1952	41,123 (31)
1953	35,663 (47)
1954	32,685 (38)
1955	29,771 (65)
1956	28,199 (64)
1957	31,015 (30)
1958	29,538 (46)
1959	34,888
1960	28,665

Mileage at 12/36: 84,941
Mileage at 31/12/50: 613,270

Sheds

Crewe	25/5/35
Patricroft	1/6/35
Bletchley	22/12/51
Crewe South	8/8/53
Springs Branch	21/11/53
Holyhead	13/11/54 (loan)
Springs Branch	27/11/54
Southport	17/8/63
Carlisle Kingmoor	14/11/64

Withdrawn w.e. 7/10/67

45135 doing a spot of shunting at Southport where it was shedded from August 1963 until November 1964. It acquired AWS in May 1960 and was domed from October 1960. Photograph A.W. Battson, www.transporttreasury.co.uk

45136

Built as 5136 at Armstrong Whitworth 22/5/35
Renumbered 45136 w.e. 15/1/49

Improvements and modifications

31/3/38	Removal of vacuum pump
12/7/47	Steam sanding
8/8/58	Modernisation

Repairs

10/10/36-26/10/36	LS
30/6/37-20/7/37	LO
18/2/38-31/3/38	HG
24/11/39-11/12/39	LS
14/8/40-10/9/40	LO
12/6/41-28/6/41	HG
10/9/42-3/10/42	HS
19/11/43-11/12/43	LS
8/5/44-3/6/44	HO
22/5/45-23/6/45	LS
7/12/45-19/1/46	LO
14/9/46-17/10/46	LS
15/9/47-19/11/47	HG
6/12/48-6/1/49	LI
8/11/49-30/12/49	LI
19/3/51-27/4/51	HI
19/11/51-21/11/51	LC
16/6/52-8/8/52	HI
14/11/53-31/12/53	G
11/12/54-9/2/55	LI
11/3/55-22/3/55	NC(EO)
14/12/55-23/12/55	NC(EO)
25/6/56-30/6/56	NC(EO)
10/8/56-23/8/56	NC(EO)
18/9/56-25/9/56	NC
28/9/56-4/10/56	NC
3/1/57-8/2/57	LI
12/9/57-19/9/57	NC
25/12/57-31/12/57	NC(EO)
29/5/58-8/8/58	G
16/11/60-9/12/60	LC(EO)
1/8/61-15/9/61	HI
10/4/63-2/5/63	LC
10/5/63-15/6/63	G
2/7/63-4/7/63	NC
16/12/63-25/1/64	LC

Boilers

New	8916
17/3/38	8641 from 5024 (domed)
12/7/41	8667 from 5055 (domed)
3/6/44	8999 from 5056
19/11/47	8920 from 5120
31/12/53	8667 from 45123 (domed)
8/8/58	8933 from 45023
15/6/63	8686 (domed)

Tenders

New	9240
10/12/45	10046
23/12/45	9240
9/7/51	9275
28/12/52	9181 (riveted)

Mileage/(weekdays out of service)

1935	32,200 (16)
1936	49,929 (51)
1937	46,011 (43)
1938	50217 (74)
1939	44,865 (82)
1940	40,915 (55)
1941	36,437 (37)
1942	36,875 (56)
1943	44,409 (49)
1944	39,377 (48)
1945	40,964 (79)
1946	44,068 (67)
1947	40,602 (91)
1948	52,557 (42)
1949	51,418 (82)
1950	45,674 (50)
1951	39,390 (76)
1952	38,973 (72)
1953	35,090 (68)
1954	37,646 (41)
1955	24,497 (77)
1956	26,375 (57)
1957	27,806 (77)
1958	18,529 (128)
1959	24,134
1960	32,094
1961	30,028
1962	26,885

Mileage at 12/36: 82,129
Mileage at 31/12/50: 696,518

Sheds

Crewe	25/5/35
Patricroft	8/6/35
Carlisle W	25/9/37
Crewe	21/3/42
Aviemore	28/11/42
Inverness	3/11/45
Aviemore	18/10/52
Perth	1/8/60

Withdrawn 30/10/64

45136 on 20 August 1962 pulls out of the sidings at Grangemouth with an oil tank train. It was allocated to Perth from August 1960 until withdrawn and had a domeless boiler up to June 1963. Photograph www.rail-online.co.uk

45137

Built as 5137 at Armstrong Whitworth 29/5/35
Renumbered 45137 w.e. 25/9/48

Improvements and modifications

?	Removal of vacuum pump
7/8/42	Steam sanding
8/8/61	Fitting BR ATC equipment

Repairs

9/11/36-24/11/36	LS
27/5/37-8/6/37	LO
31/12/37-7/2/38	HG
31/7/39-14/8/39	LS
6/5/41-24/5/41	LS
25/8/41-5/9/41	TRO
2/2/42-19/2/42	LO
6/7/42-7/8/42	HG
4/2/43-20/2/43	LO
25/2/44-17/3/44	LS
24/11/45-22/12/45	LS
13/8/46-20/9/46	LO
13/12/46-15/1/47	HG
19/8/48-22/9/48	HS
14/11/49-8/12/49	LI
21/3/51-9/5/51	HG
19/5/53-6/6/53	LI
14/5/55-11/6/55	HG
22/8/56-26/9/56	HI
22/10/58-15/11/58	LI
16/3/59-27/4/59	LC(EO)
7/11/60-22/12/60	HG
24/7/61-8/8/61	NC(EO)
17/10/63-19/11/63	HI

Boilers

New	8917
19/1/38	8674 from 5057 (domed)
7/8/42	8970 from 5128
15/1/47	8985 from 5141
9/5/51	8960 from 5184
11/6/55	8979 from 45181
22/12/60	8637 from 45193 (domed)

Tenders

New	9241
29/12/45	9632
29/7/52	9467
20/4/57	10086
9/10/58	10446
14/11/60	9485

Mileage/(weekdays out of service)

1935	31,451 (12)
1936	47,245 (48)
1937	45,640 (46)
1938	46,712 (63)
1939	39,595 (33)
1940	37,654 (38)
1941	35,407 (65)
1942	32,497 (77)
1943	30,203 (44)
1944	28,136 (58)
1945	25,112 (82)
1946	24,368 (73)
1947	42,686 (43)
1948	33,680 (65)
1949	34,342 (49)
1950	40,264 (19)
1951	40,691 (59)
1952	36,965 (39)
1953	36,171 (45)
1954	34,897 (33)
1955	36,065 (51)
1956	43,445 (70)
1957	38,959 (40)
1958	29,042 (86)
1959	36,773
1960	29,396

Mileage at 12/36: 78,696
Mileage at 31/12/50: 574,992

Sheds

Crewe	1/6/35
Patricroft	8/6/35
Springs Branch	19/6/37
Patricroft	2/10/37
Carlisle W	12/4/41
Springs Branch	19/9/42
Patricroft	8/6/46
Bedford	22/10/55 (loan)
Bedford	10/12/55
Willesden	6/2/60
Crewe North	19/3/60
Willesden	2/4/60
Edge Hill	14/5/60
Speke Jcn	14/1/61

Withdrawn w.e. 31/12/66

45137 in final condition at Willesden on 29 August 1964 with lowered top lamp iron, overhead warning flashes and AWS which was fitted in August 1961. It was at Speke Junction from January 1961 until withdrawn in December 1966 and was domed from December 1960.

45138

Built as 5138 at Armstrong Whitworth 29/5/35
Renumbered 45138 w.e. 20/11/48

Improvements and modifications

19/10/38	Removal of vacuum pump
7/9/45	Steam sanding
?	Fitting BR ATC equipment

Repairs

13/11/36-27/11/36	LS
1/2/38-18/2/38	LS
29/8/38-19/10/38	HG
6/1/40-20/1/40	LS
29/3/41-24/4/41	HG
15/5/41-31/5/41	LO
8/11/41-22/11/41	TO
17/8/42-12/9/42	LS
6/11/43-15/12/43	LS
17/4/44-17/5/44	LO
22/8/45-7/9/45	HG
14/2/46-16/3/46	LO
23/12/46-25/1/47	HS
9/10/47-7/11/47	LO
24/1/48-9/2/48	LO
5/10/48-18/11/48	LS
21/4/49-13/5/49	LC
17/10/49-3/12/49	G
29/11/50-29/12/50	HI
4/1/52-7/2/52	HI
26/3/52-15/5/52	LC
8/6/53-27/6/53	G
27/9/54-28/10/54	LI
27/10/55-26/11/55	LC(EO)
31/8/56-29/9/56	HI(EO)
13/9/57-28/9/57	LC(EO)
12/5/58-3/7/58	G
7/3/60-16/4/60	LI
20/1/62-24/2/62	HI
8/4/63-9/5/63	HG

Boilers

New	8918
29/10/38	9038 from 5108
17/5/41	8654 from 5046 (domed)
7/9/45	8915 from 5215
3/12/49	8917 from 5165
27/6/53	8975 from 45177
3/7/58	8664 from 45030 (domed)

Tenders

New	9242
17/5/44	9031 (riveted)
28/1/48	9364 (riveted)
10/2/48	9031 (riveted)
27/10/54	10592 (part-welded)
29/9/56	9277
10/2/58	10527
3/7/58	10598 (part-welded)

Mileage/(weekdays out of service)

1935	36,467 (8)
1936	50,988 (49)
1937	54,355 (37)
1938	40,446 (99)
1939	54,836 (31)
1940	40,099 (53)
1941	30,652 (86)
1942	41,556 (39)
1943	44,682 (50)
1944	36,441 (42)
1945	38,309 (57)
1946	45,243 (59)
1947	38,927 (81)
1948	39,919 (94)
1949	40,488 (100)
1950	49,198 (60)
1951	50,756 (31)
1952	43,116 (94)
1953	42,104 (54)
1954	45,459 (54)
1955	45,764 (78)
1956	23,861 (65)
1957	46,727 (54)
1958	41,801 (76)
1959	48,606
1960	45,389

Mileage at 12/36: 87,455
Mileage at 31/12/50: 682,606

Sheds

Crewe	1/6/35
Patricroft	8/6/35
Carlisle W	25/9/37
Aviemore	28/11/42
Inverness	11/5/46
Carlisle Kingmoor	25/10/52

Withdrawn w.e. 1/10/66

Kingmoor's 45138 on 9 June 1962 at Aylesbury. The domeless boiler was not recorded on the History Card, nor the fitting of the AWS although it does show a part-welded tender from July 1958.

45139

Built as 5139 at Armstrong Whitworth 29/5/35
Renumbered 45139 w.e. 9/10/48

Improvements and modifications

28/3/38	Removal of vacuum pump
16/12/38	Steam sanding
22/8/61	Fitting BR ATC equipment

Repairs

21/10/36-4/11/36	LS
11/6/37-24/6/37	LO
28/2/38-28/3/38	LS
10/11/38-16/12/38	HG
6/6/40-21/6/40	LS
10/3/41-26/3/41	LS
10/2/42-28/2/42	HS
31/3/43-28/4/43	HG
5/8/44-19/8/44	HS
26/10/45-17/11/45	HS
30/11/46-28/12/46	HS
24/9/47-18/10/47	LO
22/9/48-7/10/48	LS
30/3/50-5/5/50	HG
28/12/51-1/2/52	HI
3/5/53-27/5/53	HI
20/5/55-18/6/55	HG
26/10/56-29/11/56	LI
21/11/58-24/12/58	LI
29/8/59-23/10/59	HC
8/5/61-6/6/61	HG
11/8/61-22/8/61	NC(EO)
29/11/62-2/1/63	LC
6/11/63-7/12/63	LI
20/7/64-31/8/64	LC
21/12/65-29/1/66	LC

Boilers

New	8919
16/12/38	8665 from 5048 (domed)
28/4/43	8928 from 5125
17/11/45	8654 from 5138 (domed)
5/5/50	8949 from 5079
18/6/55	9013 from 45221
6/6/61	9039 from 45108

Tenders

New	9243
2/12/58	10480
5/9/64	10483

Mileage/(weekdays out of service)

1935	27,994 (35)
1936	50,214 (43)
1937	50,717 (37)
1938	40,712 (102)
1939	55,971 (36)
1940	42,466 (50)
1941	37,843 (55)
1942	34,067 (42)
1943	32,998 (56)
1944	39,550 (47)
1945	36,131 (72)
1946	38,616 (59)
1947	38,097 (67)
1948	37,244 (53)
1949	43,291 (42)
1950	43,041 (56)
1951	41,520 (48)
1952	37,763 (67)
1953	42,169 (52)
1954	47,527 (38)
1955	41,236 (79)
1956	31,714 (128)
1957	37,920 (89)
1958	26,371 (148)
1959	38,180
1960	39,397

Mileage at 12/36: 78,205
Mileage at 31/12/50: 648,949

Sheds

Crewe	1/6/35
Patricroft	8/6/35
Carlisle W	25/9/37
Patricroft	23/7/55
Bedford	22/10/55 (loan)
Bedford	10/12/55
Willesden	6/2/60
Rugby	18/6/60
Edge Hill	21/7/62
Stoke	4/8/62 (loan)
Edge Hill	18/8/62
Trafford Park	23/2/63
Stockport	6/11/65

Withdrawn w.e. 19/8/67

45139 passes through the Sheffield suburbs at Millhouses in the early 1960s with a stopping train. It was allocated to 9E Trafford Park from February 1963 until October 1965 and was fitted with AWS in September 1961. It always had a welded tender and had been domeless since 1950. Photograph Colourrail.co.uk

45140

Built as 5140 at Armstrong Whitworth 3/6/35
Renumbered 45140 w.e. 22/1/49

Improvements and modifications

29/11/38	Steam sanding
29/11/38	Removal of vacuum pump
5/3/59	Fitting BR ATC equipment

Repairs

21/2/36-17/12/36	LS
13/10/37-27/10/37	HS
11/10/38-29/11/38	HG
13/5/40-27/5/40	LS
20/7/40-1/8/40	LO
12/10/42-24/10/42	HS
8/11/43-20/11/43	HG
14/6/45-30/6/45	LS
19/9/47-27/10/47	LS
31/12/48-22/1/49	HG
21/2/51-17/3/51	HI
30/4/52-10/6/52	LI
9/6/53-3/7/53	HG
8/5/54-28/5/54	HC
23/5/55-16/6/55	HI
10/11/56-15/12/56	HI
8/6/58-1/7/58	HI
25/2/59-5/3/59	NC(EO)
1/1/60-5/2/60	HI
11/2/60-24/2/60	NC(EO)
13/3/61-18/4/61	HI

Boilers

New	8920
29/11/38	8963 from 5183
20/11/43	8992 from 5209
22/1/49	9059 from 5056
3/7/53	8833 from 45217
15/12/56	8832 from 45096

Tenders

New	9244
30/6/45	9630
21/3/64	9203 (riveted)

Mileage/(weekdays out of service)

1935	28,569 (44)
1936	50,104 (48)
1937	48,755 (52)
1938	38,546 (89)
1939	44,811 (28)
1940	21,506 (65)
1941	25,896 (55)
1942	28,789 (38)
1943	38,556 (38)
1944	33,862 (25)
1945	31,739 (48)
1946	33,078 (39)
1947	23,507 (79)
1948	31,278 (60)
1949	34,602 (65)
1950	25,985 (57)
1951	41,440 (43)
1952	36,161 (62)
1953	41,197 (56)
1954	43,572 (54)
1955	46,332 (62)
1956	40,753 (70)
1957	47,671 (41)
1958	45,390 (46)
1959	47,589
1960	35,675

Mileage at 12/36: 78,673
Mileage at 31/12/50: 539,583

Sheds

Patricroft	8/6/35
Springs Branch	16/9/39
Edge Hill	6/4/40
Shrewsbury	1/6/40 (loan)
Edge Hill	27/7/40
Springs Branch	20/3/43
Crewe	27/3/43
Aston	8/4/44
Bescot	6/5/44
Willesden	28/10/44
Carlisle Upperby	19/1/52
Preston	27/8/60 (loan)
Speke Jcn	10/9/60
Springs Branch	21/7/62

Withdrawn w.e. 1/10/66

45140 blowing off at Carlisle on 1 August 1959 was an Upperby engine from 1952 until 1960. It was always domeless and was equipped with AWS in March 1959. Photograph D. Forsyth, Colourrail.co.uk

45141

Built as 5141 at Armstrong Whitworth 3/6/35
Renumbered 45141 w.e. 4/9/48

Improvements and modifications

7/4/38	Removal of vacuum pump
27/9/39	BTH speed indicator
29/8/46	Steam sanding
15/5/56	Modification
22/4/59	Fitting BR ATC equipment

Repairs

27/3/36-9/4/36	LS
5/4/37-20/4/37	HS
12/2/38-7/4/38	HG
1/9/39-27/9/39	LS
29/11/39-23/12/39	LO
11/8/41-23/8/41	HG
27/12/41-13/1/42	HO
24/9/43-23/10/43	LS
30/3/45-3/5/45	LS
8/8/46-29/8/46	HG
2/8/48-31/8/48	HS
26/10/49-26/11/49	LC
31/10/50-7/12/50	HG
19/11/52-11/12/52	LI
10/3/53-23/4/53	NC
5/3/54-3/4/54	LI
9/4/56-15/5/56	HG
26/3/58-26/4/58	LI
13/3/59-22/4/59	LI
3/6/60-29/7/60	LC(EO)
8/2/62-6/3/62	HG

Boilers

New	8921
24/3/38	9039 from 5109
23/8/41	8985 from 5180
29/8/46	8674 from 5158
7/12/50	8909 from 5204
15/5/56	8992 from 45044

Tenders

New	9245

Mileage/(weekdays out of service)

1935	32,679 (15)
1936	48,776 (53)
1937	47,115 (52)
1938	43,904 (76)
1939	40,449 (77)
1940	38,369 (34)
1941	41,138 (39)
1942	30,629 (41)
1943	30,112 (50)
1944	31,716 (32)
1945	23,761 (77)
1946	28,042 (55)
1947	29,647 (35)
1948	24,779 (56)
1949	24,131 (52)
1950	28,435 (48)
1951	26,601 (35)
1952	45,945 (52)
1953	46,195 (26)
1954	45,832 (67)
1955	40,506 (58)
1956	40,945 (53)
1957	40,930 (33)
1958	43,596 (54)
1959	36,302
1960	40,492

Mileage at 12/36: 81,455
Mileage at 31/12/50: 543,682

Sheds

Patricroft	8/6/35
Springs Branch	1/11/41
Carlisle W	26/4/47 (loan)
Springs Branch	21/6/47
Carlisle Canal	2/6/51 (loan)
Barrow	30/6/51
Carlisle Kingmoor	17/12/66
Lostock Hall	28/1/67

Withdrawn w.e. 11/3/67

45141 ready to leave Carnforth with a mixed freight on 22 June 1961 was always domeless and kept its original welded tender throughout. It was a local engine, having been at Barrow since June 1951, and received its AWS in May 1959. Photograph A. Swain, www.transporttreasury.co.uk

45142

Built as 5142 at Armstrong Whitworth 3/6/35
Renumbered 45142 w.e. 22/10/49

Improvements and modifications

17/12/37	Sloping throatplate boiler
9/1/39	Removal of vacuum pump
25/2/43	Steam sanding
23/5/59	Fitting BR ATC equipment

Repairs

17/8/36-27/8/36	LS
30/4/37-15/5/37	LO
10/12/37-4/1/38	HG
9/12/38-9/1/39	HS
28/3/40-12/4/40	LS
28/10/41-12/11/41	LS
28/4/42-16/5/42	LO
9/2/43-25/2/43	HG
2/8/44-19/8/44	LS
9/8/46-24/8/46	LS
24/11/47-24/12/47	HG
23/9/49-19/10/49	LI
3/5/51-23/5/51	LI
20/4/52-22/5/52	HG
10/12/52-17/1/53	LC(EO)
21/10/53-18/11/53	HI
3/11/55-3/12/55	HG
14/5/57-5/6/57	LI
10/4/59-23/5/59	HG
21/4/61-23/5/61	HI
26/10/62-20/11/62	LI
19/8/63-16/9/63	LC

Boilers

New	8922
17/12/37	10126 new (sloping throatplate)
25/2/43	9738 from 5285 (sloping throatplate)
24/12/47	9404 from 5348 (sloping throatplate)
22/5/52	9738 (sloping throatplate)
3/12/55	9360 (sloping throatplate)
23/5/59	9548 (sloping throatplate)

Tenders

New	9246
17/3/52	9320

Mileage/(weekdays out of service)

1935	34,189 (9)
1936	50,845 (37)
1937	45,062 (56)
1938	50,431 (66)
1939	47,824 (38)
1940	37,727 (43)
1941	36,540 (51)
1942	31,567 (39)
1943	34,719 (35)
1944	29,580 (83)
1945	36,275 (32)
1946	36,284 (41)
1947	36,440 (74)
1948	38,926 (59)
1949	35,681 (52)
1950	40,601 (33)
1951	35,865 (45)
1952	40,305 (65)
1953	39,086 (81)
1954	36,546 (30)
1955	27,028 (85)
1956	39,744 (29)
1957	33,458 (50)
1958	33,661 (45)
1959	38,726
1960	40,218

Mileage at 12/36: 85,034
Mileage at 31/12/50: 622,691

Sheds

Patricroft	8/6/35
Edge Hill	7/3/36
Crewe	3/7/37
Patricroft	14/8/37
Preston	25/9/37
Patricroft	2/7/38
Preston	24/9/38
Patricroft	28/5/49
Mold Jct	15/9/56
Crewe South	22/11/58
Holyhead	10/6/61
Crewe North	23/9/61
Crewe South	6/1/62
Crewe North	9/2/63
Crewe South	14/9/63

Withdrawn w.e. 24/4/65

45142 on 16 April 1952 with a Bangor to Manchester train at Llandudno Junction. It was allocated to 10C Patricroft from May 1949 to September 1956 and had been converted to a sloping throatplate boiler in December 1937. Photograph E.R. Morten, courtesy J.R. Morten

45143

Built as 5143 at Armstrong Whitworth 14/6/35
Renumbered 45143 w.e. 27/8/49

Improvements and modifications

?	Steam sanding
?	Removal of vacuum pump
2/11/40	BTH speed indicator

Repairs

22/12/36-5/1/37	LS
17/9/37-12/10/37	HS
1/4/39-18/5/39	HG
21/10/40-2/11/40	LS
3/3/42-1/4/42	HS
31/5/43-16/6/43	HG
17/5/45-16/6/45	LS
10/12/46-1/1/47	HG
2/2/48-2/3/48	HS
1/8/49-24/8/49	LI
4/12/50-28/12/50	LI
28/3/52-17/5/52	HG
17/11/53-15/12/53	LI
16/12/53-23/12/53	NC(Rect)EO
27/7/55-26/8/55	HI
26/9/55-17/10/55	NC(Rect)EO
28/12/56-30/1/57	HG
8/2/58-1/3/58	LI
16/11/59-23/12/59	LI
18/3/64-18/4/64	G
24/4/64	NC(EO)
20/8/64-22/8/64	Rect
7/3/65-9/4/65	Rect
18/5/65-31/5/65	Rect

Boilers

New	8923
18/5/39	8912 from 5132
16/6/43	9050 from 5064
1/1/47	8980 from 5035
17/5/52	9026 from 45144
30/1/57	9051 from 45208

Tenders

New	9247
16/6/43	9600

Mileage/(weekdays out of service)

1935	31,178 (11)
1936	50,541 (36)
1937	43,790 (57)
1938	36,755 (82)
1939	39,578 (64)
1940	35,532 (67)
1941	37,619 (26)
1942	38,401 (57)
1943	40,994 (33)
1944	29,441 (41)
1945	30,037 (47)
1946	32,698 (47)
1947	38,910 (36)
1948	38,119 (65)
1949	37,243 (67)
1950	38,095 (62)
1951	43,633 (57)
1952	42,329 (73)
1953	41,534
1954	43,163
1955	33,207
1956	37,723
1957	42,762

Mileage at 12/36: 81,719
Mileage at 31/12/50: 598,931

Sheds

Crewe	15/6/35
Shrewsbury	6/7/35
Patricroft	5/10/35
Crewe South	1/1/44
Stafford	12/6/48
Shrewsbury	17/7/48
Llandudno Jct	10/10/64
Shrewsbury	2/10/65

Withdrawn w.e. 11/12/65

45143 on 8 September 1960 at Shrewsbury, where it had been shedded since 1948. It stayed there until withdrawn in late-1965 and was a frequent performer on the Central Wales line. The History Cards for the engines at sheds not on the LMR from the 1950s petered out long before the others and hence the domed boiler pictured was not recorded. Photograph www.transporttreasury.co.uk

45144

Built as 5144 at Armstrong Whitworth 14/6/35
Renumbered 45144 w.e. 25/3/50

Improvements and modifications

3/6/38	Removal of vacuum pump
22/8/46	Steam sanding
3/7/59	Fitting BR ATC equipment

Repairs

5/10/36-22/10/36	LS
21/6/37-2/7/37	LO
30/3/38-3/6/38	HG
3/10/39-14/11/39	LS
3/11/41-18/11/41	HG
27/5/43-10/6/43	HS
14/7/44-9/8/44	LS
25/6/45-9/8/45	LS
23/7/46-22/8/46	HG
20/9/48-29/10/48	LS
1/3/50-21/3/50	HI
11/2/52-21/3/52	HG
15/4/52-1/5/52	NC(Rect)
10/2/53-12/3/53	LC (EO)
1/10/53-30/10/53	LI
3/11/53-11/11/53	NC(Rect)
21/12/53-27/1/54	LC(EO)
4/3/54-31/3/54	LC
10/1/55-3/2/55	LC(EO)
31/3/56-21/4/56	LI
21/5/57-22/6/57	HG
3/6/59-3/7/59	HI
25/7/60-14/9/60	LC
22/1/62-21/2/62	LI

Boilers

New	8924
18/5/38	8996 from 5215
18/11/41	8962 from 5035
22/8/46	9026 from 5214
21/3/52	9030 from 45024
22/6/57	8673 from 45004 (domed)

Tenders

New	9248
30/6/45	9000 (prototype)
9/8/45	9055 (riveted)

Mileage/(weekdays out of service)

1935	29,807 (11)
1936	48,693 (55)
1937	48,098 (55)
1938	42,248 (84)
1939	40,009 (78)
1940	39,046 (32)
1941	29,525 (80)
1942	42,906 (18)
1943	40,230 (51)
1944	41,054 (53)
1945	40,962 (75)
1946	35,099 (77)
1947	26,110 (50)
1948	20,300 (68)
1949	24,194 (50)
1950	28,354 (66)
1951	28.447 (54)
1952	31,033 (99)
1953	27,403 (107)
1954	29,072 (89)
1955	28,290 (76)
1956	30,233 (79)
1957	30,884 (78)
1958	33,547 (60)
1959	36,607
1960	29,541

Mileage at 12/36: 78,500
Mileage at 31/12/50: 576,635

Sheds

Crewe	15/6/35
Shrewsbury	6/7/35
Patricroft	5/10/35
Longsight	16/10/43
Bushbury	19/10/46
Bescot	17/5/47
Bangor	25/6/49
Cricklewood	25/5/63
Derby	16/5/64

Withdrawn w.e. 13/6/64

45144 pictured on 28 July 1956 at Saltney on the ex-GWR main line from Chester to Wrexham remained domeless until June 1957. It received a riveted tender from August 1945 and was shedded at 6H Bangor from June 1949 until transferred to Cricklewood in 1963. Photograph www.transporttreasury.co.uk

45145

Built as 5145 at Armstrong Whitworth 14/6/35
Renumbered 45145 w.e. 2/4/49

Improvements and modifications

?	Steam sanding
?	Removal of vacuum pump
12/10/40	BTH speed indicator

Repairs

30/9/36-20/10/36	LS
13/8/37-8/9/37	HS
24/5/38-1/6/38	LO
24/4/39-7/6/39	HG
26/9/40-12/10/40	LS
1/3/43-17/3/43	LS
24/2/44-11/3/44	HG
5/10/45-3/11/45	HS
29/12/47-28/1/48	LS
1/3/49-28/3/49	HG
11/9/50-19/10/50	HG
22/1/52-25/2/52	HI
4/11/52-19/12/52	LC(EO)
19/10/53-17/11/53	LI
21/2/55-28/4/55	HG
19/6/56-28/7/56	HI
7/11/57-18/12/57	LI
11/8/59-17/9/59	HI
29/9/59	NC Rect(EO)

Boilers

New	8925
7/6/39	9033 from 5103
11/3/44	8678 from 5212 (domed)
28/3/49	8992 from 5140
17/4/50	8661 from 5204 (domed)
28/4/55	9058 from 45224

Tenders

New	9249

Mileage/(weekdays out of service)

1935	26,853 (12)
1936	46,158 (50)
1937	46,740 (30)
1938	37,994 (45)
1939	33,451 (75)
1940	30,281 (53)
1941	35,990 (41)
1942	26,791 (30)
1943	32,450 (45)
1944	32,994 (49)
1945	24,358 (93)
1946	39,330 (48)
1947	23,255 (47)
1948	37,866 (68)
1949	45,813 (53)
1950	38,617 (61)
1951	46,293 (42)
1952	42,041 (98)
1953	39,116
1954	45,391
1955	38,551
1956	42,268
1957	35,676

Mileage at 12/36: 73,011
Mileage at 31/12/50: 558,941

Sheds

Crewe	15/6/35
Stoke	6/7/35
Bangor	20/7/35
Shrewsbury	31/8/35
Warrington	5/10/35
Crewe	30/11/40
Edge Hill	18/10/41
Shrewsbury	17/4/43 (loan)
Edge Hill	24/7/43
Crewe North	9/3/46 (loan)
Crewe North	4/5/46
Bushbury	19/10/46
Shrewsbury	17/7/48
Bangor	20/6/64
Holyhead	19/6/65
Shrewsbury	2/10/65
Crewe South	11/3/67

Stored
17/4/67-15/9/67

Withdrawn w.e. 11/11/67

45145 in February 1960 at Gowerton North, between Llanelli and Swansea, with the 11.10am Shrewsbury-Swansea, was a stalwart of the Central Wales line. It was shedded at Shrewsbury from 17 July 1948 until transferred to Bangor in June 1964. The detail of its original welded tender is shown well in this picture; 45145 had a domeless boiler from April 1955. Photograph www.rail-online.co.uk

45146

Built as 5146 at Armstrong Whitworth 18/6/35
Renumbered 45146 w.e. 8/5/48

Improvements and modifications

5/5/39	Removal of vacuum pump
5/5/39	Steam sanding
6/11/40	BTH speed indicator
3/2/59	Fitting BR ATC equipment

Repairs

30/9/36-16/10/36	LS
13/8/37-30/8/37	LO
26/11/37-14/12/37	LS
14/4/39-5/5/39	HG
24/10/40-6/11/40	LS
16/3/42-7/5/42	LS
30/9/43-23/10/43	HG
29/12/45-19/1/46	LS
13/4/48-8/5/48	HG
30/11/49-21/12/49	HI
18/8/51-10/10/51	LI
2/6/52-21/6/52	LC(EO)
26/11/53-1/1/54	HG
21/4/55-20/5/55	HI
17/10/56-10/11/56	HI
13/5/58-10/6/58	HG
27/1/59-3/2/59	NC(EO)
8/4/59-23/5/59	HI
10/4/61-6/5/61	LI
28/8/62-22/9/62	HI

Boilers

New	8926
5/5/39	8968 from 5182
23/10/43	9032 from 5150
8/5/48	9015 from 5064
1/1/54	9059 from 45140
10/6/58	8935 from 45024

Tenders

New	9250
19/1/46	9001 (prototype)

Mileage/(weekdays out of service)

1935	26,602 (17)
1936	48,951 (55)
1937	48,424 (52)
1938	54,141 (28)
1939	51,141 (47)
1940	35,917 (38)
1941	35,570 (36)
1942	24,966 (67)
1943	34,896 (54)
1944	34,021 (29)
1945	33,187 (48)
1946	34,270 (46)
1947	33,274 (61)
1948	33,760 (52)
1949	28,633 (66)
1950	39.904 (33)
1951	29,371 (73)
1952	35,935 (56)
1953	33,154 (86)
1954	48,182 (23)
1955	46,838 (57)
1956	43,760 (53)
1957	44,277 (27)
1958	27,807 (65)
1959	39,997
1960	40,850

Mileage at 12/36: 75,553
Mileage at 31/12/50: 597,057

Sheds

Crewe	22/6/35
Stoke	6/7/35
Crewe North	3/5/41
Crewe South	25/10/41
Crewe North	26/6/42
Crewe South	4/3/44
Willesden	28/5/49
Carlisle Upperby	27/6/53
Patricroft	12/6/54
Longsight	18/9/54
Crewe North	21/9/57
Longsight	5/10/57
Camden	29/11/58 (loan)
Longsight	27/12/58
Rugby	10/1/59
Willesden	19/9/59
Rugby	26/9/59 (loan)
Willesden	5/12/59
Bescot	7/5/60
Stoke	9/3/63

Withdrawn w.e. 19/6/65

45146 at Shrewsbury in the mid-1950s. It was at Longsight from September 1954 until 1959. It was always domeless and had one of the three prototype Stanier 4000 gallon tenders from 1946 onwards.

45147

Built as 5147 at Armstrong Whitworth 18/6/35
Renumbered 45147 w.e. 15/1/49

Improvements and modifications

8/9/38	Removal of vacuum pump
31/1/40	BTH speed indicator
10/4/45	Steam sanding
12/2/59	Fitting BR ATC equipment

Repairs

5/10/36-23/10/36	LS
1/10/37-18/10/37	LO
24/8/38-8/9/38	LS
5/1/40-31/1/40	HG
26/12/41-10/1/42	LS
4/1/43-16/2/43	LS
29/3/44-18/4/44	HS
23/3/45-10/4/45	HG
8/1/46-14/2/46	HO
8/7/47-14/8/47	LS
11/12/48-11/1/49	HG
21/6/50-20/7/50	HI
11/3/52-21/4/52	LI
1/2/54-2/3/54	HG
4/4/55-2/5/55	LI
19/10/55-16/11/55	LC
19/11/56-30/11/56	LC(EO)
26/7/57-21/8/57	HI
2/10/58-22/10/58	LC(EO)
5/2/59-12/2/59	NC(EO)
30/11/59-23/1/60	HG
21/12/61-31/1/62	HI
3/4/64-13/5/64	LI

Boilers

New	8927
31/1/40	8961 from 5187
10/4/45	8660 from 5091 (domed)
11/1/49	9007 from 5111
2/3/54	8996 from 45055
23/1/60	8973 from 45061

Mileage/(weekdays out of service)

1935	27,565 (20)
1936	48,549 (47)
1937	44,517 (67)
1938	41,556 (43)
1939	44,587 (30)
1940	34,580 (45)
1941	34,044 (38)
1942	39,399 (30)
1943	34,721 (74)
1944	36,990 (50)
1945	32,179 (56)
1946	25,524 (81)
1947	28,773 (73)
1948	28,908 (49)
1949	41,390 (48)
1950	32,283 (43)
1951	39,908 (27)
1952	36,546 (58)
1953	34,605 (32)
1954	40,599 (52)
1955	33,477 (86)
1956	44,038 (40)
1957	43,171 (49)
1958	37,164 (65)
1959	36,231
1960	39,996

Mileage at 12/36: 76,114
Mileage at 31/12/50: 575,565

Tenders

New	9251
16/2/43	9002 (prototype)
18/4/44	9504
18/10/55	10456
23/1/60	9510
13/3/63	10702 (part-welded)

Sheds

Crewe	22/6/35
Stoke	6/7/35
Crewe	3/5/41
Longsight	7/2/42
Carlisle W	5/6/43
Crewe South	15/12/45
Patricroft	23/8/47
Bangor	25/6/49
Patricroft	?
Willesden	13/11/54
Carlisle Upperby	31/8/57
Willesden	5/10/57
Northampton	22/11/58
Willesden	19/11/60
Speke Jcn	14/1/61
Holyhead	10/6/61
Northampton	23/9/61
Bletchley	4/11/61
Stafford	7/3/64
Aintree	24/7/65

Withdrawn w.e. 20/5/67

45147 pictured on 18 April 1959 at Camden had been, like many of the class, called in for a short non-classified visit to works to be fitted with AWS equipment. This was done in February 1959 while it was allocated to Northampton. It has a domeless boiler and welded tender which still has the pre-1957 crest at this late date. Photograph J.T. Robertson, www.transporttreasury.co.uk

45148

Built as 5148 at Armstrong Whitworth 18/6/35
Renumbered 45148 w.e. 31/3/51

Improvements and modifications

27/10/38	Removal of vacuum pump
?	Steam sanding
27/11/59	Fitting BR ATC equipment

Repairs

23/11/36-8/12/36	LS
18/5/37-4/6/37	LO
26/10/37-26/11/37	LS
7/5/38-18/5/38	LO
23/8/38-27/10/38	HG
14/8/40-29/8/40	LS
15/8/41-9/9/41	LS
15/12/42-28/1/43	HG
28/6/44-19/7/44	HS
30/7/46-23/8/46	HS
23/10/47-13/12/47	HG
4/11/49-13/12/49	LI
8/3/51-29/3/51	HI
6/12/52-3/1/53	HG
28/5/53-18/6/53	LC(EO)
14/1/54-6/2/54	LC(EO)
15/4/55-4/5/55	HI
21/9/55-14/10/55	LC(EO)
24/4/56-9/6/56	HG
9/2/58-7/3/58	HI
22/3/59-2/4/59	LC(EO)
14/10/59-27/11/59	HG
6/4/60-20/5/60	LC(EO)
13/2/61-22/3/61	LI

Boilers

New	8928
27/10/38	9048 from 5118
28/1/43	9031 from 5127
13/12/47	8682 from 5131 (domed)
3/1/53	8939 from 45182
9/6/56	9025 from 45107
27/11/59	8928 from 45210

Tenders

New	9252
28/1/43	9318
?	9058 (riveted)
5/9/64	10518

Mileage/(weekdays out of service)

1935	26,834 (23)
1936	45,290 (52)
1937	37,820 (59)
1938	33,900 (91)
1939	42,403 (24)
1940	34,005 (33)
1941	34,488 (52)
1942	34,352 (30)
1943	35,378 (47)
1944	30,955 (69)
1945	34,845 (33)
1946	29,016 (60)
1947	28,508 (89)
1948	36,311 (35)
1949	29,095 (71)
1950	37,719 (40)
1951	37,082 (35)
1952	34,214 (55)
1953	42,103 (51)
1954	42,542 (70)
1955	39,067 (80)
1956	44,256 (62)
1957	46,373 (28)
1958	40,645 (49)
1959	27,592
1960	41,921

Mileage at 12/36: 72,124
Mileage at 31/12/50: 550,919

Sheds

Crewe	22/6/35
Warrington	5/10/35
Longsight	29/4/39
Stockport	30/9/39
Stoke	6/1/40
Crewe North	3/5/41
Crewe South	26/8/44
Crewe North	18/4/53
Holyhead	14/4/56
Crewe North	28/4/56
Rugby	19/4/58
Crewe North	5/7/58
Crewe South	17/9/60
Holyhead	18/6/61
Crewe North	23/9/61
Edge Hill	3/3/62
Carlisle Kingmoor	10/11/62

Withdrawn w.e. 25/12/65

Crewe North's 45148 at Carlisle Upperby in 1958/9 before it was fitted with AWS in November 1959. It has a domeless boiler and welded tender. Photograph www.rail-online.co.uk

45149

Built as 5149 at Armstrong Whitworth 24/6/35
Renumbered 45149 w.e. 29/1/49

Improvements and modifications

20/4/38	Removal of vacuum pump
12/12/46	Steam sanding
25/5/57	Modernisation
3/3/60	Fitting BR ATC equipment

Repairs

2/9/36-17/9/36	LS
14/6/37-28/6/37	HS
5/3/38-20/4/38	HG
25/4/40-9/5/40	LS
8/10/41-25/10/41	HG
2/6/43-17/6/43	HG
27/1/44-12/2/44	LO
29/2/44-7/3/44	LO
2/2/45-6/3/45	LS
1/10/45-27/10/45	LO
9/11/46-12/12/46	HG
3/12/48-25/1/49	HG
28/11/50-28/12/50	LI
1/10/51-24/10/51	HI
22/8/53-29/9/53	HG
3/6/55-1/7/55	LI
15/4/57-25/5/57	HG
25/1/60-3/3/60	HI
10/5/61-25/5/61	NC(EO)
12/4/65-12/5/65	LI

Boilers

New	8929
30/3/38	8659 from 5042 (domed)
25/10/41	8913 from 5109
12/12/46	9010 from 5037
25/1/49	8665 from 5089 (domed)
29/9/53	9016 from 45111
25/5/57	8993 from 45042
3/3/60	8959 from 45134

Tenders

New	9253
27/10/45	9119 (riveted)

Mileage/(weekdays out of service)

1935	30,242 (15)
1936	48,299 (30)
1937	42,630 (47)
1938	43,387 (55)
1939	43,581 (23)
1940	35,334 (36)
1941	25,505 (69)
1942	33,666 (30)
1943	27,940 (51)
1944	27,111 (59)
1945	28,049 (85)
1946	23,570 (104)
1947	30,344 (45)
1948	29,901 (69)
1949	42,413 (61)
1950	33,745 (65)
1951	34,373 (50)
1952	40,144 (39)
1953	35,853 (51)
1954	39,467 (35)
1955	35,833 (53)
1956	38,428 (28)
1957	35,902 (52)
1958	36,512 (37)
1959	39,240
1960	37,168

Mileage at 12/36: 78,541
Mileage at 31/12/50: 545,717

Sheds

Crewe	29/6/35
Warrington	5/10/35
Stoke	5/7/52
Crewe South	8/3/58
Chester	10/6/61
Longsight	24/6/61
Llandudno Jct	10/3/62
Shrewsbury	17/9/66
Lostock Hall	11/3/67 (loan)
Lostock Hall	1/4/67

Stored
13/9/66-2/3/67

Withdrawn w.e. 22/6/68

5149 in original condition with domeless boiler and welded tender. It had a domed boiler from March 1938 to October 1941 and a riveted tender from October 1945 It was shedded at Warrington from October 1935 until transferred to Stoke in 1952.

45150

Built as 5150 at Armstrong Whitworth 25/6/35
Renumbered 45150 w.e. 18/9/48

Improvements and modifications

8/8/38	Removal of vacuum pump
24/12/41	Steam sanding
9/6/59	Fitting BR ATC equipment

Repairs

21/2/36-16/4/36	HS
10/9/37-29/9/37	HS
14/6/38-8/8/38	HG
3/2/40-16/2/40	LS
28/11/41-24/12/41	HG
1/9/43-17/9/43	HS
27/2/44-16/3/44	LO
19/4/45-5/5/45	LS
10/6/46-19/7/46	HG
18/4/47-11/6/47	LO
24/8/48-13/9/48	HS
21/9/49-21/10/49	HI
9/8/50-1/9/50	HG
26/4/52-16/5/52	LI
23/10/53-18/11/53	LI
6/6/55-8/7/55	HG
16/1/57-9/2/57	HI
3/12/57-31/12/57	LC(EO)
5/5/59-9/6/59	HI
29/6/60-9/9/60	LC
12/4/61-10/5/61	LC
16/7/62-8/8/62	HG
6/9/63-26/9/63	LC
20/10/65-23/11/65	HI

Boilers

New	8930
8/8/38	9009 from 5079
24/12/41	9032 from 5205
17/9/43	8955 from 5115
19/7/46	8833 from 5062
1/9/50	9050 from 5223
8/7/55	9020 from 45061

Tenders

New	9254
18/11/53	9307

Mileage/(weekdays out of service)

1935	27,051 (26)
1936	39,627 (72)
1937	42,625 (37)
1938	38,983 (71)
1939	41,096 (33)
1940	33,240 (53)
1941	24,169 (72)
1942	29,744 (33)
1943	23,527 (68)
1944	40,699 (50)
1945	43,265 (60)
1946	40,537 (78)
1947	41,796 (93)
1948	35,536 (72)
1949	42,268 (84)
1950	40,356 (56)
1951	43,635 (34)
1952	38,891 (59)
1953	34,575 (55)
1954	39,573 (41)
1955	37,356 (67)
1956	44,053 (40)
1957	42,392 (60)
1958	43,586 (49)
1959	39,967
1960	29,058

Mileage at 12/36: 66,678
Mileage at 31/12/50: 584,519

Sheds

Crewe	29/6/35
Warrington	5/10/35
Edge Hill	25/3/44
Crewe North	13/5/44
Rugby	10/6/44
Shrewsbury	1/3/47
Rugby	8/3/47
Northampton	23/8/47
Rugby	27/8/49
Crewe North	3/3/56
Longsight	29/6/57
Monument Lane	31/8/57
Longsight	21/9/57
Preston	12/9/59
Warrington	9/9/61
Newton Heath	20/6/64
Trafford Park	14/11/64

Withdrawn w.e. 2/3/68

45150 in 1959 at Willesden before it received AWS in June of that year. It was a 9A Longsight engine from September 1957 until it moved to Preston in September 1959. The records show that it was always domeless with a welded tender. Photograph www.rail-online.co.uk

45151

Built as 5151 at Armstrong Whitworth 25/6/35
Renumbered 45151 w.e. 21/8/48

Improvements and modifications

17/3/38	Removal of vacuum pump
20/5/45	Steam sanding
9/6/51	Sloping throatplate boiler
10/10/59	Fitting BR ATC equipment

Repairs

15/3/37-24/4/37	LS
15/10/37-24/11/37	LO
7/3/38-17/3/38	LS
10/2/39-15/2/39	LO
6/3/39-31/3/39	HG
8/4/40-18/5/40	LS
21/7/41-23/8/41	LS
30/3/42-8/5/42	HG
8/2/43-13/3/43	HS
4/4/44-29/4/44	LS
30/5/45-14/7/45	LS
7/5/46-31/5/46	HG
17/11/47-6/12/47	LS
26/7/48-21/8/48	HO
25/10/48-26/11/48	LO
29/11/49-12/1/50	LI
27/3/51-9/6/51	G
18/6/52-9/8/52	HI
26/11/53-19/12/53	LI
5/4/55-30/4/55	HI
16/5/55-21/5/55	HC(EO)
16/1/56-25/1/56	NC(EO)
25/2/57-30/3/57	G
12/9/57-10/10/57	LC
12/5/58-5/6/58	LI
14/9/59-10/10/59	LI
22/2/61-13/4/61	HI

Boilers

New	8931
31/3/39	9017 from 5087
8/5/42	8959 from 5155
21/5/46	9046 from 5095
9/6/51	10139 from 45362 (sloping throatplate)
30/3/57	12877 from 45320 (sloping throatplate)

Tenders

New	9255
15/3/38	9261
18/7/40	9709
31/7/40	9261
23/7/41	9212 (riveted)
29/4/44	9719
2/5/47	9024 (riveted)
23/5/51	10675 (part-welded)
17/12/53	10597 (part-welded)
20/2/57	9672
5/6/58	9069 (riveted)

Mileage/(weekdays out of service)

1935	36,548 (7)
1936	69,262 (29)
1937	46,056 (86)
1938	58,943 (58)
1939	52,802 (54)
1940	40,152 (79)
1941	50,105 (62)
1942	53,864 (53)
1943	57,054 (50)
1944	47,438 (81)
1945	49,562 (78)
1946	50,101 (76)
1947	48,229 (68)
1948	33,270 (86)
1949	42,427 (81)
1950	47,320 (50)
1951	36,504 (102)
1952	44,671 (81)
1953	46,644 (54)
1954	49,985 (32)
1955	38,728 (85)
1956	36,265 (66)
1957	36,422 (101)
1958	38,099 (93)
1959	35,651
1960	47,711
1961	42,964
1962	21,218

Mileage at 12/36 105,810
Mileage at 31/12/50: 783,133

Sheds

Crewe	29/6/35
Carlisle N	18/1/36
Motherwell	4/3/50
Carlisle Kingmoor	25/3/50
Motherwell	29/4/50

Stored
13/8/62-29/12/62

Withdrawn w.e. 29/12/62

45151 was domeless until March 1951 when it was converted to a sloping throatplate boiler at St. Rollox. It is in one of the early BR livery variations with the 4 added on in August 1948 ahead of and spaced further away from what appear to be hand-painted cab numbers and the riveted tender acquired in May 1947 still has LMS insignia. 45151 was shedded at Carlisle North (Kingmoor) from 1936 until March 1950.

45152

Built as 5152 at Armstrong Whitworth 28/6/35
Renumbered 45152 w.e. 22/1/49

Improvements and modifications

22/2/41	Removal of vacuum pump
9/10/42	Steam sanding
21/11/59	Fitting BR ATC equipment

Repairs

7/11/36-4/12/36	LS
21/4/37-27/4/37	LO
27/12/37-15/1/38	LS
27/7/38-6/8/38	LO
14/9/38-14/10/38	LO
22/5/39-6/7/39	HG
8/8/40-17/8/40	LO
8/4/41-28/4/41	HS
14/10/41-20/11/41	LS
3/9/42-9/10/42	HG
15/10/43-20/11/43	LS
6/5/44-22/5/44	HO
11/4/45-19/5/45	LS
31/5/46-9/8/46	HS
29/7/47-17/9/47	HG
1/12/48-22/1/49	LI
9/11/49-17/12/49	LI
10/10/50-1/11/50	LC
29/6/51-4/8/51	LI
30/4/52-6/5/52	LC
17/6/52-20/8/52	G
1/9/52-3/9/52	NC(EO)
24/6/54-10/7/54	HI
28/10/54-9/12/54	LC(EO)
10/8/55-10/9/55	HI
14/5/56-26/5/56	NC(EO)
17/11/56-1/12/56	LC
4/3/57-12/4/57	G
3/7/58-17/7/58	LC
30/9/58-10/10/58	LC(EO)
17/11/58-29/11/58	LC(EO)
10/12/58-26/12/58	LC(EO)
15/6/59-4/7/59	LI
17/11/59-21/11/59	NC(EO)
12/12/60-20/1/61	HI

Boilers

New	8932
6/7/39	8829 from 5012
9/10/42	8818 from 5198 (domed)
22/5/44	8686 from 5132 (domed)
17/9/47	9048 from 5029
20/8/52	8824 from 45119
12/4/57	8656 from 45036 (domed)

Tenders

New	9256
27/5/44	9169 (riveted)
7/1/46	9273
31/7/47	9213 (riveted)
14/9/47	9209 (riveted)
3/8/51	10507
17/6/52	9502
9/7/54	10578 (part-welded)
26/2/57	9821

5152 a wartime repaint with serif cab numbers but in a size and position similar to the 1936 livery. It is domeless but with a St Rollox style 'incorrect' top feed cover. The date of the photograph is not recorded but is between September 1947, when 5152 had a riveted tender and domeless boiler with domed covers on the firebox shoulders, and renumbering in January 1949. It was allocated to Carlisle North (Kingmoor) and has a holder for a train staff below the cab window.

Mileage/(weekdays out of service)

1935	31,264 (18)
1936	59,757 (62)
1937	61,366 (42)
1938	48,427 (97)
1939	47,041 (72)
1940	49,843 (45)
1941	49,966 (75)
1942	52,760 (54)
1943	50,259 (65)
1944	58,229 (36)
1945	47,793 (70)
1946	34,053 (148)
1947	45,288 (78)
1948	37,225 (85)
1949	40,356 (103)
1950	39,291 (74)
1951	35,997 (72)
1952	38,680 (110)
1953	51,667 (31)
1954	40,618 (80)
1955	46,131 (53)
1956	40,013 (75)
1957	41,325 (73)
1958	36,030 (117)
1959	43,193
1960	41,066
1961	43,542
1962	7,987

Mileage at 12/36: 91,021
Mileage at 31/12/50: 752,918

Sheds

Crewe	29/6/35
Chester	12/10/35
Carlisle N	18/1/36
Motherwell	4/3/50

Stored
26/3/62-29/12/62

Withdrawn w.e. 29/12/62

45153

Built as 5153 at Armstrong Whitworth 28/6/35
Renumbered 45153 w.e. 8/5/48

Improvements and modifications

15/2/39	Removal of vacuum pump
12/6/43	Steam sanding
9/5/59	Fitting BR ATC equipment

Repairs

16/11/36-15/12/36	LS
29/4/37-5/5/37	LO
1/11/37-20/11/37	LS
27/12/37-21/1/38	LO
4/8/38-12/8/38	LO
24/1/39-15/2/39	LS
8/4/39-27/4/39	LO
2/8/39-7/9/39	HO
15/2/40-9/3/40	HS
26/2/41-27/3/41	LS
1/10/41-8/11/41	HG
28/9/42-10/10/42	LS
30/9/43-3/11/43	LS
14/2/44-17/3/44	LO
5/8/44-6/9/44	HS
3/10/45-3/11/45	HG
27/1/47-28/2/47	LS
13/4/48-11/5/48	LS
6/7/49-20/8/49	HI
4/1/50-18/1/50	LC
7/11/50-9/12/50	G
1/2/52-1/3/52	LI
23/2/53-21/3/53	HI
16/12/53-18/12/53	LC
18/1/54-28/1/54	LC(EO)
28/4/54-28/5/54	G
16/11/55-3/12/55	HI
5/1/57-26/1/57	HI
28/8/57-31/8/57	LC(EO)
10/12/57-19/12/57	LC(EO)
31/3/58-2/5/58	HI
20/4/59-9/5/59	G
26/1/60-30/1/60	NC
4/8/60-27/8/60	LI
29/1/62-2/3/62	LI
15/6/62-19/6/62	NC
11/10/62-7/11/62	LC
23/1/63-12/2/63	LC
15/3/63-3/4/63	LC

Boilers

New	8933
7/9/39	8947 from 5167
8/11/41	9030 from 5197
3/11/45	8653 from 5046 (domed)
9/12/50	9024 from 45122
28/5/54	9004
20/4/59	8950 from 45172

Tenders

New	9257
8/8/39	9212 (riveted)
23/7/41	9261
12/8/44	9877
4/10/44	9261
9/1/45	9659
25/6/47	9314
21/3/53	9214 (riveted)
21/10/55	9838
3/12/55	9534
26/1/57	10676 (part-welded)

Mileage/(weekdays out of service)

1935	29,330 (16)
1936	68,208 (51)
1937	61,468 (50)
1938	52,746 (81)
1939	43,800 (89)
1940	46,581 (51)
1941	44,547 (95)
1942	55,700 (39)
1943	54,586 (53)
1944	38,564 (86)
1945	45,109 (74)
1946	56,149 (18)
1947	45,513 (75)
1948	41,239 (64)
1949	42,026 (90)
1950	29,049 (97)
1951	51,723 (54)
1952	46,690 (74)
1953	44,633 (67)
1954	37,919 (74)
1955	36,385 (63)
1956	44,977 (38)
1957	40,762 (65)
1958	34,271 (77)
1959	39,445
1960	39,751
1961	29,334
1962	9,013

Mileage at 12/36: 97,538
Mileage at 31/12/50: 754,115

Sheds

Crewe	29/6/35
Carlisle N	18/1/36
St Rollox	5/6/43
Dumfries	13/1/64

Withdrawn w.e. 12/6/64

5153 at Ayr in 1937 was still as delivered from Armstrong Whitworth with its crosshead vacuum pump. It was allocated to Carlisle North from January 1936 until moved to St Rollox in 1943. Note the Caledonian Railway semaphore train indicator above the bufferbeam. Photograph E.R. Morten.

45154

Built as 5154 at Armstrong Whitworth 28/6/35
Named LANARKSHIRE YEOMANRY 8/4/37
Renumbered 45154 w.e. 22/1/49

Improvements and modifications

28/3/38	Removal of vacuum pump
?	Steam sanding
29/6/56	Modernisation
10/10/61	Fitting BR ATC equipment

Repairs

22/3/37-8/4/37	LS
14/3/38-28/3/38	LS
28/4/39-10/6/39	HG
24/6/40-4/7/40	LO
11/2/41-4/3/41	HS
9/1/42-20/2/42	LS
22/9/42-17/10/42	HG
17/11/43-24/12/43	LS
24/7/44-23/8/44	HS
14/9/45-24/10/45	LS
12/10/46-22/11/46	LS
31/5/47-8/7/47	LO
19/12/47-30/1/48	HG
29/12/48-20/1/49	LC
20/1/49-26/2/49	HC
2/5/49-7/6/49	HI
19/9/50-21/10/50	LI
17/3/51-18/4/51	LC
5/10/51-3/11/51	LC
25/3/52-5/7/52	G
2/4/53-16/5/53	LI
2/7/53-16/7/53	LC
28/10/54-18/11/54	HI
30/5/56-29/6/56	G
20/12/57-17/1/58	LI
31/3/60-20/5/60	HG
15/9/61-10/10/61	NC(EO)
27/2/63-20/3/63	LI

Boilers

New	8934
18/6/39	8834 from 5017
17/10/42	9016 from 5169
30/1/48	8946 from 5159
5/7/52	8988 from 45082
29/6/56	8916 (domed)

Tenders

New	9258
25/11/40	9271
16/1/42	9116 (riveted)
14/10/46	9727
10/4/47	9177 (riveted)
20/1/49	9835
7/5/52	9720
5/7/52	10683 (part-welded)
15/11/54	9215 (riveted)
29/6/56	9845
20/5/60	10479
16/6/66	9289

Mileage/(weekdays out of service)

1935	26,819 (18)
1936	65,219 (39)
1937	56,455 (52)
1938	56,082 (70)
1939	46,489 (91)
1940	45,687 (53)
1941	51,225 (60)
1942	48,063 (80)
1943	45,843 (54)
1944	53,792 (63)
1945	42,096 (60)
1946	44,664 (55)
1947	37,949 (85)
1948	40,552 (66)
1949	30,439 (130)
1950	37,006 (83)
1951	29,794 (119)
1952	33,224 (126)
1953	32,076 (128)
1954	32,857 (82)
1955	38,972 (74)
1956	38,056 (60)
1957	38,352 (56)
1958	41,071 (51)
1959	36,458
1960	36,255

Mileage at 12/36: 92,038
Mileage at 31/12/50: 728,680

Sheds

Crewe	29/6/35
Carlisle N	18/1/36
St Rollox	5/6/43
Newton Heath	30/3/57
Aintree	11/1/64
Newton Heath	20/6/64
Carnforth	11/7/64
Lancaster	18/7/64
Speke Jct	6/3/65

Withdrawn w.e. 26/11/66

45154 LANARKSHIRE YEOMANRY as renumbered in January 1949 with BRITISH RAILWAYS in full on its newly acquired welded tender, having had a riveted example from April 1947. As with many St Rollox maintained engines, it had a top feed cover from a domed boiler on its domeless boiler. 45154 was shedded at St Rollox from 1943 until it moved south to Newton Heath in March 1957. It has both a Vulcan Foundry worksplate on the smokebox side and an Armstrong Whitworth plate on the front frame. This was a fairly common occurence, the plates fitted to the smokeboxes on the Vulcan engines following the boilers at Heavy Overhaul. In this case the source was 5119 whose boiler went via 45159 in 1943 and on to 45154 in January 1948.

45155

Built as 5155 at Armstrong Whitworth 16/7/35
Renumbered 45155 w.e. 11/9/48

Improvements and modifications

26/4/38	Removal of vacuum pump
20/5/45	Steam sanding
21/11/59	Fitting BR ATC equipment

Repairs

23/3/36-10/4/36	LS
8/4/37-11/5/37	LS
23/5/38-4/6/38	LO
9/4/38-26/4/38	LS
5/12/38-22/12/38	LO
15/4/39-26/5/39	HG
19/4/40-15/5/40	HS
18/4/41-17/5/41	LS
11/12/41-7/1/42	HG
29/10/42-28/11/42	LS
23/5/44-7/6/44	LS
25/3/45-22/5/45	HS
20/5/46-15/6/46	LS
16/6/47-12/8/47	HS
5/3/48-27/3/48	LO
9/8/48-11/9/48	LS
14/9/48-15/9/48	NC(R)
4/6/49-23/6/49	LC
13/1/50-25/2/50	G
6/6/51-29/6/51	LI
23/7/52-9/8/52	LC
26/1/53-21/2/53	HI
8/9/53	NC(TO)
7/9/54-8/10/54	G
21/10/54-22/10/54	NC(TO)
30/8/55-10/9/55	LC(EO)
12/1/56-21/1/56	NC(EO)
10/7/56	NC(EO)
31/10/56-3/11/56	NC(EO)
22/9/56-20/10/56	HI(EO)
23/11/56-29/11/56	LC
7/6/57	LC(EO)
21/9/57-8/11/57	LI
3/12/57-27/12/57	NC(EO)
9/1/58-21/1/58	NC(EO)
10/7/58-21/8/58	HC
21/10/59-21/11/59	G
7/9/61-13/10/61	LI
13/8/63-19/10/63	HI

Boilers

New	8935
26/5/39	8959 from 5179
7/1/42	8995 from 5144
3/5/45	8940 from 5016
25/2/50	8957 from 5081
8/10/54	8653 from 45049 (domed)
21/11/59	8951

Tenders

New	9259
11/2/44	9283
9/8/47	9279
8/3/48	10547 (part-welded)
26/3/48	9276
1/4/48	10547 (part-welded)
4/7/49	9545
16/2/50	9279
21/2/53	10598 (part-welded)
4/10/54	9015 (riveted)
20/12/54	9022 (riveted)
20/10/56	9668
29/11/56	9269
?	10594 (part-welded)

Mileage/(weekdays out of service)

1935	29,528 (13)
1936	70,119 (45)
1937	50,584 (81)
1938	52,729 (83)
1939	52,154 (69)
1940	47,162 (41)
1941	43,293 (85)
1942	52,536 (59)
1943	46,743 (40)
1944	46,700 (34)
1945	40,301 (59)
1946	48,594 (48)
1947	36,684 (89)
1948	35,576 (88)
1949	30,952 (104)
1950	40,070 (85)
1951	39,273 (74)
1952	35,273 (94)
1953	39,356 (85)
1954	34,422 (85)
1955	34,534 (65)
1956	29,027 (85)
1957	36,986 (90)
1958	39,431 (62)
1959	32,699
1960	46,937
1961	28,977
1962	39,258

Mileage at 12/36: 99,644
Mileage at 31/12/50: 723,722

Sheds

Crewe	20/7/35
Carlisle N	18/1/36
St Rollox	4/7/36
Carlisle N	3/10/36
St Rollox	5/6/43
St Margarets	3/1/58
Dalry Road	17/2/58

Withdrawn 12/11/64

45155 on 23 July 1960 at Carlisle has large 10in cab numbers and a St Rollox cast numberplate with LMS 1946 pattern numbers. The AWS was fitted in November 1959 when it also changed from a domed to a domeless boiler. 45155 had been allocated to 64C Dalry Road since September 1958 and remained there until withdrawn in November 1964. Photograph D. Forsyth, Colourrail.co.uk

45156

Built as 5156 at Armstrong Whitworth 16/7/35
Named AYRSHIRE YEOMANRY 19/9/36
Renumbered 45156 w.e. 18/9/48

Improvements and modifications

22/4/38	Removal of vacuum pump
20/5/45	Steam sanding
27/4/56	Modernisation
9/2/62	Fitting BR ATC equipment

Repairs

10/6/36-18/6/36	LS
10/6/37-2/7/37	LS
11/4/38-22/4/38	LS
6/10/38-29/10/38	HO
16/11/38-15/12/38	LS
3/7/39-2/8/39	LS
15/5/40-1/6/40	HS
23/6/41-29/7/41	LO
18/12/41-8/1/42	LO
18/1/42-14/2/42	HG
10/8/43-8/9/43	LS
24/5/44-18/6/44	HS
25/5/45-29/6/45	LS
29/5/46-11/7/46	HG
23/10/47-21/11/47	LS
9/8/48-16/9/48	HG
11/3/49-2/4/49	LC
22/8/49-1/9/49	LC
28/2/50-8/4/50	LI
6/3/51-5/4/51	LC
30/7/51-25/8/51	HI
3/9/51-4/9/51	NC(R)
22/10/51-2/11/51	LC
15/7/52-6/8/52	LC
9/10/52-29/11/52	G
18/12/52-19/12/52	NC
31/5/54-1/6/54	NC
28/9/54-16/10/54	HI
27/7/55-18/8/55	LC(EO)
7/11/55	NC(EO)
14/3/56-27/4/56	G
8/5/58-29/5/58	HI
22/6/60-5/8/60	LI
25/1/62-9/2/62	NC
4/6/62-28/6/62	HG
13/1/66-18/2/66	LI

Boilers

New	8936
29/10/38	9011 from 5081
14/2/42	9009 from 5180
10/6/44	8675 from 5093
11/7/46	9044 from 5122
16/9/46	9000 from 5177
29/11/52	8668 from 45183 (domed)
27/4/56	8976

Tenders

New	9260
18/6/36	9277
17/9/48	9260
7/4/50	9266
21/12/50	10508
24/8/51	10674 (part-welded)
28/11/52	9266
15/10/54	10510
27/4/56	9832

Mileage/(weekdays out of service)

1935	31,579 (7)
1936	69,934 (34)
1937	51,634 (68)
1938	47,803 (94)
1939	52,793 (45)
1940	49,819 (38)
1941	47,859 (63)
1942	55,850 (56)
1943	50,462 (48)
1944	46,142 (38)
1945	47,580 (59)
1946	42,072 (82)
1947	44,237 (58)
1948	39,879 (70)
1949	41,404 (73)
1950	35,718 (74)
1951	32,423 (92)
1952	28,877 (129)
1953	45,930 (45)
1954	37,402 (85)
1955	40,148 (60)
1956	37,958 (93)
1957	38,751 (59)
1958	31,415 (81)
1959	25,586
1960	28,381

Mileage at 12/36: 101,513
Mileage at 31/12/50: 753,468

Sheds

Crewe	20/7/35
Carlisle N	18/1/36
St Rollox	13/2/43
Newton Heath	30/3/57
Bolton	22/12/62
Warrington	18/5/63
Edge Hill	22/6/63
Patricroft	11/5/68
Rose Grove	6/7/68

Stored
5/12/66-27/5/67
13/1/68-26/2/68

Withdrawn w.e. 10/8/68

On 4 August 1968 45156 hauled a GC Enterprises/Stockport (Bahamas) Locomotive Society 'Farewell to Steam' Tour from Stockport to Carnforth and back. This picture was taken at Bolton Trinity Street during a water stop. Named in 1936, it lost its AYRSHIRE YEOMANRY nameplates in the early 1960s after it was transferred from Scotland to Newton Heath in 1957. The enthusiasts have restored its 65B St Rollox shedplate in place of the Rose Grove one. 45156 was always domeless apart from one spell between 1952 and 1956 and received AWS in February 1962. Photograph www.rail-online.co.uk

45156 AYRSHIRE YEOMANRY, soon after its transfer from Scotland to Newton Heath in March 1957, at Deal Street Salford on the 8.10am Leeds-Liverpool. Photograph www.rail-online.co.uk

BRITISH RAILWAYS

45157

Built as 5157 at Armstrong Whitworth 17/7/35
Named THE GLASGOW HIGHLANDER 6/3/36
Renumbered 45157 w.e. 8/5/48

Improvements and modifications

3/3/38	Removal of vacuum pump
20/5/45	Steam sanding
21/5/59	Fitting BR ATC equipment

Repairs

16/2/37-20/3/37	LS
21/2/38-3/3/38	LS
13/10/38-3/11/38	LO
8/5/39-17/6/39	HG
6/12/39-6/1/40	LO
5/10/40-25/10/40	LS
1/11/40-13/11/40	LO
21/11/40-29/11/40	LO
25/1/41-25/2/41	LO
22/5/41-23/6/41	LS
9/12/41-29/12/41	LO
14/5/42-1/7/42	HG
20/4/43-22/5/43	LS
9/9/44-10/10/44	LS
7/12/45-11/1/46	HG
10/6/46-28/9/46	HO
12/4/48-8/5/48	LS
22/9/48-1/10/48	LO
4/7/49-20/8/49	HI
18/10/50-2/12/50	G
28/1/52-20/2/52	LI
20/3/52-25/3/52	NC(TO)
9/7/53-15/8/53	HI
23/11/54	LC(EO)
24/12/54-22/1/55	G
6/8/56-25/8/56	LI
6/1/58-6/2/58	HI
3/12/58-19/12/58	LC(EO)
18/5/59-21/5/59	NC(EO)
16/10/59-11/12/59	G
31/5/60-7/6/60	NC(EO)
20/10/60	NC(TO)
1/3/61-1/4/61	LI
5/4/61-7/4/61	NC(EO)

Boilers

New	8937
1/7/42	8950 from 5117
11/1/46	9011 from 5008
2/12/50	8907 from 45010
22/1/55	8936 from 45100
11/12/59	8915 from 45010

Tenders

New	9261
20/3/37	9269
21/9/44	9281
13/4/48	9545
4/7/49	10547 (part-welded)
19/2/52	9022 (riveted)
20/12/54	9015 (riveted)
20/1/55	9287
25/8/56	9679
20/12/62	9209 (riveted)

45157 THE GLASGOW HIGHLANDER at St Rollox on 14 August 1962, one of the first withdrawals at the end of that year. It was one of the two 'namers' to remain in Scotland and was shedded at St Rollox from November 1935 onwards. 45157 was always domeless but had had all three different patterns of tender and received AWS in May 1959.

Mileage/(weekdays out of service)

1935	21,920 (20)
1936	55,399 (71)
1937	58,749 (58)
1938	52,177 (88)
1939	63,322 (84)
1940	48,650 (65)
1941	47,544 (86)
1942	46,214 (59)
1943	51,779 (55)
1944	34,819 (82)
1945	42,076 (54)
1946	31,354 (127)
1947	41,558 (79)
1948	35,427 (79)
1949	38,860 (87)
1950	32,906 (107)
1951	46,411 (61)
1952	39,098 (81)
1953	35,507 (72)
1954	42,567 (65)
1955	40,692 (65)
1956	36,182 (82)
1957	40,862 (56)
1958	34,838 (72)
1959	33,296
1960	46,261
1961	30,271
1962	17,065

Sheds

Edge Hill	20/7/35
St Rollox	2/11/35

Mileage at 12/36: 77,319
Mileage at 31/12/50: 702,754

Stored
1/10/62-29/12/62

Withdrawn w.e. 29/12/62

45158

Built as 5158 at Armstrong Whitworth 17/7/35
Named GLASGOW YEOMANRY 22/5/36
Renumbered 45158 w.e. 26/6/48

Improvements and modifications

4/2/38	Removal of vacuum pump
13/6/43	Steam sanding
18/2/56	Modernisation
2/5/59	Fitting BR ATC equipment

Repairs

29/4/37-19/5/37	LS
24/1/38-4/2/38	LO
26/3/38-6/4/38	LS
19/1/39-28/1/39	LS
20/6/39-22/8/39	HG
28/6/40-13/7/40	LS
28/5/41-17/6/41	HS
23/8/41-15/10/41	LO
12/8/42-12/9/42	HG
17/12/43-31/12/43	LS
6/10/44-21/10/44	LS
18/8/45-13/9/45	LO
3/4/46-11/5/46	HG
2/10/46-14/11/46	LO
8/9/47-17/10/47	LS
12/6/48-25/6/48	LO
18/10/48-1/12/48	LS
25/5/49-11/6/49	LC
19/12/49-27/1/50	HI
18/10/50-17/11/50	LC
1/10/51-24/11/51	G
10/12/51-13/12/51	NC(EO)
13/4/53-27/5/53	HI
12/8/54-28/8/54	HI
4/10/54-9/10/54	LC(EO)
26/10/54-30/10/54	LC(EO)
23/11/54	LC(EO)
18/8/55-25/8/55	NC(EO)
18/1/56-18/2/56	G
19/10/57-9/11/57	HI
30/10/58-5/11/58	NC
27/2/59-20/3/59	LI
24/4/59-2/5/59	NC(EO)
23/2/60-26/3/60	LI
12/5/60-27/5/60	LC(EO)
11/9/61-28/10/61	HI

Boilers

New	8938
22/8/39	9047 from 5117
12/9/42	8674 from 5137 (domed)
11/5/46	8822 from 5221 (domed)
24/11/51	9057 from 45169
18/2/56	9011 from 45087
28/10/61	8958 (domed)

Tenders

New	9262
22/5/36	9268
26/8/41	9727
31/12/41	9709
18/6/42	9268
8/10/48	10621 (part-welded)
15/10/48	9268
14/11/51	9023 (riveted)
23/3/53	9364 (riveted)
27/8/54	10685 (part-welded)
18/2/56	9282
9/11/57	9117 (riveted)

Mileage/(weekdays out of service)

1935	21,782 (21)
1936	52,433 (55)
1937	60,191(68)
1938	61,398(78)
1939	40,215(102)
1940	58,069(36)
1941	43,927(91)
1942	37,867(89)
1943	49,109(24)
1944	43,299(40)
1945	39,425(51)
1946	39,801(87)
1947	37,122(81)
1948	34,984(90)
1949	44,258(67)
1950	35,192(90)
1951	24,548(117)
1952	43,611(73)
1953	37,849(95)
1954	33,902(89)
1955	37,273(47)
1956	37,097(60)
1957	34,233(71)
1958	42,911(54)
1959	41,472
1960	37,996
1961	26,888
1962	7,683

Mileage at 12/36: 74,215
Mileage at 31/12/50: 699,072

Sheds

Edge Hill	20/7/35
St Rollox	2/11/35
Ardrossan	13/1/64
Dumfries	5/5/64

Stored
12/3/62-24/12/62

Withdrawn 23/7/64

45158 GLASGOW YEOMANRY on 28 August 1957 at St Rollox where it was shedded from 1935 until 1964. It has a domeless boiler but with domed type top feed cover, and Manson tablet exchange apparatus for single working in the north. The missing domed covers from the firebox shoulders and the scorched smokebox contribute to its neglected appearance. Photograph Peter Groom.

45159

Built as 5159 at Armstrong Whitworth 21/7/35
Renumbered 45159 w.e. 18/6/49

Improvements and modifications

2/41	Removal of vacuum pump
20/5/45	Steam sanding
8/5/59	Fitting BR ATC equipment

Repairs

7/5/36-21/5/36	LO
22/10/36-11/11/36	LS
22/4/37-28/4/37	LO
5/11/37-25/11/37	LS
2/5/38-4/5/38	LO
4/9/39-18/10/39	HG
20/7/40-19/8/40	LO
31/3/41-7/5/41	LS
6/3/42-24/3/42	LO
25/3/42-21/4/42	HS
18/12/42-8/1/43	HG
15/9/43-7/10/43	LS
10/7/44-5/8/44	LS
28/4/45-2/6/45	HS
24/6/46-12/8/46	LS
14/10/47-22/11/47	HG
5/12/47-10/12/47	NC(R)
7/5/49-10/6/49	LI
24/3/50-14/4/50	LC
24/8/50-4/10/50	HI
30/3/51-13/4/51	LC
28/9/51-19/10/51	LC
23/10/51-5/12/51	G
23/5/52-4/6/52	NC(EO)
21/8/52-4/9/52	NC(EO)
6/3/53-27/4/53	HI
15/7/53-16/7/53	LC
22/3/54-10/4/54	HI
20/4/54-24/4/54	NC(EO)
28/6/55-12/8/55	G
27/10/56-23/11/56	LI
25/10/57-21/11/57	LI
26/8/58-13/9/58	HC(EO)
4/5/59-8/5/59	NC(EO)
13/7/59-29/5/59	G
8/2/61-3/4/61	HI
22/5/62-23/5/62	NC(TO)

Boilers

New	8939
18/10/39	8948 from 5168
8/1/43	8946 from 5119
22/11/47	9001 from 5178
5/12/51	8831 from 45160
12/8/55	8915 from 45010
29/8/59	9004 from 45153

Tenders

New	9263
16/12/46	9258
25/11/51	10686 (part-welded)
9/4/54	9061 (riveted)
12/8/55	10582 (part-welded)
21/11/57	10581 (part-welded)

Mileage/(weekdays out of service)

1935	28,792 (7)
1936	60,000 (49)
1937	60,424 (45)
1938	58,267 (58)
1939	43,097 (83)
1940	58,791 (36)
1941	60,494 (55)
1942	56,135 (66)
1943	57,441 (42)
1944	55,825 (62)
1945	51,895 (70)
1946	41,861 (72)
1947	35,090 (88)
1948	49,986 (34)
1949	43,442 (69)
1950	31,661 (100)
1951	31,752 (111)
1952	41,350 (72)
1953	37,333 (93)
1954	39,755 (63)
1955	32,603 (78)
1956	36,611 (79)
1957	29,421 (84)
1958	31,026 (70)
1959	37,431
1960	39,661
1961	32,066
1962	23,883

Mileage at 12/36: 88,792
Mileage at 31/12/50: 793,201

Sheds

St Rollox	27/7/35
Inverness	2/11/35
St Rollox	27/10/45

Withdrawn w.e. 22/4/63

45159 in the configuration with which it emerged from a General repair in August 1955 with domeless 21 element boiler and part-welded tender. It was shedded at 65B St Rollox from 1945 until withdrawn in April 1963. The Manson tablet exchange apparatus is partially obscuring the large 10in cab numbers. 45159 has both a Vulcan Foundry oval worksplate on the smokebox side and a rectangular Armstrong Whitworth plate on the frames.

45160

Built as 5160 at Armstrong Whitworth 21/7/35
Renumbered 45160 w.e. 7/8/48

Improvements and modifications

8/2/38	Removal of vacuum pump
20/5/45	Steam sanding
?	Fitting BR ATC equipment

Repairs

11/12/36-31/12/36	LS
13/4/37-19/4/37	LO
20/1/38-8/2/38	LS
28/8/39-24/10/39	HG
10/7/40-31/7/40	HS
5/4/41-1/5/41	HS
21/11/41-3/12/41	LO
26/1/42-2/5/42	HS
10/8/42-16/10/42	HO
23/3/43-19/4/43	LS
11/2/44-13/3/44	LS
4/7/44-6/7/44	LO
16/4/45-2/6/45	LS
30/3/46-2/5/46	HG
19/4/47-16/5/47	HS
12/6/48-7/8/48	HS
23/6/49-13/7/49	LC
25/1/50-2/3/50	LI
31/10/50-6/12/50	LI
28/4/51-1/9/51	G
20/10/51-7/11/51	LC
4/12/51-15/12/51	LC(EO)
21/1/52-7/2/52	LC(EO)
6/4/53-27/4/53	HI
28/9/53-17/10/53	LC(EO)
3/11/53-13/11/53	NC(EO)
11/2/54-13/2/54	HI
23/11/55-17/12/55	G
25/5/57-31/7/57	LI
14/10/57-19/10/57	NC(EO)
12/1/59-6/2/59	HI
8/4/59-29/4/59	LC(EO)
28/8/59-19/9/59	LC(EO)
30/5/60-2/7/60	LC(EO)
6/7/60-12/7/60	LC(EO)
20/7/60-5/8/60	LC(EO)
24/10/60-10/12/60	G
22/12/60-4/3/61	HC(EO)
18/8/62-14/9/62	HI
22/6/65-10/7/65	LC(EO)

Boilers

New	8940
24/10/39	9045 from 5115
1/5/41	8945 from 5173
16/10/42	8942 from 5165
2/5/46	8831 from 5165

Tenders

New	9264
8/2/38	9245
?	9240
?	9553
17/12/55	10503
?	9726

Mileage/(weekdays out of service)

1935	35,738 (2)
1936	60,568 (44)
1937	59,465 (34)
1938	49,548 (66)
1939	44,183 (79)
1940	63,532 (26)
1941	48,367 (104)
1942	37,108 (153)
1943	56,618 (46)
1944	40,645 (103)
1945	51,433 (82)
1946	53,407 (58)
1947	57,063 (56)
1948	50,673 (71)
1949	42,182 (87)
1950	41,742 (102)

Mileage at 12/36: 96,306
Mileage at 31/12/50: 792,272

Sheds

St Rollox	27/7/35
Inverness	2/11/35
Corkerhill	1/1/52
Ayr	10/11/59

Withdrawn 2/9/66

5160, an Inverness engine from 1935 until 1952, has high positioned post-war cab numbers to clear the Manson tablet exchange apparatus. It was always domeless and was photographed with a later pattern boiler with domed covers on the firebox, probably after a Heavy overhaul completed in May 1947 since the previous boiler exchange in 1946 gave it one without the covers.

45161

Built as 5161 at Armstrong Whitworth 21/7/35
Renumbered 45161 w.e. 7/5/49

Improvements and modifications

24/1/39	Removal of vacuum pump
?	Steam sanding
?	Fitting BR ATC equipment

Repairs

13/11/36-4/12/36	LS
16/4/37-23/4/37	LO
8/11/37-9/12/37	LS
3/1/39-24/1/39	LS
7/11/39-15/12/39	HG
17/10/40-1/11/40	HS
30/8/41-6/10/41	LS
13/4/42-15/5/42	HG
8/8/42-6/9/42	LO
25/3/43-8/5/43	LS
13/1/44-12/2/44	LS
15/1/45-21/2/45	HS
16/5/45-16/6/45	LO
14/11/45-15/12/45	LS
31/12/46-15/2/47	HG
4/2/48-9/3/48	LS
11/3/49-29/4/49	HI
10/8/49-13/10/49	LC
20/3/50-29/4/50	LC
27/7/50-8/8/50	LC
17/11/50-13/1/51	G
4/2/52-1/3/52	LI
31/1/53-6/3/53	HI
8/11/54-4/12/54	HI
10/8/55-25/8/55	LC
4/1/56-4/2/56	G
11/6/56-22/6/56	LC(EO)
20/2/57-15/3/57	HI
20/8/58-15/10/58	HI
27/3/59-3/4/59	NC(EO)
17/12/59-30/12/59	LC(EO)
6/2/61-18/3/61	G
1/5/61-11/5/61	LC(EO)
10/12/62-19/1/63	HI
6/4/66-30/4/66	LC(EO)
16/5/66-20/5/66	NC(LO)

Boilers

New	8941
15/12/39	8943 from 5163
15/5/42	9043 from 5054
15/2/47	9022 from 5066

Tenders

New	9265
17/10/40	9280
16/8/42	9005 (riveted)
20/2/45	9015 (riveted)
13/1/51	9185 (riveted)
?	10697 (part-welded)
6/3/53	9097 (riveted)
2/12/54	10502
12/8/55	9620
4/2/56	9511
14/3/57	9209 (riveted)
20/12/62	9679
9/5/65	9593
21/10/66	9531

Mileage/(weekdays out of service)

1935	30,965 (12)
1936	59,727 (48)
1937	60,406 (58)
1938	65,235 (34)
1939	44,697 (80)
1940	54,067 (51)
1941	50,554 (83)
1942	57,732 (77)
1943	54,215 (54)
1944	48,949 (57)
1945	49,371 (114)
1946	50,924 (26)
1947	49,855 (69)
1948	47,442 (75)
1949	30,067 (116)
1950	19,829 (138)

Mileage at 12/36: 90,692
Mileage at 31/12/50: 769,335

Sheds

St Rollox	27/7/35
Inverness	2/11/35
St Rollox	27/10/45
Perth	17/8/46
Inverness	12/6/48
Perth	3/7/48
Inverness	25/6/49
Carstairs	22/10/49
Dalry Road	6/10/51 (PE)
Corkerhill	17/7/58 (loan)
Carstairs	13/11/59
Ayr	22/6/64
Carstairs	8/10/66 (PE)

Withdrawn 29/11/66

45161 on a parcels train of just three vehicles at Hilton Junction near Perth on 21 August 1962. It was allocated to Carstairs at the date of this picture and spent three spells there, being finally withdrawn from there in November 1966. It has a domeless boiler, welded tender and AWS. Photograph www.rail-online.co.uk

45162

Built as 5162 at Armstrong Whitworth 29/7/35
Renumbered 45162 w.e. 17/7/48

Improvements and modifications

22/2/38	Removal of vacuum pump
?	Steam sanding

Repairs

15/1/37-6/2/37	LS
9/4/37-15/4/37	LO
1/2/38-22/2/38	LS
22/3/38-16/4/38	HS
9/6/38-29/6/38	LO
6/11/39-22/12/39	HG
17/8/40-7/9/40	HS
16/6/41-19/7/41	LO
5/12/41-24/12/41	LS
19/10/42-3/12/42	HG
6/8/43-8/9/43	LS
30/11/44-22/12/44	HS
24/4/46-23/5/46	HG
11/8/47-20/9/47	LS
16/6/48-15/7/48	HS
29/12/48-13/1/49	LC
8/8/49-23/9/49	HI
14/10/49-19/10/49	NC(R)
5/6/50-14/7/50	HG
24/9/51-20/10/51	LI
7/11/51-1/12/51	LC(EO)
2/12/52-10/1/53	LI
4/8/53-12/8/53	NC(EO)
27/11/53-9/1/54	G
16/5/55-24/6/55	HI
25/6/56-17/8/56	LI
31/5/57-11/6/57	LC(EO)
13/12/57-26/12/57	LC(EO)
11/8/58-11/10/58	G
12/10/60-18/11/60	LI
1/11/62-7/12/62	G
11/3/63-17/4/63	LC(EO)
19/8/65-18/9/65	LC

Boilers

New	8942
22/12/39	9013 from 5083
3/12/42	8969 from 5121
15/6/46	8916 from 5213
24/7/50	9014 from 5016

Tenders

New	9266
10/3/39	9556
21/4/39	9266
5/12/41	9530
24/12/41	9914
23/9/49	9064 (riveted)
9/1/51	9277
?	10595 (part-welded)

Mileage/(weekdays out of service)

1935	29,847 (6)
1936	70,729 (25)
1937	52,463 (76)
1938	42,758 (105)
1939	44,687 (75)
1940	65,129 (30)
1941	47,520 (97)
1942	50,149 (65)
1943	57,008 (43)
1944	44,053 (46)
1945	41,749 (55)
1946	43,177 (78)
1947	54,302 (57)
1948	50,505 (63)
1949	38,517 (104)
1950	43,559 (74)

Mileage at 12/36: 100,576
Mileage at 31/12/50: 776,152

Sheds

Crewe	4/8/35
Carlisle N	28/9/35
Inverness	4/7/36
St Rollox	4/9/43
Perth	17/8/46
Polmadie	11/7/53 (PE)
Ferryhill	23/8/54
Dalry Road	9/8/64
St Margarets	4/10/65

Withdrawn 19/11/66

5162 at Crewe in original condition as built in July 1935 before permanent allocation to the Northern Division at Carlisle. It has the Armstrong Whitworth worksplate on the frames, the small access cover on the cylinders and the 60in tender letter spacing.

45163

Built as 5163 at Armstrong Whitworth 29/7/35
Renumbered 45163 w.e. 30/10/48

Improvements and modifications

24/3/38	Removal of vacuum pump
20/5/45	Steam sanding
30/3/56	Modernisation
?	Fitting BR ATC equipment
26/5/61	Sloping throatplate boiler

Repairs

10/3/37-9/4/37	LS
14/3/38-24/3/38	LS
2/10/39-25/11/39	HG
15/8/40-31/8/40	LS
22/3/41-17/4/41	LO
21/10/41-4/12/41	HS
19/5/42-18/7/42	LS
17/9/42-5/11/42	HO
12/4/43-11/5/43	HS
4/3/44-28/3/44	LS
4/1/45-10/2/45	LS
22/8/45-21/9/45	LS
11/12/45-27/12/45	LO
29/7/46-21/9/46	HG
13/8/47-20/9/47	LS
27/9/48-28/10/48	LS
19/11/48-25/11/48	NC
25/6/49-29/6/49	NC
20/7/49-16/8/49	LC
22/12/49-28/1/50	HI
7/6/51-13/10/51	G
26/5/52-25/6/52	HC
13/3/53-11/4/53	LI
7/7/54-14/8/54	LI
16/12/54-14/1/55	LC(EO)
22/2/56-30/3/56	G
15/5/56-16/6/56	HC
28/6/56-4/7/56	LC(EO)
30/10/57-23/11/57	LI
30/4/58-6/5/58	LC
8/8/59-5/9/59	HI
18/4/61-26/5/61	G
8/6/61	NC(EO)

Boilers

New	8943
25/11/39	8957 from 5177
5/11/42	9005 from 5223
21/9/46	9009 from 5156
13/10/51	8652 from 45172 (domed)
30/3/56	8938
26/5/61	9459 from 44900 (sloping throatplate)

Tenders

New	9267
10/8/42	9298
16/11/42	9267
27/7/49	9164 (riveted)
8/1/51	10686 (part-welded)
18/7/51	9329
3/10/51	9194 (riveted)
14/8/54	10593 (part-welded)
30/3/56	10601 (part-welded)
16/6/56	10692 (part-welded)
4/7/56	9823
23/11/57	10582 (part-welded)
1/8/61	10695 (part-welded)

Mileage/(weekdays out of service)

1935	27,080 (16)
1936	69,687 (40)
1937	65,054 (55)
1938	57,277 (72)
1939	44,594 (117)
1940	68,752 (34)
1941	52,454 (89)
1942	45,255 (128)
1943	62,960 (47)
1944	48,370 (50)
1945	42,682 (119)
1946	51,807 (76)
1947	51,921 (49)
1948	47,744 (69)
1949	39,316 (84)
1950	55,311 (54)
1951	29,362 (143)
1952	43,882 (73)
1953	40,713 (59)
1954	45,208 (75)
1955	27,244 (84)
1956	38,194 (94)
1957	41,994 (86)
1958	44,222 (96)
1959	46,606
1960	52,087

Mileage at 12/36: 96,767
Mileage at 31/12/50: 830,264

Sheds

Crewe	3/8/35
Perth	5/10/35
Inverness	4/7/36
Perth	10/10/36
Corkerhill	1/4/50
Carlisle Kingmoor	17/5/52

Withdrawn w.e 15/5/65

Kingmoor allocated 45163 on 10 June 1961 at Balornock after a short Non Classified visit to St Rollox for adjustment after a General repair when it was fitted with a sloping throatplate boiler. It has its sixth different part-welded tender; AWS and 8in cab numbers positioned lower than normal. Photograph G.H. Robin.

45164

Built as 5164 at Armstrong Whitworth 29/7/35
Renumbered 45164 w.e. 21/8/48

Improvements and modifications

24/5/38	Removal of vacuum pump
20/5/45	Steam sanding
?	Fitting BR ATC equipment

Repairs

11/5/36-23/5/36	LS
4/6/37-22/6/37	LS
14/5/38-24/5/38	LO
7/3/39-7/4/39	HG
22/2/40-16/3/40	HS
28/10/40-16/11/40	LS
25/8/41-17/9/41	LS
22/7/42-29/8/42	LS
8/3/43-17/4/43	LS
21/2/44-4/3/44	HG
8/8/44-16/9/44	HO
23/1/45-3/3/45	LS
27/2/46-23/3/46	LS
4/5/46-18/5/46	LO
15/1/47-8/3/47	LS
1/9/47-27/10/47	HG
21/12/48-11/2/49	HI
25/2/50-7/4/50	LI
28/1/52-15/3/52	G
2/4/52-10/4/52	NC(EO)
?-11/4/53	HI
18/5/54-18/6/54	LI
2/2/55-17/2/55	NC(EO)
8/9/55-7/10/55	HI
30/11/55-7/12/55	NC(EO)
21/8/56-7/9/56	LC(EO)
25/9/56-4/10/56	NC(EO)
10/10/56-16/11/56	G
5/12/56-15/12/56	NC
9/5/58-25/6/58	LI
16/6/59-19/6/59	NC(EO)
30/5/60	NC(TO)
24/6/60-15/7/60	LC(EO)
23/11/60	NC(TO)
28/12/60	NC(TO)
10/3/61-13/5/61	G
15/5/61-19/5/61	LC(EO)
23/1/62-2/2/62	LC(EO)
18/3/63-27/4/63	LI
11/8/65-21/8/65	NC

Boilers

New	8944
7/4/39	8824 from 5007
4/3/44	8988 from 5194 (domed)
16/9/44	8667 from 5136 (domed)
1/11/47	8686 from 5152 (domed)

Tenders

New	9268
22/5/36	9262
22/5/46	9708
24/10/47	9663
29/10/48	9708
?	10556 (part-welded)
16/11/56	10695 (part-welded)
12/5/61	10690 (part-welded)
16/3/54	9242

Mileage/(weekdays out of service)

1935	31,426 (5)
1936	68,247 (42)
1937	64,534 (43)
1938	61,423 (51)
1939	55,955 (62)
1940	57,456 (60)
1941	62,610 (43)
1942	49,434 (73)
1943	55,041 (79)
1944	41,676 (89)
1945	57,606 (67)
1946	49,071 (80)
1947	39,591 (137)
1948	51,885 (47)
1949	47,471 (75)
1950	48,489 (82)

Mileage at 12/36: 99,673
Mileage at 31/12/50: 841,915

Sheds

Crewe	3/8/35
Carlisle N	28/9/35
Perth	@23/5/36
Polmadie	11/7/53 (PE)
Perth	15/9/54
Dundee Tay Bridge	31/1/55
Corkerhill	18/4/60
Ayr	13/8/62

Withdrawn 9/8/66

45164, renumbered on 21 August 1948, after a Heavy Intermediate overhaul completed in February 1949. It has large BR serif numbers in a high position but the tender has no insignia. 45164 had a domed boiler between 1944 and 1952 and had been shedded at 63A Perth since 1936. Photograph R.K. Blencowe.

45165

Built as 5165 at Armstrong Whitworth 5/8/35
Renumbered 45165 w.e. 6/11/48

Improvements and modifications

14/3/38	Removal of vacuum pump
20/5/45	Steam sanding
13/5/60	Fitting BR ATC equipment

Repairs

10/2/37-25/3/37	LS
2/3/38-14/3/38	LS
21/4/38-9/4/38	LO
16/11/39-5/1/40	HG
28/2/40-22/3/40	HS
19/12/40-11/1/41	LS
21/1/41-1/2/41	LO
11/9/41-13/10/41	LS
5/5/42-26/6/42	HG
19/4/43-15/5/43	LS
3/4/44-26/4/44	LS
12/3/45-18/4/45	HS
4/12/45-12/1/46	HG
31/12/46-8/2/47	LS
16/2/48-13/3/48	LS
20/9/48-3/11/48	LO
10/6/49-13/8/49	G
3/11/49-12/11/49	LC
4/8/50-21/9/50	LI
12/4/51-11/5/51	LC
1/6/51-7/6/51	NC
25/12/51-25/1/52	LI
21/8/52-13/9/52	LC(EO)
25/2/53-18/4/53	G
3/9/53-24/9/53	LC
1/12/53-25/12/53	HI
4/1/55-23/2/55	LI
28/4/55-11/5/55	NC(EO)
24/11/55-24/12/55	HI
17/8/56	NC
19/12/56-31/1/57	G
15/2/57-22/2/57	LC(EO)
29/8/57-7/9/57	LC(EO)
18/11/57-13/12/57	LI
17/2/58-14/3/58	LC(EO)
9/5/58-23/5/58	NC(EO)
17/1/59-6/2/59	HI
6/4/59-2/5/59	LC(EO)
18/8/59-5/9/59	LC(EO)
8/4/60-13/5/60	HI
2/5/61-1/6/61	LC

Boilers

New	8945
5/1/40	8942 from 5162
26/6/42	8831 from 5116
12/1/46	9817 from 5055 (domed)
13/8/49	8937 from 45167
18/4/53	9000
31/1/57	9003

Tenders

New	9269
26/3/37	9261
15/3/38	9181 (riveted)
6/5/42	9270
26/4/44	9212 (riveted)
10/1/46	9250
15/4/53	10688 (part-welded)
22/12/53	9216 (riveted)
24/12/55	9594
23/2/57	10712
8/5/63	10510 (part-welded)

Mileage/(weekdays out of service)

1935	20,859 (15)
1936	75,086 (31)
1937	61,514 (58)
1938	55,374 (75)
1939	51,356 (90)
1940	62,084 (58)
1941	47,629 (84)
1942	51,239 (74)
1943	55,951 (47)
1944	50,805 (70)
1945	45,763 (110)
1946	58,084 (49)
1947	54,362 (58)
1948	47,582 (90)
1949	31,752 (128)
1950	46,169 (71)
1951	43,879 (51)
1952	38,385 (87)
1953	40,025 (113)
1954	54,722 (34)
1955	40,871 (115)
1956	45,689 (87)
1957	43,518 (110)
1958	48,452 (63)
1959	39,836
1960	42,558
1961	33,720
1962	8,759

Mileage at 12/36: 95,945
Mileage at 31/12/50: 815,612

Sheds

Crewe	10/8/35
Perth	26/10/35
Hamilton	25/9/61
Motherwell	10/12/62

Stored
13/8/62-29/12/62

Withdrawn w.e. 29/12/62

5165 in a picture which contradicts the History Cards which show it with a domed boiler from January 1946 until August 1949. However it is shown here domeless with the M prefix which it received on 11/3/48 before it was renumbered as 45165 in November 1948. It was allocated to Perth, hence the Manson tablet exchange apparatus, from 1935 until 1961 and was one of the early withdrawals in December 1962. Photograph R.K. Blencowe.

45166

Built as 5166 at Armstrong Whitworth 5/8/35
Renumbered 45166 w.e. 1/5/48

Improvements and modifications

18/5/38	Removal of vacuum pump
20/5/45	Steam sanding
21/11/59	Fitting BR ATC equipment

Repairs

5/5/37-26/5/37	LS
9/5/38-18/5/38	LS
6/5/39-15/6/39	HG
26/10/39-28/11/39	LO
19/6/40-23/7/40	LS
9/11/40-6/12/40	LS
10/7/41-16/8/41	LS
27/8/41-3/9/41	LO
1/6/42-4/9/42	HG
31/12/43-27/1/44	LS
1/3/45-7/4/45	LS
22/6/45-11/7/45	LO
1/4/46-27/4/46	LS
8/5/46-28/5/46	LO
11/11/46-25/1/47	HG
7/4/47-22/4/47	LO
2/4/48-1/5/48	LS
1/6/49-2/7/49	HI
6/2/50-27/2/50	LC
24/5/50-10/6/50	LC
1/7/50-6/7/50	LC
28/7/50-24/8/50	LC
12/6/51-7/7/51	HI
23/9/52-20/12/52	G
10/12/53-11/12/53	LC
24/5/54-23/6/54	HI
21/8/55-1/10/55	HI
12/7/56-23/7/56	NC(EO)
6/2/57-16/3/57	G
26/9/57-8/10/57	NC(EO)
25/4/58-24/5/58	HI
8/10/59-21/11/59	LI
2/3/60-9/4/60	LC(EO)
27/9/60-15/10/60	LC(EO)
8/8/61-22/9/61	G

Boilers

New	8946
15/6/39	9012 from 5082
4/9/42	8934 from 5157
25/1/47	8932 from 5117
20/12/52	9048 from 45152
16/3/57	8962
20/9/61	8652 from 45112 (domed)

Tenders

New	9270
6/5/42	9181 (riveted)
8/6/42	9179 (riveted)
2/4/46	9210 (riveted)
2/7/49	9712
28/7/50	10602 (part-welded)
15/12/52	9164 (riveted)
10/3/57	9268
?	10815 (part-welded)
18/11/63	9836

Mileage/(weekdays out of service)

1935	32,135 (4)
1936	74,039 (36)
1937	61,940 (55)
1938	60,501 (51)
1939	49,632 (92)
1940	51,816 (73)
1941	48,323 (72)
1942	40,904 (113)
1943	53,509 (56)
1944	54,666 (74)
1945	52,163 (75)
1946	44,275 (114)
1947	49,902 (82)
1948	50,248 (50)
1949	43,534 (83)
1950	31,620 (114)
1951	49,864 (51)
1952	34,731 (132)
1953	57,017 (31)
1954	48,022 (40)
1955	46,882 (27)
1956	44,640 (58)
1957	46,355 (87)
1958	43,826 (84)
1959	35,740
1960	42,683
1961	30,192
1962	41,015

Mileage at 12/36: 106,174
Mileage at 31/12/50: 799,207

Sheds

Crewe	10/8/35
Perth	12/10/35
Corkerhill	13/10/51
Carstairs	15/2/56

Withdrawn 16/9/63

An immaculate 45166 at Carstairs in July 1958 with an Edinburgh-Crewe train. It has a domeless boiler and a part-welded tender.

45167

Built as 5167 at Armstrong Whitworth 2/8/35
Renumbered 45167 w.e. 1/5/48

Improvements and modifications

12/4/38	Removal of vacuum pump
20/5/45	Steam sanding

Repairs

31/3/36-21/4/36	LO
4/3/37-3/4/37	LS
30/3/38-12/4/38	LS
20/6/39-16/8/39	HG
24/11/39-30/12/39	LS
10/5/40-30/5/40	HS
4/4/41-25/4/41	LS
22/9/41-30/10/41	LS
2/10/42-17/10/42	HG
29/9/43-3/11/43	LS
8/6/44-30/6/44	HS
10/7/44-29/7/44	LO
31/5/45-29/6/45	HG
12/6/46-10/7/46	LS
21/8/47-27/9/47	LS
5/4/48-1/5/48	LO
8/2/49-26/3/49	G
18/1/50-17/2/50	LI
6/3/50-10/3/50	NC
20/3/51-20/4/51	INT
28/4/52-29/4/52	LC(TO)
26/8/52-4/10/52	HI
11/9/53-31/10/53	G
18/10/54-25/11/54	LI
10/11/55-2/12/55	LI
16/10/56-8/11/56	HC
12/12/56-20/12/56	LC(EO)
30/3/57-17/5/57	LI
25/6/57-27/6/57	NC(EO)
7/11/57-19/11/57	NC(EO)
4/1/58-23/1/58	LC(EO)
9/5/58-31/5/58	LC(EO)
13/10/58-22/11/58	G
3/4/59-16/4/59	LC(EO)
4/3/60-25/3/60	LC(EO)
7/2/61-10/3/61	LI
5/4/61-21/4/61	LC(EO)
18/8/61-2/9/61	LC(EO)
3/12/62-19/12/62	HC
8/4/66-7/5/66	LC

Boilers

New	8947
16/8/39	8958 from 5178
17/10/42	9028 from 5087
29/6/45	8937 from 5170
26/3/49	9044 from 5156

Tenders

New	9271
2/4/37	9211 (riveted)
1/10/41	9179 (riveted)
8/6/42	9255
?	10677 (part-welded)
3/11/53	10533
15/10/54	9122 (riveted)
2/12/55	9015 (riveted)
20/9/61	9716
5/11/63	10684 (part-welded)

Mileage/(weekdays out of service)

1935	25,373 (11)
1936	62,715 (65)
1937	59,581 (62)
1938	56,900 (85)
1939	38,230 (137)
1940	62,271 (39)
1941	53,246 (88)
1942	51,405 (65)
1943	54,930 (49)
1944	41,959 (130)
1945	52,718 (83)
1946	58,465 (65)
1947	51,331 (70)
1948	50,993 (51)
1949	54,220 (61)
1950	51,083 (56)

Mileage at 12/36: 88,088
Mileage at 31/12/50: 825,420

Sheds

Crewe	10/8/35
Perth	13/6/36
Ferryhill	16/6/56
Kittybrewster	4/6/60
Ardrossan	15/5/61
Ayr	15/2/65
Carstairs	8/10/66 (PE)
Motherwell	13/11/66

Withdrawn 1/5/67

The welded tender paired with 45167 from September 1961 to November 1963 still has a pre-1957 BR crest. Allocated to Ardrossan from 1961 until 1965, the covers are missing on the firebox shoulders. Photograph www.rail-online.co.uk

45168

Built as 5168 at Armstrong Whitworth 17/8/35
Renumbered 45168 w.e. 3/4/48

Improvements and modifications

7/38	Removal of vacuum pump
13/6/43	Steam sanding
?	Fitting BR ATC equipment

Repairs

29/10/36-14/11/36	LS
17/5/37-21/5/37	LO
6/12/37-23/12/37	LS
16/8/39-2/10/39	HG
19/2/41-8/3/41	HS
19/1/42-20/2/42	LS
18/1/43-8/2/43	HG
10/1/44-9/2/44	LS
22/8/45-29/9/45	LS
22/4/46-24/5/46	HS
24/2/47-12/4/47	LS
7/3/48-3/4/48	HG
30/11/48-8/1/49	LC
31/1/49-5/3/49	LI
20/3/50-21/4/50	LI
1/3/52-17/5/52	G
12/11/52-18/12/52	NC(EO)
22/8/53-2/10/53	LI
10/11/53-14/11/53	LC(EO)
13/1/54-29/1/54	NC
10/1/55-5/2/55	LI
11/2/55-16/2/55	NC(EO)
12/3/56-14/4/56	HI
17/6/57-8/7/57	G
27/3/58-12/4/58	NC(EO)
4/11/58-22/11/58	LC(EO)
7/1/59-28/1/59	LC(EO)
26/2/59-6/3/59	LC(EO)
14/8/59-12/9/59	LI
31/7/61-15/9/61	G
14/8/63-21/8/63	LC(EO)
4/9/64-26/9/64	LI

Boilers

New	8948
2/10/39	9015 from 5085
8/2/42	8924 from 5075
3/4/48	8958 from 5127

Tenders

New	9272
6/12/44	9062 (riveted)
15/12/44	9298
29/9/45	9538
25/2/47	9837
7/1/49	9175 (riveted)
21/4/50	10506
9/2/51	9176 (riveted)
?	9032 (riveted)
5/2/55	10448
14/4/56	10605 (part-welded)
8/7/57	9545
10/11/58	10620 (part-welded)
27/2/59	9545

Mileage/(weekdays out of service)

1935	23,975 (6)
1936	59,343 (66)
1937	60,544 (57)
1938	61,052 (55)
1939	53,998 (85)
1940	65,455 (31)
1941	59,286 (63)
1942	51,907 (77)
1943	62,131 (45)
1944	28,967 (136)
1945	36,245 (106)
1946	51,745 (62)
1947	41,205 (114)
1948	39,125 (88)
1949	51,324 (69)
1950	40,824 (91)

Mileage at 12/36: 83,318
Mileage at 31/12/50: 787,126

Sheds

Perth	17/8/35
Corkerhill	29/4/44
Perth	23/2/53
Polmadie	28/5/60
Hamilton	26/9/61
Motherwell	29/10/62
Dalry Road	26/8/63
St Margarets	4/10/65

Withdrawn 26/9/66

45168 in the 1950s at Corkerhill has St Rollox large cab numbers above the tablet holder. Always a Scottish engine it was at Perth from March 1953 until transferred to Polmadie in June 1960. The domeless boiler, power class '5' and the riveted tender suggest the photo was taken between February 1951 and February 1955. Note that it has acquired a Vulcan Foundry worksplate on the smokebox above the steam pipe. Photograph www.rail-online.co.uk

45169

Built as 5169 at Armstrong Whitworth 13/8/35
Renumbered 45169 w.e. 25/9/48

Improvements and modifications

21/4/37	Removal of vacuum pump
20/5/45	Steam sanding
13/7/51	Sloping throatplate boiler
28/10/61	Fitting BR ATC equipment

Repairs

6/1/37-30/1/37	LS
15/4/37-21/4/37	LO
29/12/37-21/1/38	LS
14/4/39-20/5/39	HG
15/12/39-16/1/40	HS
15/5/41-16/6/41	LS
22/9/41-10/10/41	LO
10/7/42-20/8/42	HG
20/7/43-19/8/43	LS
3/1/44-3/2/44	LO
14/2/45-14/3/45	HS
21/3/45-14/4/45	LO
22/11/46-25/1/47	HG
26/8/47-17/10/47	LO
19/8/48-23/9/48	LS
15/3/49-18/5/49	HC
13/12/49-2/2/50	LI
9/8/50-19/8/50	LC
1/9/50-13/9/50	LC
28/3/51-13/7/51	G
17/9/52-18/10/52	LI
14/8/53-12/9/53	LI
24/2/54-6/3/54	LC(EO)
14/5/54-8/6/54	LC(EO)
27/6/55-15/7/55	G
29/12/56-19/1/57	HI
5/12/57-28/1/58	LI
24/4/58-14/5/58	LC(EO)
9/1/59-31/1/59	HI
18/2/60-25/3/60	G
31/8/61-28/10/61	HI

Boilers

New	8949
20/5/39	9016 from 5086
20/8/42	8965 from 5003
25/1/47	9057 from 5015
13/7/51	8638 from 45087 (sloping throatplate)
15/7/55	12125 from 44961 (sloping throatplate)
25/3/60	12442 from 45049 (sloping throatplate)

Tenders

New	9273
7/1/46	9169 (riveted)
18/10/52	9206 (riveted)
12/9/53	10582 (part-welded)
21/7/55	9722
19/1/57	9724
11/2/63	9598

Mileage/(weekdays out of service)

1935	28,931 (2)
1936	66,805 (38)
1937	60,599 (59)
1938	61,171 (71)
1939	51,833 (85)
1940	58,181 (61)
1941	38,713 (120)
1942	54,800 (78)
1943	47,306 (59)
1944	43,454 (82)
1945	41,455 (75)
1946	45,480 (100)
1947	35,441 (127)
1948	44,365 (72)
1949	34,906 (147)
1950	42,254 (83)
1951	41,286 (107)
1952	38,123 (98)
1953	45,108 (62)
1954	35,633 (77)
1955	29,450 (112)
1956	37,435 (44)
1957	43,050 (67)
1958	41,691 (82)
1959	50,910
1960	43,591
1961	33,175
1962	45,618

Mileage at 12/36: 95,736
Mileage at 31/12/50: 755,694

Sheds

Perth	17/8/35
Carlisle	28/8/43
Perth	3/12/49
Dumfries	13/10/51

Withdrawn 13/5/63

45169 at Carlisle around 1959/60 has St Rollox large cab numbers and 1946 style smokebox numberplate. It was converted to sloping throatplate in July 1951 and allocated to Dumfries from November 1951 until withdrawn in May 1963. Photograph B.G. Tweed.

45170

Built as 5170 at Armstrong Whitworth 12/8/35
Renumbered 45170 w.e. 22/5/48

Improvements and modifications

14/4/38	Removal of vacuum pump
20/5/45	Steam sanding
?	Modernisation
13/1/61	Fitting BR ATC equipment

Repairs

23/4/36-16/5/36	LO
4/5/37-29/5/37	LS
4/4/38-14/4/38	LS
22/5/39-31/7/39	HG
15/4/40-22/5/40	HS
17/3/41-12/4/41	LS
27/12/41-31/1/42	HG
6/2/42-25/2/42	LO
5/11/42-28/11/42	LS
11/1/44-3/2/44	HS
12/1/45-28/2/45	HG
4/3/46-6/4/46	LS
27/11/46-9/1/47	LS
24/1/47-20/2/47	LO
2/8/47-16/8/47	NC
5/4/48-21/5/48	LS
14/6/48-10/7/48	LO
1/6/49-15/7/49	G
7/4/50-11/5/50	LI
28/2/51-20/4/51	HI
31/7/51-4/8/51	NC
13/8/51-19/9/51	LC
16/4/52-10/5/52	LC
24/9/52-1/11/52	LC
3/7/53-9/7/53	LC
4/9/53-31/10/53	G
3/7/54-14/7/54	LC
15/12/54-14/1/55	LI
24/1/55-27/1/55	NC(EO)
8/9/55-23/9/55	LC(EO)
4/11/55-2/12/55	HI
30/7/56-21/9/56	LI
29/12/56-5/1/57	NC(EO)
28/1/57-5/2/57	NC(EO)
7/6/57	LC(EO)
7/11/57-20/12/57	G
17/1/59-5/2/59	HI
24/9/59-9/10/59	LC(EO)
21/11/59-12/12/59	LC
2/3/60-11/3/60	LC
8/12/60-31/12/60	LI
31/12/60-13/1/61	LI
28/1/61-8/2/61	LC(EO)
18/6/62-2/8/62	G

Boilers

New	8950
31/7/39	8932 from 5152
31/1/42	8937 from 5013 (domed)
15/7/49	8950 from 5174
31/10/53	9021 from 45213
28/12/57	8999

Tenders

New	9274
6/8/47	9712
5/7/49	9210 (riveted)
25/2/51	9064 (riveted)
1/11/52	9062 (riveted)
21/5/53	9296
30/10/53	9287
14/1/55	9015 (riveted)
2/12/55	9116 (riveted)
20/12/57	9595
14/4/64	9120 (riveted)

Mileage/(weekdays out of service)

1935	27,754 (4)
1936	62,480 (63)
1937	63,400 (45)
1938	61,147 (44)
1939	47,549 (96)
1940	59,482 (53)
1941	47,920 (83)
1942	42,821 (120)
1943	57,549 (50)
1944	54,333 (54)
1945	49,149 (100)
1946	40,958 (97)
1947	40,883 (114)
1948	47,875 (98)
1949	52,039 (61)
1950	46,314 (81)
1951	29,762 (118)
1952	40,266 (89)
1953	40,586 (115)
1954	55,271 (48)
1955	46,341 (87)
1956	49,762 (75)
1957	40,855 (105)
1958	60,720 (45)
1959	49,225
1960	39,148
1961	37,114
1962	27,492

Mileage at 12/36: 90,234
Mileage at 31/12/50: 801,653

Sheds

Perth	17/8/35
Dalry Road	25/9/61

Withdrawn 31/3/64

An audience watches two men dressing coal on the tender of 45170 at Helmsdale on 26 August 1949. It was renumbered 45170 during w.e. 22/5/48 with close-spaced large cab numbers set high to clear the Manson tablet exchange equipment and BRITISH RAILWAYS in full on the tender. The domeless boiler was fitted during a General repair completed in the previous month when its domed boiler was replaced and it also acquired a riveted tender at the same time. 45170 only had two sheds, Perth from new and Dalry Road in September 1961.

45171

Built as 5171 at Armstrong Whitworth 15/8/35
Renumbered 45171 w.e. 22/5/48

Improvements and modifications

1/2/38	Removal of vacuum pump
20/5/45	Steam sanding
?	Fitting BR ATC equipment

Repairs

24/12/36-30/1/37	LS
20/4/37-24/4/37	LO
14/1/38-1/2/38	LS
3/4/39-6/5/39	HG
30/4/40-10/5/40	HS
24/2/41-23/3/41	LS
3/12/41-10/1/42	HG
24/9/42-7/11/42	LS
15/11/43-3/12/43	HS
12/7/44-12/8/44	HG
17/8/45-29/9/45	LS
23/10/45-1/12/45	LO
6/3/46-30/3/46	LO
30/1/47-1/3/47	LS
18/11/47-20/12/47	LS
5/5/48-21/5/48	LO
29/11/48-7/1/49	HG
14/7/49-1/9/49	LI
24/6/50-12/8/50	LI
30/8/51-29/9/51	HI
26/7/52-9/9/52	HI
27/11/52-9/12/52	LC(EO)
29/6/53-15/8/53	G
16/12/53-29/12/53	LC
18/5/54-24/5/54	LC(EO)
17/8/54-4/9/54	LI
9/8/55-3/9/55	HI
19/9/55-21/9/55	NC(EO)
5/4/56-25/5/56	LC(EO)
28/5/56-2/6/56	NC(EO)
7/6/56-21/6/56	NC(EO)
29/10/56-11/12/56	HI
3/1/57-5/1/57	NC(EO)
16/1/57-17/1/57	NC(EO)
23/9/57-11/10/57	LC(EO)
9/12/57-30/1/58	G
16/2/59-7/3/59	HI
28/1/60-20/2/60	HI
18/4/60-6/5/60	LC(EO)
8/8/61-17/8/61	LC(EO)
13/2/62-17/3/62	HI
9/7/62	NC(TO)
26/7/62-6/8/62	NC(EO)
23/1/63-8/2/63	LC(EO)
9/8/63-12/10/63	G
4/11/63-21/12/63	LC(EO)
30/12/63-9/1/64	LC(EO)
2/7/64-9/7/64	NC(TO)
5/8/64-7/8/64	NC(TO)
31/8/64-12/9/64	NC(EO)
13/10/64-17/10/64	LC
4/11/64-14/11/64	NC
1/6/65-5/6/65	NC(EO)

Boilers

New	8951
6/5/39	9014 from 5084
10/1/42	8659 from 5149 (domed)
12/8/44	8657 from 5192
7/1/49	8994 from 5126

Tenders

New	9275
29/1/38	9244
20/9/44	9194 (riveted)
?	9713
6/9/54	9364 (riveted)
8/8/55	10808 (part-welded)
3/9/55	10525
8/8/64	9198 (riveted)

Mileage/(weekdays out of service)

1935	25,048 (9)
1936	67,704 (27)
1937	54,962 (63)
1938	55,816 (64)
1939	56,329 (74)
1940	61,617 (54)
1941	55,943 (61)
1942	61,396 (62)
1943	54,841 (42)
1944	42,205 (71)
1945	44,358 (102)
1946	52,211 (51)
1947	35,821 (102)
1948	37,954 (89)
1949	58,039 (65)
1950	53,880 (63)

Mileage at 12/36: 92,752
Mileage at 31/12/50: 821,124

Sheds

Carlisle	31/8/35
Perth	2/11/35
Corkerhill	10/6/61
Carstairs	13/6/65

Withdrawn w.e. 30/10/65

45171, pictured on 11 September 1954 at Balornock, had left St Rollox the previous week after a Light Intermediate overhaul emerging with a riveted tender and a domed boiler. It was allocated to Perth from November 1935 until transferred to Corkerhill in June 1961 and was withdrawn in October 1965. It has St Rollox trademark 10in cab numbers with the power classification positioned unusually below.

45172

Built as 5172 at Armstrong Whitworth 15/8/35
Renumbered 45172 w.e. 18/12/48

Improvements and modifications

26/2/38	Removal of vacuum pump
20/5/45	Steam sanding

Repairs

17/2/37-17/3/37	LS
15/2/38-26/2/38	LS
12/9/39-16/11/39	HG
8/1/41-31/1/41	HS
17/10/41-6/12/41	HG
2/10/42-21/10/42	LS
18/11/42-24/12/42	LO
28/12/42-15/2/43	HO
27/10/43-19/11/43	LS
17/10/44-4/11/44	HS
27/8/45-3/10/45	LS
29/7/46-13/9/46	HG
14/10/46-8/11/46	LO
20/11/46-14/12/46	LO
21/8/47-9/10/47	LS
20/2/48-21/2/48	NC
1/11/48-18/12/48	LS
21/12/48-24/12/48	NC(R)
18/10/49-19/11/49	HI
13/3/51-19/5/51	G
13/3/52-15/4/52	HI
5/1/53-7/2/53	HI
17/2/53-26/2/53	LC
22/10/53-6/11/53	LC
1/2/54-20/2/54	HI
17/3/54-10/4/54	HC(EO)
3/8/55-27/8/55	LI
26/6/56-3/8/56	HI
7/11/56-15/11/56	LC(EO)
3/6/57-11/6/57	LC(EO)
24/8/57-8/10/57	HI
17/2/58-5/3/58	LC(EO)
13/11/58-27/12/58	G
23/2/60-18/3/60	LI
7/12/60-16/12/60	LC(EO)
13/9/62-6/10/62	LI

Boilers

New	8952
16/11/39	8833 from 5016
6/12/41	8994 from 5134
15/2/43	8938 from 5085
13/9/46	8652 from 5179 (domed)
19/5/51	9022 from 45161
10/4/54	8950 from 45170
27/12/58	8917

Tenders

New	9276
11/9/46	9247
15/12/48	9277
28/10/49	9107 (riveted)
30/10/49	9277
19/11/49	9725
7/5/51	10579 (part-welded)
15/4/52	9209 (riveted)
7/2/53	9727
27/8/55	9283
3/8/56	9777
6/11/56	9269
15/11/56	9365 (riveted)
19/11/56	10673 (part-welded)

Mileage/(weekdays out of service)

1935	21,996 (6)
1936	69,880 (15)
1937	41,424 (57)
1938	62,891 (55)
1939	40,067 (119)
1940	65,863 (34)
1941	43,620 (95)
1942	53,092 (86)
1943	55,334 (78)
1944	49,853 (43)
1945	53,791 (78)
1946	37,704 (118)
1947	49,359 (66)
1948	40,126 (91)
1949	45,614 (68)
1950	56,926 (30)
1951	43,176 (76)
1952	49,796 (50)
1953	39,824 (82)
1954	42,308 (78)
1955	52,194 (59)
1956	44,503 (97)
1957	39,032 (115)
1958	36,231 (100)
1959	47,074
1960	39,188
1961	40,353
1962	29,185

Mileage at 12/36: 91,876
Mileage at 31/12/50: 807,843

Sheds

Carlisle	31/8/35
Perth	2/11/35
Polmadie	28/5/60
Carstairs	16/10/61

Withdrawn 18/6/64

45172 was domeless apart from 1946 to 1951 and had a part-welded tender from May 1951 until April 1952, which narrows down the date of this picture. Large cab numbers positioned to clear the tablet exchange apparatus. 45172 has no shedplate but was at Perth from 1935 until 1960. Photograph R.K. Blencowe.

Perth's 45172 double heading another Black 5 arrives at Ballinluig Junction, the junction for the on Aberfeldy branch, on the Perth to Inverness main line. The picture was taken during the period it was paired with a riveted tender between April 1952 and February 1953. Photograph www.rail-online.co.uk

45173

Built as 5173 at Armstrong Whitworth 15/8/35
Renumbered 45173 w.e. 18/9/48

Improvements and modifications

26/1/38	Removal of vacuum pump
20/5/45	Steam sanding
4/10/57	Modernisation
18/6/60	Fitting BR ATC equipment

Repairs

6/6/36-24/6/36	LS
17/2/37-19/3/37	LS
3/1/38-26/1/38	LS
4/6/38-14/6/38	LO
10/1/39-31/1/39	LS
25/12/39-12/2/40	HG
24/1/41-25/2/41	HS
8/7/41-19/8/41	HS
25/5/42-25/7/42	HS
30/9/43-23/10/43	HS
23/9/44-28/10/44	HS
13/9/45-20/10/45	LS
29/10/45-31/10/45	LO
10/12/46-18/1/47	HS
3/11/47-19/12/47	HG
18/8/48-17/9/48	LS
4/8/49-3/9/49	LI
31/12/49-14/1/50	LC
7/4/50-19/4/50	LC
11/10/50-17/11/50	LI
23/1/51-2/3/51	LC
24/10/51-17/11/51	LC
26/3/52-12/7/52	G
28/7/52-22/8/52	LC
2/11/53-28/11/53	LI
9/11/54-18/11/54	NC(EO)
21/1/55-12/2/55	LI
6/7/55-15/7/55	LC(EO)
1/8/55-6/8/55	NC(EO)
12/8/55-16/8/55	LC(EO)
14/3/56-14/4/56	HI
19/5/56-1/6/56	NC(EO)
21/6/56-23/6/56	NC(NO)
16/8/57-4/10/57	G
11/5/60-18/6/60	LI
5/7/60-8/7/60	NC(EO)
17/8/62-8/9/62	G
20/8/63-30/8/63	LC
26/9/63-10/10/63	LC
13/1/64-22/2/64	LC(EO)

Boilers

New	8953
12/2/40	8945 from 5165
25/2/41	8684 (domed)
28/10/44	8988 from 5164
19/12/47	9003 from 5098
12/7/52	9052 from 45120
10/9/57	8929 from 45119
8/9/62	9049

Tenders

New	9277
18/6/36	9260
2/9/42	9723
16/9/42	9260
17/9/48	9277
18/11/48	9273
3/7/52	9059 (riveted)
27/11/53	10585 (part-welded)
11/1/56	10605 (part-welded)
14/4/56	10618 (part-welded)
4/10/57	9636

Mileage/(weekdays out of service)

1935	27,526 (4)
1936	70,917 (39)
1937	45,839 (51)
1938	58,397 (70)
1939	53,834 (70)
1940	55,880 (76)
1941	49,224 (82)
1942	55,090 (72)
1943	57,451 (50)
1944	50,666 (79)
1945	63,858 (59)
1946	44,547 (89)
1947	40,159 (96)
1948	56,729 (54)
1949	50,091 (60)
1950	43,977 (94)
1951	38,418 (97)
1952	35,333 (159)
1953	42,570 (100)
1954	45,872 (51)
1955	36,600 (93)
1956	38,388 (96)
1957	42,998 (87)
1958	45,933 (88)
1959	33,226
1960	26,464
1961	40,391
1962	32,323

Mileage at 12/36: 98,443
Mileage at 31/12/50: 843,179

Sheds

Carlisle	31/8/35
Perth	2/11/35
Polmadie	10/1/53
Perth	5/9/53
Polmadie	5/10/53
Corkerhill	28/8/54
Carstairs	27/2/56

Withdrawn 23/7/64

45173 seen at Kingmoor was always domeless apart from 1941-44. The picture was taken between March 1956 when it was transferred to 64D Corkerhill and October 1957 when its part-welded tender was replaced by a welded example. It has Scottish Region style large cab numbers with the power classification 5MT above and a serif 1946 type smokebox plate. Photograph www.rail-online.co.uk

45174

Built as 5174 at Armstrong Whitworth 26/8/35
Renumbered 45174 w.e. 26/2/49

Improvements and modifications

27/5/39	Removal of vacuum pump
20/5/45	Steam sanding
?	Fitting BR ATC equipment

Repairs

30/12/36-22/1/37	LS
13/4/37-27/4/37	LS
22/3/38-4/4/38	LO
22/4/39-27/5/39	HG
27/4/40-21/5/40	HS
17/9/41-11/10/41	LS
11/7/42-19/9/42	HG
11/6/43-3/7/43	HS
28/2/44-11/3/44	LS
13/12/44-13/1/45	HS
24/10/45-24/11/45	LS
16/2/46-19/3/46	HO
21/10/46-3/12/46	LS
13/11/47-16/12/47	LS
30/12/47-7/1/48	NC(R)
15/1/49-26/2/49	G
11/1/50-16/2/50	HI
10/7/50-11/8/50	LC
1/5/51-8/6/51	LI
14/10/52-1/11/52	LC(EO)
9/12/52-14/2/53	G
9/3/53-21/3/53	LC(EO)
9/7/54	NC(EO)
6/9/54-24/9/54	HI
13/12/54-25/12/54	LC(EO)
12/4/55-20/4/55	NC(EO)
8/3/56-31/3/56	HI
19/10/56-20/10/56	NC(EO)
1/2/57-16/2/57	LC(EO)
14/11/57-28/12/57	G
29/8/58-11/9/58	LC
8/12/58-9/1/59	LI
4/8/59	NC
10/12/59-15/1/60	HI
28/4/61-27/5/61	LI

Boilers

New	8954
27/5/39	8949 from 5169
19/9/42	8648 from 5037 (domed)
19/3/46	8950 from 5157
26/2/49	8659 from 5090 (domed)
14/2/53	8658 from 45086 (domed)
28/12/57	9053 from 45098

Tenders

New	9278
3/2/41	9255
17/2/50	9181 (riveted)
14/2/53	9672
24/9/54	9538
31/3/56	10812 (part-welded)

Mileage/(weekdays out of service)

1935	23,703 (4)
1936	67,644 (33)
1937	54,574 (76)
1938	64,598 (43)
1939	52,067 (73)
1940	64,795 (42)
1941	57,873 (62)
1942	41,102 (114)
1943	65,228 (42)
1944	49,966 (64)
1945	57,143 (57)
1946	39,133 (109)
1947	48,068 (59)
1948	44,386 (59)
1949	55,888 (68)
1950	46,033 (87)
1951	43,519 (85)
1952	35,238 (134)
1953	42,155 (110)
1954	30,734 (125)
1955	51,090 (39)
1956	40,210 (84)
1957	31,385 (105)
1958	45,089 (83)
1959	32,474
1960	43,369
1961	28,672
1962	26,655

Mileage at 12/36: 91,347
Mileage at 31/12/50: 835,201

Sheds

Crewe	31/8/35
Perth	5/10/35
Corkerhill	1/4/50
Carstairs	9/4/56

Withdrawn 13/5/63

45174 was near the end when photographed at Carstairs, where it had been shedded since April 1956 until withdrawn in May 1963. It had a domeless boiler from December 1957 and a part-welded tender from March 1956. The date of the AWS fitting was not recorded on the surviving History Card but is likely to have been at the Heavy Intermediate repair completed in January 1960.

45175

Built as 5175 at Armstrong Whitworth 26/8/35
Renumbered 45175 w.e. 18/6/49

Improvements and modifications

14/4/37	Removal of vacuum pump
28/9/39	Steam sanding
23/9/60	Fitting BR ATC equipment

Repairs

1/2/37-20/2/37	LS
8/4/37-14/4/37	LO
25/1/38-14/2/38	LS
3/11/38-16/11/38	LO
14/8/39-28/9/39	HG
6/3/40-22/3/40	HS
23/5/40-4/6/40	LS
16/5/41-3/7/41	HG
6/7/42-25/8/42	LS
17/6/43-14/7/43	LS
7/4/44-11/5/44	HS
3/5/45-9/6/45	HG
7/6/46-27/6/46	HS
8/7/47-30/8/47	LS
31/12/47-26/1/48	LO
25/4/49-11/6/49	G
3/1/50-20/1/50	LC
1/8/50-7/9/50	LI
9/7/51-17/8/51	HI
8/12/52-7/2/53	G
4/5/53-16/5/53	LC
28/7/53-8/8/53	LC
17/8/53-29/8/53	LC
8/10/53-27/10/53	LC
22/12/53-25/12/53	LC
22/2/54-3/4/54	HI
13/8/54-31/8/54	LC(EO)
22/9/54-9/10/54	LC
18/10/54-29/10/54	LC(EO)
10/1/55-19/1/55	LC(EO)
6/8/55-27/8/55	LI
3/10/55-8/10/55	LC
14/11/55-22/11/55	NC(EO)
28/5/56-14/6/56	NC(EO)
19/10/56-16/11/56	HI
3/4/57-10/4/57	NC(EO)
26/2/58-27/3/58	G
25/5/59-12/6/59	HI
7/7/59-9/7/59	LC(EO)
29/8/60-23/9/60	LI
16/1/61-9/2/61	LC(EO)
18/5/62-9/6/62	LI
13/6/62-29/6/62	LC
26/2/63-27/2/63	NC

Boilers

New	8955
28/9/39	8933 from 5153
3/7/41	9048 from 5160
9/6/45	9021 from 5065
11/6/49	8657 from 5171 (domed)
7/2/53	8944 from 45126
29/3/58	9052 from 45173

Tenders

New	9279
17/5/44	9712
19/7/47	10586 (part-welded)
2/1/50	10503
23/1/50	9216 (riveted)
31/1/53	10783 (riveted)
20/1/55	9835
8/10/55	10718 (part-welded)
11/6/56	10695
16/11/56	10511
27/3/58	9283

Mileage/(weekdays out of service)

1935	26,407 (3)
1936	70,579 (31)
1937	57,534 (63)
1938	55,664 (65)
1939	54,821 (73)
1940	61,660 (44)
1941	46,734 (116)
1942	56,299 (75)
1943	51,165 (59)
1944	53,208 (82)
1945	50,607 (80)
1946	58,919 (66)
1947	40,541 (80)
1948	46,218 (67)
1949	46,001 (96)
1950	45,282 (76)
1951	44,566 (69)
1952	42,227 (53)
1953	46,053 (109)
1954	38,495 (110)
1955	26,955 (98)
1956	34,385 (89)
1957	46,747 (75)
1958	38,320 (87)
1959	47,919
1960	40,662
1961	33,036
1962	25,545

Mileage at 12/36: 96,986
Mileage at 31/12/50: 821,639

Sheds

Crewe	31/8/35
Perth	16/11/35
Motherwell	10/10/42
Perth	31/10/42
Corkerhill	10/7/54
Carstairs	15/2/56

Withdrawn 26/7/63

45175 after fitting with AWS in September 1960. It always had a domeless boiler except between 1949 and 1953, and was allocated to Carstairs from February 1956 until withdrawn in July 1963.

45176

Built as 5176 at Armstrong Whitworth 26/8/35
Renumbered 45176 w.e. 4/6/49

Improvements and modifications

19/2/38	Removal of vacuum pump
20/5/45	Steam sanding
?	Fitting BR ATC equipment

Repairs

20/1/37-17/2/37	LS
12/4/37-20/4/37	LO
5/2/38-19/2/38	LS
8/3/39-11/4/39	HG
17/2/40-13/3/40	LS
9/1/41-1/2/41	HG
3/9/41-2/10/41	LS
31/10/42-1/12/42	HS
28/4/44-20/5/44	HG
15/11/44-9/12/44	HO
9/1/45-26/1/45	LO
11/9/45-17/10/45	LS
30/3/46-4/5/46	LO
8/4/47-9/5/47	HG
16/4/49-1/6/49	HI
12/9/49-12/10/49	LC
21/6/50-6/9/50	LC
19/2/52-22/3/52	G
10/12/53-20/1/54	HI
5/7/54-16/7/54	HC
16/6/55-9/7/55	LI
9/1/56-28/1/56	LC(EO)
10/8/56-22/9/56	G
13/3/58-3/4/58	HI
31/12/58-8/1/59	LC(TO)
7/5/59-21/5/59	LC(EO)
15/12/59-9/1/60	LC(EO)
10/10/60-11/11/60	G
12/5/62-18/5/62	LC(EO)
18/9/62-11/10/62	LC(EO)
4/6/63-5/7/63	LI
22/8/63-3/10/63	LC(EO)
19/11/63-14/12/63	LC(EO)
16/4/65-24/4/65	LC(EO)
30/7/65-7/8/65	NC(EO)
18/2/66-15/3/66	NC(EO)

Boilers

New	8956
11/4/39	8931 from 5151
1/2/41	8944 from 5016 (domed)
9/5/47	8978 from 5216

Tenders

New	9280
14/11/38	9177 (riveted)
10/4/47	9727
14/7/50	9724
?	10814 (part-welded)
28/1/56	9277
22/9/56	10713 (part-welded)
3/4/58	10511
8/1/59	9005 (riveted)
?	9665
12/3/66	9594

Mileage/(weekdays out of service)

1935	23,797 (4)
1936	75,453 (20)
1937	43,054 (58)
1938	62,830 (48)
1939	55,535 (55)
1940	62,327 (47)
1941	49,587 (103)
1942	63,401 (55)
1943	45,163 (39)
1944	39,167 (78)
1945	36,326 (61)
1946	45,970 (67)
1947	49,143 (65)
1948	41,824 (42)
1949	35,247 (103)
1950	33,145 (103)

Mileage at 12/36: 99,250
Mileage at 31/12/50: 781,969

Sheds

Crewe	31/8/35
Perth	5/10/35
Motherwell	10/10/42
Perth	31/10/42
St Rollox	13/2/43
Motherwell	6/11/48

Withdrawn 17/8/66

45176 was always a Scottish loco, allocated to Motherwell from 1948 until withdrawn in August 1966. The boiler is one of the early rebuilt ones with no domed covers, hence the low atomiser with the small cover. It has several St Rollox trademarks including the 'double domed' effect, close spaced large cab numbers plus painted background to the smokebox numberplate and shedplate. The picture was taken in the late 1950s before 45176 received AWS equipment.

45177

Built as 5177 at Armstrong Whitworth 6/9/35
Renumbered 45177 w.e. 15/5/48

Improvements and modifications

2/3/38	Removal of vacuum pump
20/5/45	Steam sanding
17/1/53	Sloping throatplate boiler
?	Fitting BR ATC equipment

Repairs

6/4/37-28/4/37	LS
19/2/38-2/3/38	LS
13/9/39-9/11/39	HG
25/3/40-15/4/40	HS
19/11/40-7/12/40	LS
5/5/41-31/5/41	HG
31/7/41-5/8/41	LO
17/2/42-31/3/42	LS
1/12/42-14/1/43	HS
26/8/43-25/9/43	LS
23/1/45-7/3/45	HG
3/1/46-9/2/46	LS
18/1/47-13/3/47	LS
7/10/47-28/10/47	LO
13/4/48-15/5/48	HG
11/2/50-15/3/50	LI
12/5/50-24/5/50	LC
9/10/50-13/10/50	NC
12/11/52-17/1/53	G
8/5/53-20/5/53	LC(EO)
1/2/54-13/2/54	HI
16/2/54-18/2/54	NC(EO)
2/2/55-8/2/55	LC(EO)
28/9/55-10/11/55	HI
16/2/57-16/3/57	G
19/4/58-10/5/58	LI
20/6/58	LC(EO)
9/2/59-28/2/59	HI
28/8/59-11/9/59	NC(EO)
21/9/59-3/10/59	LC(EO)
16/3/60-19/3/60	NC(EO)
12/4/60-14/5/60	HI
28/2/61-18/3/61	NC(EO)
14/10/61-25/11/61	G
1/5/64-20/6/64	LI

Boilers

New	8957
9/11/39	8940 from 5160
31/5/41	9024 from 5081
15/5/48	8975 from 5018
17/1/53	12915 (sloping throatplate)

Tenders

New	9281
21/9/44	9269
7/7/47	9659
15/3/50	10527
?	9005 (riveted)
12/2/54	9268
16/3/57	9229
10/5/58	10670 (part-welded)
6/6/66	9679

Mileage/(weekdays out of service)

1935	20,077 (5)
1936	70,470 (25)
1937	60,188 (61)
1938	61,710 (46)
1939	47,243 (103)
1940	65,765 (47)
1941	54,338 (74)
1942	43,012 (75)
1943	50,631 (60)
1944	46,548 (27)
1945	48,931 (60)
1946	44,563 (57)
1947	31,870 (112)
1948	31,867 (98)
1949	41,586 (49)
1950	33,412 (98)

Mileage at 12/36: 90,547
Mileage at 31/12/50: 752,211

Sheds

Crewe	7/9/35
Carlisle N	5/10/35
Perth	28/10/35
Carlisle	10/10/42
Perth	31/10/42
St Rollox	13/2/43
Grangemouth	1/10/60
Ayr	18/10/65

Withdrawn 14/7/66

45177 at Balornock soon after it was renumbered in May 1948, had no tender markings, LMS pattern large high cab numbers and smokebox numberplate. 45177 has its final domeless boiler which was taken off in 1953 when it was converted to sloping throatplate configuration. It allocated to St. Rollox until October 1960. Photograph www.rail-online.co.uk

45178

Built as 5178 at Armstrong Whitworth 5/9/35
Renumbered 45178 w.e. 4/12/48

Improvements and modifications

19/5/38	Removal of vacuum pump
17/2/44	BTH speed indicator
17/2/44	Steam sanding
?	Fitting BR ATC equipment

Repairs

7/1/36-20/1/36	LS
30/3/36-16/4/36	LS
19/6/37-14/7/37	LS
13/1/38-17/2/38	LO
10/5/38-19/5/38	LS
6/2/39-25/2/39	LO
9/6/39-8/8/39	HG
23/1/41-15/2/41	LS
17/2/42-13/3/42	LS
12/11/42-19/12/42	HS
8/1/44-17/2/44	HG
31/1/45-10/3/45	LS
17/7/45-21/9/45	LO
20/6/46-8/8/46	LS
2/6/47-25/6/47	LO
15/8/47-11/10/47	HS
23/10/47-7/11/47	LO
18/10/48-1/12/48	LS
27/4/49-2/5/49	NC
4/8/49-10/9/49	HI
19/10/49-22/10/49	NC(R)
12/9/52-22/11/52	G
16/12/52-26/12/52	LC(EO)
29/1/53-14/2/53	LC
21/2/53-6/3/53	LC
15/4/53-24/4/53	LC(EO)
16/5/53-22/5/53	LC(EO)
5/1/54-7/1/54	NC(EO)
10/6/54-26/6/54	LI
1/8/55-12/10/55	HI
5/11/56-1/12/56	G
22/1/57-2/2/57	LC(EO)
15/3/58-11/4/58	LI
23/4/59-12/6/59	LI
29/6/59-8/7/59	NC(EO)
7/6/60-25/6/60	LC(EO)
18/11/60-22/12/60	G
1/3/62	NC(TO)
6/3/63-17/4/63	HC
23/5/63-15/6/63	LC(EO)
5/7/63-10/7/63	LC(EO)
12/8/63-15/8/63	LC(EO)

Boilers

New	8958
8/8/39	8855 from 5018
17/2/44	9001 from 5044
1/11/47	8933 from 5192

Tenders

New	9282
?	9122 (riveted)
26/6/54	10671 (part-welded)
1/12/56	9663
11/4/58	10586 (part-welded)
1/3/62	10445
17/4/63	9261
11/11/64	9835

Mileage/(weekdays out of service)

1935	24,025 (5)
1936	62,997 (57)
1937	58,964 (43)
1938	54,448 (80)
1939	47,007 (111)
1940	48,220 (53)
1941	48,703 (49)
1942	43,465 (77)
1943	51,141 (23)
1944	56,559 (49)
1945	39,506 (108)
1946	44,069 (64)
1947	29,407 (142)
1948	41,698 (68)
1949	35,229 (108)
1950	45,487 (48)

Mileage at 12/36: 87,022
Mileage at 31/12/50: 730,925

Sheds

Crewe	7/9/35
Carlisle	16/11/35
Corkerhill	15/4/39
St Rollox	25/11/39
Grangemouth	1/10/60
Motherwell	29/12/62

Withdrawn 30/1/65

St. Rollox allocated 45178 on 22 November 1952 at its home shed with a domeless boiler and riveted tender. It had just completed a General overhaul and has the usual Scottish 10in cab numbers.

45179

Built as 5179 at Armstrong Whitworth 4/9/35
Renumbered 45179 w.e. 19/6/48

Improvements and modifications

3/3/38	Removal of vacuum pump
28/11/42	Steam sanding
26/5/61	Fitting BR ATC equipment

Repairs

1/2/37-26/2/37	LS
9/2/38-3/3/38	LS
31/12/38-12/1/39	LO
22/4/39-17/5/39	HG
9/11/39-2/12/39	HS
20/9/40-3/10/40	LS
28/12/40-18/1/41	LO
7/4/41-19/4/41	LO
7/8/41-9/9/41	LS
24/8/42-30/9/42	HG
15/11/43-8/12/43	LS
14/2/44-13/4/44	HO
27/6/45-21/7/45	LS
11/6/46-27/6/46	HG
24/6/47-14/8/47	LS
27/5/48-18/6/48	LO
29/12/48-12/2/49	HI
2/5/49-19/5/49	LC
25/7/49-5/8/49	LC
4/2/50-18/3/50	G
19/8/50-25/9/50	LC
21/7/51-24/8/51	LI
25/10/52-22/11/52	HI
24/7/53-24/8/53	LC
17/10/53-19/11/53	HC(EO)
11/5/54-12/6/54	HI
26/1/55-11/2/55	LC(EO)
11/8/55-23/9/55	HI
10/5/56-25/5/56	NC(EO)
1/12/56-28/12/56	LI
24/1/57	NC(EO)
31/1/57-13/2/57	LC(EO)
7/6/57	NC(TO)
18/7/57-29/7/57	NC(EO)
3/10/57-23/10/57	LC(EO)
22/1/58-29/1/58	NC(EO)
8/3/58-3/5/58	G
10/11/58-15/12/58	HC(EO)
5/9/59-26/9/59	LI
30/9/59-3/10/59	NC(EO)
12/10/60-22/10/60	LC(EO)
24/4/61-26/5/61	HI
29/9/62-23/10/62	LC

Boilers

New	8959
17/5/39	8825 from 5008
30/9/42	8652 from 5124 (domed)
27/6/46	8648 from 5174 (domed)
18/3/50	8991 from 5008
19/11/53	8994 from 45171
3/5/58	8984 from 45100

Tenders

New	9283
7/8/41	9727
18/8/41	9283
11/2/44	9259
21/7/45	9314
25/6/47	9659
7/7/47	9269
9/8/47	9283
11/2/49	9067 (riveted)
5/9/50	9242
1/10/50	9067 (riveted)
23/7/53	10813 (part-welded)
18/11/53	9317
3/5/58	9275

Mileage/(weekdays out of service)

1935	21,619 (2)
1936	69,196 (29)
1937	53,178 (68)
1938	59,990 (56)
1939	33,732 (105)
1940	55,397 (39)
1941	54,249 (70)
1942	45,287 (65)
1943	42,110 (50)
1944	38,850 (86)
1945	41,819 (59)
1946	42,607 (56)
1947	43,153 (77)
1948	38,726 (48)
1949	33,578 (117)
1950	41,483 (89)
1951	43,124 (61)
1952	43,130 (62)
1953	29,421 (105)
1954	46,984 (68)
1955	40,003 (103)
1956	39,964 (68)
1957	40,329 (76)
1958	32,931 (120)
1959	45,088
1960	37,989
1961	36,677
1962	20,746

Mileage at 12/36: 90,815
Mileage at 31/12/50: 714,974

Sheds

Crewe	7/9/35
Carlisle North	5/10/35
Corkerhill	15/4/39
St Rollox	28/10/39
Motherwell	6/11/48
Inverness	10/12/49
Perth	1/8/60
Hamilton	25/9/61
Motherwell	5/11/62

Withdrawn 13/5/63

5179 recently delivered from Armstrong Whitworth in September 1935 with motion and wheels still burnished. It was always a Northern Division engine, lasting until May 1963.

45180

Built as 5180 at Armstrong Whitworth 10/9/35
Renumbered 45180 w.e. 16/4/49

Improvements and modifications

20/2/38	BTH speed indicator
18/5/38	Removal of vacuum pump
19/5/45	Steam sanding
16/9/59	Fitting BR ATC equipment

Repairs

2/4/36-20/4/36	LO
3/8/36-18/8/36	LO
6/9/37-24/9/37	LO
25/2/38-18/5/38	HG
19/1/39-21/2/39	HG
24/6/40-8/7/40	LS
30/5/41-12/7/41	HG
29/4/42-20/5/42	LO
18/10/42-14/11/42	LS
12/12/43-20/1/44	LS
28/4/45-19/5/45	HG
17/12/46-18/1/47	LS
6/10/47-2/12/47	HS
25/3/49-13/4/49	HG
8/9/50-29/9/50	LI
23/7/52-30/8/52	HI
6/1/54-5/2/54	G
4/11/55-23/11/55	HI
30/8/56-28/9/56	LC(EO)
26/1/58-15/2/58	LI
11/8/59-16/9/59	HG
26/8/61-30/9/61	LI
30/9/61-6/10/61	NC
31/10/62-28/11/62	LI

Boilers

New	8960
28/4/38	8964 from 5184
21/2/39	8985 from 5205
12/7/41	8662 from 5079 (domed)
19/5/45	8993 from 5218
23/4/49	9040 from 5103
5/2/54	8834 from 45073
16/9/59	8972 from 45074

Tenders

New	9284

Mileage/(weekdays out of service)

1935	26,090 (20)
1936	59,174 (99)
1937	39,025 (136)
1938	44,630 (136)
1939	52,385 (74)
1940	34,858 (58)
1941	38,691 (67)
1942	30,706 (78)
1943	39,964 (44)
1944	45,215 (63)
1945	41,164 (49)
1946	40,949 (58)
1947	28,138 (117)
1948	41,064 (46)
1949	43,684 (63)
1950	33,639 (58)
1951	48,194 (41)
1952	22,730 (89)
1953	33,956 (57)
1954	45,941 (50)
1955	38,755 (60)
1956	37,861 (47)
1957	39,954 (38)
1958	40,718 (49)
1959	31,212
1960	37,305

Mileage at 12/36: 85,264
Mileage at 31/12/50: 639,376

Sheds

Crewe	14/9/35
Derby	5/10/35
Saltley	7/11/36
Derby	11/9/37
Shrewsbury	16/10/43
Crewe South	19/5/45
Shrewsbury	14/7/45
St Margarets	7/10/51
Chester	19/9/53
Holyhead	12/6/54
Carlisle Upperby	8/1/55
Crewe South	14/1/56
Holyhead	14/6/58
Llandudno Jct	4/10/58
Monument Lane	21/5/60
Bescot	25/6/60
Saltley	3/4/65
Crewe South	19/6/65

Withdrawn w.e. 25/9/65

45180 at Willesden while shedded at 12A Carlisle Upperby between January 1955 and January 1956. It kept the same welded tender throughout and was always domeless apart from one boiler during the war. Photograph www.rail-online.co.uk

45181

Built as 5181 at Armstrong Whitworth 10/9/35
Renumbered 45181 w.e. 22/5/48

Improvements and modifications

31/5/38	Removal of vacuum pump
?	Steam sanding
23/1/59	Fitting BR ATC equipment

Repairs

1/6/36-15/7/36	LS
1/7/37-22/7/37	LO
1/4/38-31/5/38	HG
13/10/39-3/11/39	LS
5/10/40-9/11/40	LS
8/1/42-27/1/42	LS
11/5/43-27/5/43	HG
10/5/44-24/5/44	LO
7/5/46-28/5/46	LS
22/4/48-20/5/48	HG
4/2/50-25/2/50	HI
30/10/50-24/11/50	LC
10/7/51-11/8/51	HG
31/1/53-26/2/53	HI
14/8/53-4/9/53	LC(EO)
25/11/54-23/12/54	HG
18/6/55-23/7/55	LC
4/8/56-30/8/56	HI
18/12/57-11/1/58	LI
20/12/58-23/1/59	LI
29/11/59-22/1/60	HC(EO)
19/7/60-19/8/60	LC(EO)
23/8/61-29/9/61	HG

Boilers

New	8961
16/5/38	8929 from 5149
27/5/43	9041 from 5186
20/5/48	9036 from 5105
11/8/51	8979 from 45214
23/12/54	8990 from 45186
29/9/61	8674 from 45203 (domed)

Tenders

New	9285
18/4/64	9487

Mileage/(weekdays out of service)

1935	26,445 (13)
1936	64,197 (91)
1937	33,801 (51)
1938	31,860 (69)
1939	35,752 (46)
1940	30,226 (60)
1941	32,990 (28)
1942	33,907 (42)
1943	37,671 (46)
1944	36,500 (36)
1945	34,113 (33)
1946	34,791 (54)
1947	33,396 (54)
1948	31,079 (53)
1949	36,250 (51)
1950	36,458 (55)
1951	41,246 (45)
1952	46,678 (25)
1953	38,479 (70)
1954	37,629 (63)
1955	44,231 (51)
1956	43,978 (43)
1957	38,699 (49)
1958	40,682 (43)
1959	39,580
1960	40,923

Mileage at 12/36: 90,642
Mileage at 31/12/50: 569,436

Sheds

Crewe	14/9/35
Kentish Town	12/10/35
Crewe North	20/12/36
Crewe South	26/8/44
Edge Hill	4/12/48
Rugby	17/2/51
Edge Hill	24/3/51
Holyhead	23/6/62
Speke Junction	13/10/62
Springs Branch	22/6/63
Carnforth	13/7/63
Speke Junction	14/9/63

Withdrawn w.e. 15/1/66

45181 has both an 8C shedplate and painted Speke Junction on its bufferbeam; it was allocated there from October 1962 until withdrawn in January 1966, apart from a few weeks at Springs Branch and Carnforth in mid-1963. It had carried a domed boiler since its final boiler change in 1961 and received AWS in January 1959 and always had a welded tender.

45182

Built as 5182 at Armstrong Whitworth 11/9/35
Renumbered 45182 w.e. 23/10/48

Improvements and modifications

4/4/38	Removal of vacuum pump
?	Steam sanding
11/1/56	Modernisation
28/11/59	Fitting BR ATC equipment

Repairs

15/4/36-8/5/36	**LO**
5/11/36-20/11/36	**LS**
29/9/37-28/10/37	**HS**
24/2/38-4/4/38	**HG**
27/9/38-25/10/38	**LO**
31/1/39-6/3/39	**HS**
17/8/39-2/9/39	**LO**
3/8/40-4/9/40	**HS**
9/12/40-6/1/41	**LO**
7/1/42-20/2/42	**HG**
19/6/43-3/7/43	**LS**
23/7/45-25/8/45	**LS**
26/4/46-23/5/46	**LO**
21/2/47-15/3/47	**HG**
2/10/48-21/10/48	**LS**
25/7/50-15/8/50	**LI**
1/3/51-20/3/51	**LC**
23/6/52-29/8/52	**HG**
14/6/54-5/8/54	**HI**
12/12/55-11/1/56	**HG**
13/2/58-7/3/58	**HI**
21/10/59-12/12/59	**HG**
17/4/61-27/5/61	**HI**

Boilers

New	8962
21/2/38	8968 from 5188
6/3/39	9006 from 5076
20/2/42	9055 from 5208
15/3/47	8939 from 5116
29/8/52	8649 from 45101 (domed)
11/1/56	8643 from 45003 (domed)
12/12/59	8663 from 45063 (domed)

Tenders

New	9286
12/11/55	9301
13/12/60	10494

Mileage/(weekdays out of service)

1935	19,997 (13)
1936	46,566 (123)
1937	48,201 (127)
1938	58,757 (87)
1939	45,809 (94)
1940	31,611 (100)
1941	34,395 (52)
1942	35,194 (64)
1943	37,723 (50)
1944	34,342 (38)
1945	35,194 (42)
1946	30,691 (91)
1947	39,601 (47)
1948	36,552 (54)
1949	39,921 (28)
1950	34,188 (39)
1951	40,507 (37)
1952	34,862 (84)
1953	40,314 (58)
1954	29,170 (79)
1955	27,978 (64)
1956	42,976 (33)
1957	34,128 (32)
1958	38,545 (47)
1959	30,977
1960	46,008

Mileage at 12/36: 66,563
Mileage at 31/12/50: 608,742

Sheds

Crewe	14/9/35
Derby	5/10/35
Warrington	19/9/42 (loan)
Warrington	17/10/42
Patricroft	26/12/42
Carlisle Upperby	22/9/56
Patricroft	3/11/56
Trafford Park	14/11/64
Carlisle Canal	16/1/65

Withdrawn w.e. 12/3/66

5182 still with its ex-works finish at Bedford on 29 September 1935. It was allocated to 17A Derby in the week ended 7/10/35 and remained there until 1942. Photograph R.K. Blencowe.

45183

Built as 5183 at Armstrong Whitworth 17/9/35
Renumbered 45183 w.e. 1/7/50

Improvements and modifications

12/10/38	Removal of vacuum pump
23/1/43	Steam sanding
3/11/56	Modernisation
2/7/59	Fitting BR ATC equipment

Repairs

15/6/36-5/7/36	LO
5/1/37-18/1/37	LS
6/11/37-22/11/37	LO
18/8/38-12/10/38	HG
29/12/39-10/1/40	LS
21/8/41-6/9/41	LS
19/12/42-23/1/43	HG
9/2/43-6/3/43	LO
29/11/44-14/12/44	LS
9/8/46-7/9/46	LS
6/11/47-22/12/47	HG
13/6/49-22/7/49	HI
3/6/50-30/6/50	LC
1/3/51-29/3/51	HI
19/6/51-17/7/51	LC
5/12/51-20/12/51	LC
10/4/52-18/7/52	G
13/1/53-4/3/53	LC
7/9/53-9/10/53	HI
15/1/55-25/2/55	HI
10/10/56-3/11/56	G
18/6/58-12/7/58	HI
29/1/59-4/2/59	NC(EO)
29/6/59-2/7/59	NC(EO)
1/3/61-6/5/61	G
8/5/61-19/5/61	LC(EO)
15/3/63-20/3/63	LC
26/3/63-28/3/63	NC
29/6/64-6/8/64	LI
14/8/64	NC

Boilers

New	8963
29/10/38	9044 from 5114
23/1/43	8673 from 5030 (domed)
27/12/47	8668 from 5217 (domed)
18/7/52	8978 from 45176
3/11/56	9049
6/5/61	9005

Tenders

New	9287
6/10/53	9831
3/11/56	9190 (riveted)
12/5/61	9176 (riveted)
19/5/61	10719 (part-welded)

Mileage/(weekdays out of service)

1935	13,917 (28)
1936	57,280 (56)
1937	39,077 (62)
1938	37,401 (79)
1939	51,645 (33)
1940	38,003 (43)
1941	32,446 (51)
1942	32,960 (23)
1943	37,483 (60)
1944	34,270 (41)
1945	33,194 (27)
1946	36,314 (62)
1947	25,757 (89)
1948	40,796 (47)
1949	36,226 (72)
1950	33,002 (75)
1951	41,747 (74)
1952	48,088 (106)
1953	36,023 (81)
1954	49,417 (17)
1955	38,720 (67)
1956	33,168 (62)
1957	51,798 (33)
1958	38,922 (55)
1959	37,849
1960	42,743
1961	22,287
1962	23,095

Mileage at 12/36: 71,197
Mileage at 31/12/50: 579,771

Sheds

Crewe	21/9/35
Saltley	12/10/35
Aston	29/11/36
Bushbury	27/2/37
Llandudno Jct	2/7/38
Patricroft	9/7/38
Carnforth	24/9/38
Patricroft	15/7/39
Crewe South	16/12/44
Shrewsbury	17/7/48
Dalry Road	23/9/51

Withdrawn 30/10/64

45183 on 19 October 1964 at Dalry Road, where it was allocated from November 1951 until withdrawn in October 1964. It has a domeless boiler but the top feed casing from a domed boiler. 45183 ran with a part welded tender from May 1961 and had been fitted with AWS in July 1959. Other details are the lowered top lamp bracket and the polished rim on the numberplate. Photograph D.P. Rowland.

45184

Built as 5184 at Armstrong Whitworth 17/9/35
Renumbered 45184 w.e. 24/7/48

Improvements and modifications

19/4/38	Removal of vacuum pump
?	Steam sanding
12/6/59	Fitting BR ATC equipment

Repairs

18/1/37-4/2/37	LS
27/11/37-13/12/37	HS
23/2/38-19/4/38	HO
10/8/38-9/9/38	LO
30/10/39-14/11/39	LS
26/5/41-11/6/41	HG
14/10/41-24/10/41	LO
3/10/42-27/10/42	LS
3/3/43-20/3/43	LO
17/8/43-3/9/43	LO
14/3/44-29/3/44	HS
26/10/45-30/11/45	HG
5/6/47-5/7/47	LS
15/6/48-22/7/48	LS
2/9/48-12/10/48	LO
13/4/49-29/4/49	LC
13/6/50-25/7/50	HG
13/8/51-1/9/51	HI
3/3/53-26/3/53	HG
12/5/54-31/5/54	LI
28/11/55-28/12/55	LI
15/10/57-26/11/57	HG
21/11/58-4/12/58	LC(EO)
18/5/59-12/6/59	HI
21/1/61-17/2/61	HI
7/8/62-1/9/62	LI
18/6/64-18/7/64	HI

Boilers

New	8964
6/4/38	8921 from 5141
11/6/41	8984 from 5221
30/11/45	8960 from 5195
25/7/50	8971 from 5080
26/3/53	8911 from 45019
26/11/57	8919 from 45000

Tenders

New	9288
30/11/45	9543
17/4/57	9535

Mileage/(weekdays out of service)

1935	22,419 (9)
1936	41,503 (119)
1937	43,552 (59)
1938	38,197 (93)
1939	45,653 (52)
1940	33,403 (45)
1941	37,107 (44)
1942	39,318 (47)
1943	33,461 (54)
1944	36,254 (58)
1945	34,374 (80)
1946	38,444 (42)
1947	30,721 (78)
1948	33,804 (103)
1949	36,068 (53)
1950	40,616 (56)
1951	40,429 (47)
1952	47,018 (36)
1953	43,455 (65)
1954	42,934 (53)
1955	40,522 (58)
1956	52,071 (31)
1957	36,856 (70)
1958	43,628 (35)
1959	40,066
1960	30,515

Mileage at 12/36: 63,922
Mileage at 31/12/50: 584,894

Sheds

Crewe	21/9/35
Leeds	5/10/35
Derby	18/1/36
Willesden	19/12/36 (loan)
Longsight	2/1/37
Patricroft	3/7/37
Preston	25/9/37
Patricroft	2/7/38
Preston	24/9/38
Springs Branch	8/2/41
Longsight	29/3/41
Carlisle W	5/6/43
Dalry Road	21/8/48 (loan)
Carlisle Upperby	6/11/48
Holyhead	25/6/55
Carlisle Upperby	20/8/55
Patricroft	14/6/58
Bletchley	20/9/58
Rugby	7/11/59
Speke Junction	11/2/61
Holyhead	10/6/61
Northampton	23/9/61
Rugby	25/11/61
Chester	22/6/63

Withdrawn w.e. 18/9/65

45184 at Polmadie on 31 July 1948, a week after it gained its BR number during a Light Scheduled overhaul, although it still has LMS on the tender. It was one of those which was always domeless and had been shedded at Upperby since June 1943, although it would go on a three month loan to Dalry Road the following month. Photograph J.L. Stevenson.

45185

Built as 5185 at Armstrong Whitworth 18/9/35
Renumbered 45185 w.e. 21/8/48

Improvements and modifications

2/12/38	Steam sanding
2/12/38	Removal of vacuum pump
13/9/57	Modification
12/3/59	Fitting BR ATC equipment

Repairs

1/4/36-7/5/36	LO
3/12/36-17/12/36	LS
28/5/37-7/6/37	LO
17/10/38-2/12/38	HG
29/4/40-11/5/40	LS
23/2/42-11/3/42	LS
6/6/42-17/7/42	LO
14/8/43-28/8/43	HG
29/1/45-8/3/45	LS
12/2/47-19/3/47	LS
21/7/48-21/8/48	HG
12/5/50-6/6/50	LI
5/6/51-27/6/51	LI
30/10/51-24/11/51	HC EO
26/8/53-26/9/53	HG
20/8/55-10/9/55	HI
28/2/56-28/3/56	LC(EO)
25/10/56-24/11/56	HC
25/7/57-13/9/57	HG
24/3/58-17/4/58	NC(EO)
19/8/58-30/9/58	LC(EO)
3/3/59-12/3/59	NC(EO)
16/3/60-29/4/60	HI
20/7/60-27/8/60	LC(EO)
7/2/61-10/3/61	LC(EO)
19/6/61-29/7/61	LC(EO)

Boilers

New	8965
2/12/38	8976 from 5196
28/8/43	8996 from 5071
21/8/48	8666 from 5109 (domed)
26/9/53	8660 from 45042 (domed)
13/9/57	9054 from 45005

Tenders

New	9289
28/3/56	9254

Mileage/(weekdays out of service)

1935	21,089 (11)
1936	51,690 (119)
1937	39,620 (51)
1938	34,373 (87)
1939	45,986 (35)
1940	29,813 (53)
1941	37,418 (59)
1942	28,461 (82)
1943	32,138 (43)
1944	22,745 (47)
1945	31,955 (66)
1946	38,080 (39)
1947	42,184 (56)
1948	31,436 (69)
1949	36,001 (37)
1950	38,392 (50)
1951	35,377 (67)
1952	33,304 (42)
1953	36,076 (58)
1954	41,855 (34)
1955	36,917 (49)
1956	34,991 (94)
1957	41,101 (79)
1958	39,361 (79)
1959	38,408
1960	32,314

Mileage at 12/36: 72,779
Mileage at 31/12/50: 561,381

Sheds

Crewe	21/9/35
Saltley	12/10/35
Trafford Park	20/6/36
Springs Branch	21/11/36
Preston	11/3/39
Springs Branch	7/10/39
Crewe North	13/4/40
Springs Branch	15/2/41
Preston	5/4/41
Crewe South	20/11/48
Patricroft	20/11/48 (loan)
Crewe South	11/12/48
Stoke	9/6/56
Crewe South	2/2/57
Carlisle Upperby	9/2/57
Carlisle Kingmoor	22/6/63

Withdrawn w.e. 2/7/66

5185 at Oxenholme on a five coach excursion with lots of people hanging out of the windows. It remained domeless until 1948 and was in one of three periods allocated to Springs Branch when this picture was taken. Photograph R.K. Blencowe.

45186

Built 5186 at Armstrong Whitworth 20/9/35
Renumbered 45186 w.e. 2/10/48

Improvements and modifications

21/3/38	Removal of vacuum pump
24/2/40	BTH speed indicator
23/1/46	Steam sanding
8/5/58	Modification
15/6/63	Smith-Stone speed indicators

Repairs

31/10/36-11/12/36	LS
24/6/37-16/7/37	LO
16/2/38-21/3/38	HG
23/6/39-29/7/39	HS
22/4/41-13/5/41	HG
16/7/42-8/8/42	LS
8/3/43-13/4/43	HS
21/1/44-15/2/44	LO
24/10/44-10/11/44	LS
31/12/45-23/1/46	HG
2/6/47-28/7/47	LS
12/9/48-2/10/48	HS
15/9/49-24/10/49	LC
8/5/50-25/5/50	HG
14/2/52-13/3/52	LI
17/4/53-16/5/53	LI
25/6/54-19/8/54	HG
21/5/56-13/6/56	HI
8/11/56-21/11/56	LC(EO)
11/3/58-8/5/58	HG
23/3/59-15/4/39	LC(EO)
15/4/60-10/6/60	LI

Boilers

New	8966
9/3/38	8971 from 5191
13/5/41	9041 from 5195
13/4/43	8979 from 5102
23/1/46	8967 from 5200
25/5/50	8990 from 5133
19/8/54	8930 from 45032
8/5/58	8986 from 45072

Tenders

New	9290
23/1/46	9057 (riveted)

Mileage/(weekdays out of service)

1935	15,625 (23)
1936	45,349 (100)
1937	50,631 (121)
1938	45,419 (106)
1939	42,097 (70)
1940	31,689 (97)
1941	35,128 (53)
1942	42,182 (72)
1943	38,368 (55)
1944	39,777 (68)
1945	33,792 (39)
1946	43,413 (59)
1947	38,700 (82)
1948	31,183 (64)
1949	33,673 (96)
1950	50,988 (56)
1951	32,359 (57)
1952	34,609 (48)
1953	40,772 (85)
1954	32,653 (116)
1955	38,794 (64)
1956	37,054 (64)
1957	39,519 (55)
1958	46,167 (126)
1959	45,589
1960	35,343

Mileage at 12/36: 60,974
Mileage at 31/12/50: 618,014

Sheds

Crewe	21/9/35
Saltley	5/10/35
Leeds	5/9/36
Saltley	25/9/37
Derby	14/11/53
Sheffield	23/10/54
Saltley	27/11/54
Leicester Central	7/6/58 (loan)
Saltley	3/1/59
Derby	17/9/60
Saltley	4/3/61
Oxley	3/4/65
Crewe South	11/3/67

Withdrawn w.e. 9/9/67

45186 at Blackwell, the top of the Lickey incline, when shedded at Saltley. It was first transferred there in March 1961 but the shed code was not changed to 2E until September 1963 and it remained there until April 1965. The lowered top lamp iron and later steam lance piping confirm this date. Interestingly it had no AWS but was fitted with a speed indicator in October 1963. 45186 was always domeless and was paired with a riveted tender from 1946. The edges of the smokebox plate have been polished and someone has chalked three large numbers on the front frames.

45187

Built as 5187 at Armstrong Whitworth 23/9/35
Renumbered 45187 w.e. 13/11/48

Improvements and modifications

13/6/38	Removal of vacuum pump
?	Steam sanding
31/8/57	Modernisation
16/2/59	Fitting BR ATC equipment

Repairs

17/10/36-4/11/36	LS
20/4/37-1/5/37	LO
3/7/37-18/8/37	LS
12/11/37-6/12/37	LO
12/4/38-13/6/38	HG
10/5/39-6/6/39	HS
24/5/40-13/6/40	HS
30/10/41-11/12/41	HG
7/10/42-24/10/42	LS
22/4/44-11/5/44	LS
28/5/45-13/6/45	HG
6/8/46-28/8/46	HS
27/6/47-4/7/47	LO
4/2/48-2/3/48	LS
18/10/48-11/11/48	LO
26/7/49-10/9/49	HG
13/4/51-4/5/51	LI
18/6/52-26/7/52	LI
2/11/53-4/12/53	HG
28/7/54-13/8/54	LC(EO)
27/8/55-23/9/55	HI
31/7/56-18/8/56	LC
3/8/57-31/8/57	HG
3/10/58-24/10/58	LC(EO)
10/2/59-16/2/59	NC(EO)
9/11/59-1/1/60	LI
7/8/62-7/9/62	HG

Boilers

New	8967
25/5/38	8961 from 5181
6/6/39	8909 from 5129
11/12/41	9051 from 5108
13/6/45	8961 from 5147
10/9/49	8905 from 5211
4/12/53	9017 from 45113
31/8/57	9012 from 45056

Tenders

New	9291
17/11/64	9497
?	9676

Mileage/(weekdays out of service)

1935	23,854 (3)
1936	51,192 (102)
1937	37,435 (137)
1938	45,251 (124)
1939	44,827 (85)
1940	28,698 (82)
1941	25,389 (86)
1942	43,856 (77)
1943	51,070 (45)
1944	40,931 (61)
1945	40,845 (70)
1946	39,197 (84)
1947	44,562 (72)
1948	41,410 (79)
1949	37,429 (84)
1950	43,353 (45)
1951	41,419 (41)
1952	38,857 (70)
1953	35,712 (59)
1954	42,573 (58)
1955	36,940 (54)
1956	38,866 (40)
1957	41,218 (44)
1958	41,353 (62)
1959	59,644
1960	45,469

Mileage at 12/36: 75,046
Mileage at 31/12/50: 639,299

Sheds

Nottingham	5/10/35
Leeds	10/2/40
Normanton	20/4/40
Leeds	18/10/41
Rugby	24/7/48 (loan)
Rugby	6/11/48
Willesden	15/9/56
Edge Hill	14/5/60
Patricroft	11/5/68

Withdrawn w.e. 25/5/68

45187, allocated to Rugby between 1948 and 1956 after either a General overhaul completed in October 1953 or a Heavy Intermediate completed in September 1955 at Crewe. It had a 21-element domeless boiler and a welded tender throughout its life. Photograph www.rail-online.co.uk

45188

Built as 5188 at Armstrong Whitworth 23/9/35
Renumbered 45188 w.e. 30/7/49

Improvements and modifications

?	Removal of vacuum pump
15/8/39	BTH speed indicator
?	Steam sanding
24/4/59	Fitting BR ATC equipment

Repairs

16/3/36-14/4/36	HO
28/9/36-26/10/36	LS
24/5/37-25/6/37	LO
29/11/37-11/2/38	HG
10/8/38-27/8/38	LO
22/11/38-14/12/38	LS
17/2/39-24/3/39	LO
17/7/39-15/8/39	LS
10/6/40-27/7/40	HG
17/4/41-10/5/41	LS
16/12/41-14/1/42	LO
2/8/42-2/9/42	LS
10/1/44-24/1/44	HG
9/2/46-23/2/46	LS
17/7/47-30/8/47	HG
28/6/49-28/7/49	HI
19/4/51-26/5/51	HG
20/5/53-19/6/53	LI
7/2/55-12/3/55	HG
9/2/57-2/3/57	HI
1/4/59-24/4/59	LI
11/5/59-19/5/59	LC
8/1/60-19/2/60	LC(EO)
23/10/61-22/11/61	HG
11/2/64-7/3/64	INT

Boilers

New	8968
27/1/38	8660 from 5043 (domed)
27/7/40	8668 from 5038 (domed)
24/1/44	8677 from 5112 (domed)
30/8/47	8823 from 5041 (domed)
26/5/51	8674 from 45141 (domed)
12/3/55	8681 from 45045 (domed)
22/11/61	8669 from 45107 (domed)

Tenders

New	9292
7/4/38	9110 (riveted)
21/6/40	9137 (riveted)
27/7/40	9110 (riveted)
28/7/44	9166 (riveted)
22/2/64	10721 (part-welded)

Mileage/(weekdays out of service)

1935	12,858 (28)
1936	43,269 (123)
1937	43,560 (129)
1938	58,808 (115)
1939	57,538 (89)
1940	46,724 (53)
1941	49,795 (52)
1942	40,471 (72)
1943	40,620 (12)
1944	38,767 (36)
1945	27,866 (22)
1946	36,365 (34)
1947	32,810 (75)
1948	39,345 (36)
1949	36,969 (52)
1950	32,995 (33)
1951	36,186 (63)
1952	26,593 (58)
1953	33,056 (48)
1954	23,450 (53)
1955	35,071 (71)
1956	39,816 (42)
1957	42,334 (42)
1958	37,951 (50)
1959	28,555
1960	33,788

Mileage at 12/36: 56,127
Mileage at 31/12/50: 638,760

Sheds

Nottingham	12/10/35
Kentish Town	25/9/37
Warrington	26/9/42 (loan)
Warrington	17/10/42
Patricroft	26/12/42
Crewe South	31/12/55
Longsight	29/6/57
Crewe North	31/8/57
Crewe South	23/11/57
Monument Lane	18/6/60
Preston	27/8/60 (loan)
Monument Lane	10/9/60
Willesden	17/9/60
Edge Hill	22/10/60
Holyhead	23/6/62
Springs Branch	15/9/62
Edge Hill	17/8/63
Speke Junction	19/10/63

Withdrawn w.e. 22/7/67

45188 was at Crewe South but had been sent to Horwich on 10 May 1959 for attention to its axles less than three weeks after an Light Intermediate overhaul at Crewe when it received AWS equipment. It had a domed boiler from January 1938 onwards and had riveted tenders from the same date until 1964. Photograph F.A. Wycherley.

45189

Built as 5189 at Armstrong Whitworth 23/9/35
Renumbered 45189 w.e. 27/8/49

Improvements and modifications

28/3/39	Steam sanding
28/3/39	Removal of vacuum pump
13/7/40	BTH speed indicator
21/3/59	Fitting BR ATC equipment

Repairs

9/1/37-25/1/37	LS
29/8/37-12/10/37	HS
15/2/39-28/3/39	HG
22/5/40-1/6/40	LS
14/7/41-9/8/41	LO
11/3/42-22/4/42	LS
2/5/42-16/5/42	LO
14/5/43-28/5/43	HG
16/10/43-6/11/43	LO
7/7/45-18/8/45	LS
26/7/47-12/9/47	HG
28/7/49-27/8/49	HI
28/8/50-6/10/50	HI
20/6/52-12/8/52	HG
17/11/53-12/12/53	LI
29/4/55-26/5/55	HI
16/10/56-6/12/56	HG
31/7/58-5/9/58	HI
10/3/59-18/3/59	NC(EO)
7/5/59-19/6/59	LC(EO)
12/4/60-27/5/60	LI
30/5/61-31/7/61	HI
8/12/62-16/1/63	HG

Boilers

New	8969
28/3/39	9035 from 5105
28/5/43	8918 from 5061
12/9/47	9033 from 5190
12/8/52	8980 from 45143
6/12/56	8683 from 45113 (domed)
?	9043

Tenders

New	9293

Mileage/(weekdays out of service)

1935	14,981 (23)
1936	52,993 (92)
1937	43,927 (80)
1938	49,066 (36)
1939	38,558 (72)
1940	35,433 (30)
1941	26,327 (52)
1942	28,793 (79)
1943	28,294 (82)
1944	35,859 (41)
1945	30,136 (75)
1946	38,648 (45)
1947	28,561 (72)
1948	35,506 (46)
1949	34,252 (56)
1950	33,493 (76)
1951	36,635 (39)
1952	34,800 (69)
1953	39,170 (47)
1954	44,674 (24)
1955	36,121 (51)
1956	35,966 (75)
1957	44,932 (37)
1958	34,018 (67)
1959	42,377
1960	36,782

Mileage at 12/36: 67,974
Mileage at 31/12/50: 554,827

Shed

Nottingham	5/10/35
Crewe	5/12/36 (loan)
Crewe	19/12/36
Edge Hill	13/11/37
Crewe North	9/3/46 (loan)
Crewe North	4/5/46
Crewe South	26/10/46
Stoke	20/4/57 (loan)
Stoke	22/6/57
Crewe North	21/9/57
Crewe South	23/6/62
Crewe North	15/9/62

Withdrawn w.e. 13/7/63

45189 in July 1955 ascending the Lickey incline with a ten coach train is assisted by a Jinty banking engine which seems to be doing all the work. It had been shedded at Crewe South since 1946, was domeless until December 1956 and kept the same welded tender throughout. Photograph www.transporttreasury.co.uk

45190

Built as 5190 at Armstrong Whitworth 1/10/35
Renumbered 45190 w.e. 11/12/48

Improvements and modifications

22/6/38	Removal of vacuum pump
6/3/42	Steam sanding

Repairs

7/11/36-19/11/36	LS
28/4/37-13/5/37	LO
21/4/38-22/6/38	HG
3/2/40-15/2/40	LS
12/2/42-6/3/42	HG
14/1/44-29/1/44	HS
9/5/44-23/5/44	HO
27/9/45-20/10/45	LS
9/6/47-1/8/47	HG
13/11/48-6/12/48	LS
21/4/50-25/5/50	HG
28/10/51-9/11/51	LI
28/1/52-20/2/52	LC
23/8/52-26/9/52	HC(EO)
19/3/54-21/4/54	HG
28/9/55-22/10/55	LI
20/5/57-13/6/57	HI
1/59-21/2/59	HG
17/1/61-3/3/61	HI
18/10/61-30/11/61	LC
10/6/63-27/6/63	LI
21/6/65-9/8/65	INT

Boilers

New	8970
1/6/38	8956 from 5206
6/3/42	8819 from 5191 (domed)
23/5/44	9033 from 5145
1/8/47	9055 from 5182
25/5/50	8672 from 5095 (domed)
21/4/54	9010 from 45014
21/2/59	9018 from 45114

Tenders

New	9294

Mileage/(weekdays out of service)

1935	14,047 (-)
1936	62,164 (41)
1937	55,679 (58)
1938	40,817 (104)
1939	50,431 (77)
1940	40,019 (51)
1941	43,057 (58)
1942	28,428 (35)
1943	38,869 (30)
1944	44,781 (62)
1945	37,115 (51)
1946	46,333 (52)
1947	37,238 (91)
1948	44,248 (55)
1949	46,901 (36)
1950	45,942 (50)
1951	40,717 (74)
1952	49,667 (58)
1953	48,414
1954	46,314
1955	40,893
1956	44,818
1957	40,347

Mileage at 12/36: 76,211
Mileage at 31/12/50: 676,069

Sheds

Crewe	5/10/35
Swansea	25/9/37
Chester	7/5/38
Mold Jct	1/11/41
Chester	28/8/43
Mold Jct	7/7/45
Chester	1/12/45
Shrewsbury	27/7/46
Bletchley	1/3/47
Shrewsbury	19/4/47
Annesley	10/10/64
Derby	13/3/65
Annesley	14/8/65
Kirkby	23/10/65
Colwick	25/12/65 (loan)
Colwick	8/1/66
Heaton Mersey	28/5/66

Stored
11/10/65-13/12/65
10/10/66-14/8/67

Withdrawn w.e. 4/5/68

45190 at Hereford on 2 September 1962. It was shedded at Shrewsbury from 1947 until 1964 when it was transferred to Annesley. It is domeless and has its original welded tender.

45191

Built as 5191 at Armstrong Whitworth 1/10/35
Renumbered 45191 w.e 22/7/50

Improvements and modifications

22/4/39	Removal of vacuum pump
2/2/42	Steam sanding
18/2/59	Fitting BR ATC equipment

Repairs

13/12/36-4/1/37	LS
4/6/37-17/6/37	LO
13/1/38-10/2/38	HG
11/3/40-28/3/40	LS
14/1/42-2/2/42	HG
4/5/44-19/5/44	HS
12/7/44-21/7/44	LO
18/6/45-21/7/45	HG
3/10/46-19/11/46	LS
5/1/48-19/2/48	HS
15/3/49-28/4/49	LI
17/6/50-20/7/50	LI
15/11/51-22/12/51	HG
21/3/53-29/4/53	LI
6/3/54-1/4/54	HI
26/8/55-28/9/55	HG
18/9/56-5/10/56	LC(EO)
26/10/56-1/12/56	LC
21/9/57-17/10/57	HI
28/10/58-28/11/58	LI
12/2/59-18/2/59	NC(EO)
18/8/59-3/9/59	LC(EO)
15/2/60-13/4/60	HC(EO)
31/7/61-12/9/61	HG
28/8/64-10/10/64	LI

Boilers

New	8971
24/1/38	8819 from 5002 (domed)
2/2/42	8909 from 5187
21/7/45	8643 from 5220 (domed)
19/2/48	9031 from 5148
22/12/51	9019 from 45203
28/9/55	8947 from 45080
12/9/61	9019 from 45044

Tenders

New	9295

Mileage/(weekdays out of service)

1935	11,726 (17)
1936	62,773 (40)
1937	58,193 (63)
1938	50,318 (84)
1939	44,053 (36)
1940	34,738 (54)
1941	31,494 (54)
1942	42,107 (42)
1943	24,416 (41)
1944	26,043 (64)
1945	34,795 (60)
1946	37,054 (74)
1947	43,828 (65)
1948	41,544 (91)
1949	37,726 (79)
1950	32,090 (69)
1951	39,076 (88)
1952	51,501 (43)
1953	41,155 (69)
1954	39,201 (65)
1955	33,379 (74)
1956	39,784 (92)
1957	45,570 (45)
1958	37,391 (61)
1959	38,756
1960	24,317

Mileage at 12/36: 74,499
Mileage at 31/12/50: 612,898

Sheds

Crewe	5/10/35
Swansea	25/9/37
Willesden	20/8/38
Northampton	27/1/45
Rugby	17/9/60
Willesden	11/2/61
Stoke	22/2/62

Stored
17/4/67-21/4/67

Withdrawn w.e. 22/7/67

45191 waiting at Willesden in the mid-1950s. It had been a Northampton engine since 1945, the shed being recoded to 2E in March 1952. 45191 was domeless from 1948 and kept its original welded tender until withdrawn from Stoke in July 1967. Photograph R. Collins, www.transporttreasury.co.uk

45192

Built as 5192 at Armstrong Whitworth 30/9/35
Renumbered 45192 w.e. 3/7/48

Improvements and modifications

14/3/38	Removal of vacuum pump
14/3/44	Steam sanding

Repairs

5/5/36-18/5/36	LO
2/2/38-14/3/38	HG
28/3/40-20/4/40	HS
13/5/42-30/6/42	LS
1/3/43-2/4/43	HS
3/2/44-14/3/44	HG
25/1/45-3/3/45	LS
23/2/46-18/4/46	LS
31/5/47-8/7/47	HS
12/5/48-3/7/48	LS
6/7/48	NC(R)
17/7/48-2/8/48	NC
2/6/49-12/7/49	HI
11/3/50-7/4/50	LC
7/9/50-13/10/50	HI
15/1/52-16/2/52	G
21/2/52	NC(TO)
27/2/52-29/2/52	NC(TO)
28/2/53-28/3/53	LI
5/3/54-17/4/54	HI
22/4/55-27/5/55	LI
6/8/55-9/8/55	NC(EO)
17/3/56-27/3/56	NC(EO)
8/9/56-6/10/56	G
17/10/56-18/10/56	NC(EO)
15/1/57-8/2/57	LC(EO)
9/11/57-30/11/57	HI
12/5/58-19/5/58	NC(EO)
6/12/58-29/1/59	LI
7/7/59-17/7/59	NC(EO)
4/6/60-9/7/60	HI
12/5/61-9/6/61	LC
23/5/62-23/6/62	G
30/1/63-12/2/63	LC(EO)
4/3/65-10/3/65	NC

Boilers

New	8972
28/2/38	8993 from 5213
20/4/40	8657 from 5051 (domed)
18/2/44	8933 from 5007
12/7/47	8929 from 5053

Tenders

New	9296
17/5/43	9069 (riveted)
25/5/43	9296
20/2/44	9032 (riveted)
6/2/45	9060 (riveted)
6/7/45	9071 (riveted)
18/4/46	9364 (riveted)
28/1/48	9031 (riveted)
10/2/48	9364 (riveted)
7/7/49	9027 (riveted)
18/10/56	9068 (riveted)
30/11/57	9715

Mileage/(weekdays out of service)

1935	14,714 (2)
1936	59,596 (43)
1937	51,029 (49)
1938	37,934 (77)
1939	36,594 (52)
1940	26,511 (60)
1941	45,941 (34)
1942	56,762 (77)
1943	55,983 (50)
1944	50,210 (64)
1945	49,589 (60)
1946	41,017 (75)
1947	43,804 (57)
1948	42,236 (99)
1949	38,862 (99)
1950	37,112 (95)

Mileage at 12/36: 74,310
Mileage at 31/12/50: 687,894

Sheds

Crewe	5/10/35
Mold Jct	25/9/37
Farnley Jct	18/6/38
Wakefield	7/10/39
Newton Heath	30/11/40
Inverness	30/8/41
Perth	30/7/60 (PE)
Corkerhill	2/5/61
Hurlford	20/7/61
Grangemouth	21/10/63

Withdrawn 21/8/65

The fireman rakes the coal while 45192 stands at Inverness on 7 October 1952, where it was allocated from 1941 until 1960. It has large high positioned cab numbers to clear the tablet catcher but no crest on its riveted tender. Scottish touches include a domed top feed cover on its domeless boiler. An early onset of winter weather is obviously anticipated with a snowplough already fitted. Photograph J.L. Stevenson, courtesy Hamish Stevenson.

45193

Built as 5193 at Armstrong Whitworth 9/10/35
Renumbered 45193 w.e. 30/7/49

Improvements and modifications

16/9/38	Removal of vacuum pump
?	Steam sanding
17/3/56	Modification
10/5/60	Fitting BR ATC equipment

Repairs

27/11/36-17/12/36	LS
3/5/37-20/5/37	LO
18/8/37-1/10/37	LO
21/4/38-29/4/38	LO
13/8/38-16/9/38	HG
6/3/40-11/4/40	LS
11/2/41-27/2/41	LS
21/10/42-26/11/42	HG
28/12/42-23/1/43	LO
11/4/44-26/4/44	HS
19/6/45-28/7/45	HS
6/7/46-20/8/46	HS
15/11/47-10/1/48	HG
25/6/49-28/7/49	HI
30/12/50-19/1/51	HI
7/7/52-29/8/52	HG
11/12/52-17/1/53	HC(EO)
20/2/54-12/3/54	LI
18/2/56-17/3/56	HG
12/2/58-8/3/58	HI
28/4/60-10/5/60	NC(EO)
25/7/60-27/8/60	HG
20/6/62-25/7/62	LI
30/12/64-21/1/65	LI

Boilers

New	8973
16/9/38	9002 from 5222
26/11/42	8829 from 5152
28/7/45	8655 from 5108 (domed)
10/1/48	9023 from 5209
29/8/52	8655 from 45197 (domed)
17/3/56	8637 from 45050 (domed)
27/8/60	8829 from 45133

Tenders

New	9297
26/4/44	9613
?	9300

Mileage/(weekdays out of service)

1935	14,563 (1)
1936	62,405 (46)
1937	45,796 (88)
1938	36,707 (80)
1939	40,294 (46)
1940	36,359 (59)
1941	29,672 (73)
1942	32,458 (85)
1943	31,472 (46)
1944	30,900 (48)
1945	41,039 (63)
1946	35,772 (74)
1947	37,181 (72)
1948	43,535 (45)
1949	41,756 (54)
1950	44,416 (32)
1951	49,239 (43)
1952	35,813 (89)
1953	57,477 (45)
1954	42,256 (50)
1955	37,268 (45)
1956	51,963 (48)
1957	45,122 (42)
1958	47,575 (57)
1959	36,571
1960	34,966

Mileage at 12/36: 76,968
Mileage at 31/12/50: 604,325

Sheds

Crewe	12/10/35
Bushbury	13/11/37
Aston	20/1/40
Willesden	10/2/40
Edge Hill	23/8/41
Rugby	13/9/41
Springs Branch	19/9/43
Edge Hill	11/3/44
Carlisle Upperby	16/3/46
Carnforth	5/6/48
Lancaster	2/6/62
Carnforth	23/4/66

Withdrawn w.e. 23/9/67

45193 at the strangely named Pontefract Tanshelf on 16 July 1960 with a Liverpool Exchange-Scarborough SO train. It has a domed boiler but was only a few days from a Heavy General overhaul during which it reverted to a domeless boiler. The AWS had been fitted in May 1960 and it was shedded at Carnforth from June 1948 until June 1962. Photograph N.E. Preedy.

45194

Built as 5194 at Armstrong Whitworth 9/10/35
Renumbered 45194 w.e. 20/3/48

Improvements and modifications

16/3/39	Steam sanding
16/3/39	Removal of vacuum pump
?	Fitting BR ATC equipment

Repairs

14/10/36-31/10/36	LS
27/10/37-11/11/37	LS
19/9/38-30/9/38	LO
3/2/39-16/3/39	HG
21/3/40-18/4/40	LS
24/2/41-15/3/41	LS
22/4/41-8/5/41	HO
22/5/42-18/7/42	LS
16/1/43-13/2/43	LO
21/12/43-22/1/44	HG
18/12/44-27/1/45	LS
15/10/45-23/11/45	LO
1/8/46-11/9/46	HS
6/6/47-17/7/47	LO
16/2/48-18/3/48	HG
19/4/49-18/5/49	HI
6/1/50-11/2/50	HI
13/4/50-17/5/50	LC
2/7/51-11/8/51	HI
1/1/52-22/1/52	LC(EO)
11/7/52-8/8/52	NC(EO)
5/2/53-28/3/53	G
4/8/54-28/8/54	LI
5/5/55-21/5/55	NC(EO)
20/7/56-18/8/56	HI
3/6/57-14/6/57	LC(EO)
22/2/58-21/3/58	G
6/6/59-27/6/59	LI
3/8/59-12/8/59	NC(EO)
23/3/61-21/4/61	LI
24/4/62-25/5/62	G
5/11/63-15/11/63	LC
27/11/63-28/11/63	NC(TO)
19/3/64-17/4/64	LI
3/3/65-26/3/65	LC

Boilers

New	8974
16/3/39	8988 from 5208
22/1/44	8658 from 5011 (domed)
18/3/48	8664 from 5154

Tenders

New	9298
10/8/42	9267
16/11/42	9298
15/12/44	9062 (riveted)
20/6/47	9777
10/2/50	9545
8/8/56	9721
23/4/65	10509

Mileage/(weekdays out of service)

1935	14,184 (4)
1936	63,161 (38)
1937	51,171 (60)
1938	44,192 (75)
1939	51,367 (62)
1940	43,123 (51)
1941	45,663 (69)
1942	50,025 (74)
1943	55,092 (63)
1944	42,796 (88)
1945	30,011 (139)
1946	44,097 (81)
1947	43,802 (97)
1948	45,837 (73)
1949	48,288 (67)
1950	45,054 (104)

Mileage at 12/36: 77,345
Mileage at 31/12/50: 717,863

Sheds

Crewe	12/10/35
Bath	30/4/38
Leeds	16/3/40
Bath	20/4/40
Perth	14/9/41
Corkerhill	29/4/44
Ayr	9/11/59

Withdrawn 24/4/65

45194 on 11 August 1957 at Corkerhill where it was allocated from 1944 until 1959. The domed boiler is not recorded on the surviving History Card but was replaced by a domeless one in March 1958; the blanking plates on the firebox shoulders indicate that it is one of the rebuilt 14 element examples. St Rollox has fitted the top feed cover from a domeless boiler giving the 'double domed' effect. 45194 has 10in cab numbers below the tablet staff holder.

45195

Built as 5195 at Armstrong Whitworth 9/10/35
Renumbered 45195 w.e. 3/7/48

Improvements and modifications

2/7/38	Removal of vacuum pump
?	Steam sanding
14/4/59	Fitting BR ATC equipment

Repairs

2/10/36-16/10/36	LS
19/2/37-25/3/37	LO
18/5/38-2/7/38	HG
20/10/39-18/11/39	LS
27/2/40-9/3/40	LO
14/8/40-14/9/40	LO
25/2/41-24/3/41	HG
4/11/42-1/12/42	LS
10/7/44-29/7/44	HS
15/9/45-15/10/45	HG
13/8/47-9/10/47	LS
12/6/48-3/7/48	LO
30/3/49-20/4/49	LI
13/4/50-5/6/50	HG
6/6/50-17/6/50	NC(Rect)
3/1/52-23/2/52	HI
2/10/52-24/10/52	LC(EO)
23/5/53-13/6/53	LC(EO)
5/1/54-4/2/54	LI
20/6/55-30/7/55	HG
30/7/57-17/8/57	HI
6/9/58-8/10/58	LC(EO)
11/3/59-14/4/59	HI
29/3/60-28/5/60	HG
17/11/60-17/12/60	LC(EO)
25/5/62-15/6/62	HI
12/5/64-6/6/64	LI

Boilers

New	8975
15/6/38	9041 from 5111
24/3/41	8960 from 5215
15/10/45	8641 from 5074 (domed)
5/6/50	9028 from 5006
30/7/55	8640 from 45063 (domed)
28/5/60	9025 from 45148

Tenders

New	9299

Mileage/(weekdays out of service)

1935	15,521 (1)
1936	56,543 (46)
1937	47,495 (59)
1938	46,035 (73)
1939	46,520 (52)
1940	27,918 (65)
1941	36,881 (49)
1942	30,044 (45)
1943	30,658 (27)
1944	27,925 (42)
1945	32,192 (58)
1946	32,655 (58)
1947	27,949 (94)
1948	32,124 (62)
1949	34,442 (63)
1950	35,305 (78)
1951	39,871 (34)
1952	32,375 (62)
1953	39,888 (57)
1954	37,539 (62)
1955	38,981 (68)
1956	47,110 (34)
1957	40,339 (44)
1958	36,844 (59)
1959	35,698
1960	32,255

Mileage at 12/36: 72,064
Mileage at 31/12/50: 560,207

Sheds

Crewe North	12/10/35
Crewe South	25/9/37
Crewe North	19/2/38
Edge Hill	23/9/39
Warrington	8/6/40
Carlisle W	30/11/40
Carnforth	19/7/41
Willesden	4/10/41
Crewe South	21/2/42
Crewe North	1/11/52
Holyhead	6/12/52 (loan)
Crewe North	10/1/53
Crewe South	18/4/53
Walsall	3/7/54
Bletchley	19/2/55
Carlisle Upperby	31/8/57 (loan)
Bletchley	5/10/57
Patricroft	4/7/59
Agecroft	17/6/61
Carlisle Canal	12/1/63
Carlisle Kingmoor	22/6/63
Newton Heath	13/7/63
Carlisle Kingmoor	5/10/63

Withdrawn w.e. 30/7/66

45195 has both a 12A shedplate and CARLISLE KINGMOOR on the bufferbeam following a Light Intermediate repair at Cowlairs completed in June 1964. It was shedded at Kingmoor from October 1963 until withdrawn in July 1966. 45195 was domeless from May 1960, had AWS fitted in April 1959 and was only recorded with its original welded tender. Photograph Rail-Archive Stephenson.

45196

Built as 5196 at Armstrong Whitworth 9/10/35
Renumbered 45196 w.e. 9/10/48

Improvements and modifications

2010/38	Removal of vacuum pump
?	Steam sanding
9/5/59	Fitting BR ATC equipment

Repairs

19/11/36-12/12/36	LS
24/5/37-3/6/37	LO
15/9/38-20/10/38	HG
16/5/40-20/5/40	LS
18/4/41-10/5/41	LS
15/2/42-7/3/42	HG
22/5/43-5/6/43	HS
25/9/44-7/10/44	LO
13/2/45-2/3/45	HS
28/9/46-15/10/46	HS
29/10/47-24/11/47	LS
20/8/48-8/10/48	HG
14/6/49-2/7/49	LC
11/12/50-26/1/51	LI
14/9/51-19/10/51	HC
31/12/51-30/1/52	LI
4/2/52-9/2/52	NC(Rect)
14/1/53-14/2/53	LC
12/1/54-13/2/54	HG
5/3/56-6/4/56	HI
18/5/57-11/6/57	HI
10/2/58-14/3/58	LC(EO)
7/5/58-10/6/58	LC(EO)
3/4/59-9/5/59	HG
18/5/59-29/5/59	LC(EO)
17/3/61-24/4/61	LI
27/11/62-29/12/62	LI
23/5/63-14/6/63	HC
11/3/65-3/4/65	LI

Boilers

New	8976
20/10/38	8973 from 5193
7/3/42	9058 from 5062
2/3/45	8663 from 5034 (domed)
8/10/48	8912 from 5019
13/2/54	8671 from 45078 (domed)
9/5/59	8926 from 45073

Tenders

New	9300

Mileage/(weekdays out of service)

1935	14,396 (5)
1936	61,939 (47)
1937	55,329 (45)
1938	32,023 (99)
1939	44,932 (36)
1940	35,603 (71)
1941	33,970 (54)
1942	32,069 (38)
1943	30,975 (44)
1944	25,437 (64)
1945	29,713 (44)
1946	28,837 (58)
1947	27,203 (82)
1948	30,026 (82)
1949	44,046 (50)
1950	35,536 (53)
1951	31,960 (76)
1952	41,147 (73)
1953	32,196 (61)
1954	41,959 (55)
1955	35,452 (32)
1956	40,055 (52)
1957	38,720 (54)
1958	39,817 (88)
1959	40,825
1960	38,407

Mileage at 12/36: 76,335
Mileage at 31/12/50: 562,034

Sheds

Crewe	12/10/35
Bushbury	13/11/37
Patricroft	17/12/38
Springs Branch	16/9/39
Patricroft	30/9/39
Preston	9/3/40
Warrington	8/3/41
Crewe North	2/4/60 (loan)
Warrington	25/6/60
Edge Hill	9/7/60
Lancaster	16/3/63
Rose Grove	31/10/64

Stored
26/9/65-6/12/65
7/2/66-28/5/66
30/5/66-27/6/66
16/1/67-28/5/67

Withdrawn w.e. 30/12/67

45196 in 1952 with a long northbound freight waits at Tebay for banking assistance up Shap. It has a domeless boiler which it kept until February 1954 and has BRITISH RAILWAYS on its original welded tender. 45196 was shedded at 8B Warrington from 1941 until 1960. Photograph www.rail-online.co.uk

45197

Built as 5197 at Armstrong Whitworth 15/10/35
Renumbered 45197 w.e. 19/11/49

Improvements and modifications

13/6/38	Removal of vacuum pump
30/9/39	BTH speed indicator
11/11/46	Steam sanding
13/10/59	Fitting BR ATC equipment
14/5/60	Sloping throatplate boiler

Repairs

27/10/36-10/11/36	HS
16/7/37-30/7/37	LO
25/4/38-13/6/38	HG
16/9/39-30/9/39	LS
21/7/41-7/8/41	HG
5/10/41-1/11/41	LO
7/5/42-6/6/42	HO
28/5/43-12/6/43	HS
27/5/44-13/6/44	LS
17/6/44-20/7/44	LO
14/8/45-19/9/45	LO
10/10/46-11/11/46	HG
20/12/47-31/1/48	HS
31/10/49-17/11/49	HI
17/3/51-16/4/51	HI
17/4/52-17/6/52	HG
20/12/52-15/1/53	LI(EO)
14/8/54-14/9/54	LI
14/9/55-15/10/55	HG
10/9/56-11/10/56	LC(EO)
18/4/57-24/5/57	LI
16/5/58-13/6/58	LI
29/9/59-13/10/59	NC(EO)
15/10/59-13/11/59	HI
28/3/60-14/5/60	HG
23/10/61-1/12/61	HI
11/2/64-11/3/64	LI

Boilers

New	8977
26/5/38	9030 from 5100
7/6/41	9054 from 5214
6/6/42	9006 from 5183
11/11/46	8955 from 5150
31/1/48	8655 from 5193 (domed)
17/6/52	8987 from 45075
15/10/55	8997 from 45135
14/5/60	9495 from 44869 (sloping throatplate)

Tenders

New	9301
7/1/49	9244
15/12/51	9535
17/4/57	9543

Mileage/(weekdays out of service)

1935	12,742 (2)
1936	63,261 (40)
1937	53,004 (49)
1938	48,090 (77)
1939	50,808 (49)
1940	41,489 (36)
1941	34,439 (80)
1942	35,511 (60)
1943	43,163 (36)
1944	32,605 (71)
1945	32,279 (62)
1946	28,977 (69)
1947	34,126 (66)
1948	29,332 (62)
1949	34,597 (56)
1950	46,755 (30)
1951	38,491 (57)
1952	31,308 (80)
1953	40,453 (58)
1954	39,713 (79)
1955	36,468 (78)
1956	43,406 (59)
1957	33,005 (73)
1958	42,878 (48)
1959	21,528
1960	44,576

Mileage at 12/36: 76,003
Mileage at 31/12/50: 621,178

Sheds

Crewe North	26/10/35
Crewe South	1/1/38
Crewe North	19/3/38
Crewe South	31/1/42
Crewe North	7/3/42
Crewe South	9/9/44
Carlisle Upperby	17/7/48
Warrington	10/3/62
Llandudno Jct	5/5/62
Mold Jcn	9/2/63 (loan)
Llandudno Jct	11/5/63
Bedford	25/5/63
Cricklewood	6/7/63
Speke Jct	2/5/64 (loan)
Speke Jct	23/5/64
Lostock Hall	11/7/64

Withdrawn w.e. 14/1/67

45197 picks up water from the troughs at Brock on 12 June 1957. It had a domeless boiler at the time but was to be converted to a sloping throatplate type in 1960. 45197 was allocated to Carlisle Upperby from July 1948 until transferred to Warrington in March 1962. Photograph A.G. Batson, www.transporttreasury.co.uk

45198

Built as 5198 at Armstrong Whitworth 15/10/35
Renumbered 45198 w.e. 24/12/49

Improvements and modifications

5/5/38	Removal of vacuum pump
15/8/42	Steam sanding
6/5/59	Fitting BR ATC equipment
26/1/63	Smith-Stone speed indicator

Repairs

12/11/36-26/11/36	**LS**
6/5/37-30/5/37	**LO**
28/2/38-5/5/38	**HG**
24/2/40-8/3/40	**LS**
23/7/42-15/8/42	**HG**
8/6/44-21/6/44	**HS**
12/10/45-10/11/45	**HS**
4/9/47-12/11/47	**HG**
9/11/49-24/12/49	**LI**
5/1/50-20/1/50	**HC**
2/10/50-19/10/50	**LC**
2/12/50-30/12/50	**LC**
6/8/51-6/9/51	**HG**
4/9/52-1/10/52	**HI**
2/10/52-11/10/52	**NC(Rect)**
23/5/53-11/6/53	**LC(EO)**
7/4/54-11/5/54	**HG**
2/6/55-22/6/55	**LC(EO)**
24/2/57-3/4/57	**HI**
27/4/58-12/6/58	**HI**
23/4/59-6/5/59	**NC(EO)**
8/5/59-25/5/59	**LC**
1/2/61-15/3/61	**HG**

Boilers

New	8978
20/4/38	8818 from 5001 (domed)
15/8/42	8941 from 5015
12/11/47	8637 from 5068 (domed)
6/9/51	9029 from 45001
11/5/54	9039 from 45038
15/3/61	8968 from 45220

Boilers

New	8978
20/4/38	8818 from 5001 (domed)
15/8/42	8941 from 5015
12/11/47	8637 from 5068 (domed)
6/9/51	9029 from 45001
11/5/54	9039 from 45038
15/3/61	8968 from 45220

Tenders

New	9302
21/6/44	9002 (prototype)

Mileage/(weekdays out of service)

1935	13,073 (1)
1936	61,834 (50)
1937	55,918 (50)
1938	31,546 (76)
1939	38,032 (25)
1940	32,144 (40)
1941	29,191 (45)
1942	34,721 (46)
1943	38,119 (29)
1944	35,465 (43)
1945	26,790 (58)
1946	32,134 (37)
1947	26,313 (98)
1948	36,346 (46)
1949	26,432 (81)
1950	30,900 (80)
1951	34,081 (51)
1952	35,137 (55)
1953	40,805 (37)
1954	39,921 (46)
1955	37,682 (68)
1956	36,977 (42)
1957	36,487 (65)
1958	32,713 (78)
1959	29,898
1960	30,966

Mileage at 12/36: 74,907
Mileage at 31/12/50: 548,958

Sheds

Crewe	26/10/35
Crewe South	9/9/44
Bletchley	6/11/48 (loan)
Crewe South	11/12/48
Stockport	10/6/61
Willesden	7/4/62
Chester	2/11/63
Croes Newydd	2/10/65
Springs Branch	11/3/67 (loan)
Springs Branch	1/4/67

Stored
7/9/66-3/3/67

Withdrawn w.e. 30/9/67

45198 at Willesden on 2 March 1963. It ran with Stanier prototype tender no.9002 from 1944 until withdrawn. It had a domeless boiler from 1951 onwards, was fitted with AWS in May 1959 and a Smith-Stone speedometer in January 1963. 45198 was shedded at Willesden from April 1962 until transferred to Chester in November 1963.

45199

Built as 5199 at Armstrong Whitworth 15/10/35
Renumbered 45199 w.e. 2/9/50

Improvements and modifications

?	Steam sanding
?	Removal of vacuum pump
10/4/59	Fitting BR ATC equipment

Repairs

22/2/37-7/4/37	HS
26/8/38-11/10/38	HG
3/4/40-18/4/40	LS
21/5/42-4/7/42	HG
6/1/44-22/1/44	HS
9/12/44-6/1/45	HS
19/6/46-20/7/46	LS
13/3/47-14/4/47	HG
17/11/48-10/12/48	HS
11/8/50-30/8/50	LI
22/2/52-4/4/52	HG
3/2/54-25/2/54	LI
1/3/54-9/3/54	NC(Rect)
20/5/56-23/6/56	HG
11/3/59-10/4/59	LI
26/6/61-18/8/61	HG

Boilers

New	8979
11/10/38	9008 from 5078
4/7/42	9017 from 5151
14/4/47	8651 from 5067 (domed)
4/4/52	9002 from 45068
23/6/56	8654 from 45052 (domed)
18/8/61	8913 from 45106

Tenders

New	9303

Mileage/(weekdays out of service)

1935	10,432 (-)
1936	46,686 (29)
1937	39,814 (71)
1938	37,938 (75)
1939	40,299 (35)
1940	32,373 (41)
1941	34,488 (35)
1942	32,477 (61)
1943	29,660 (26)
1944	36,816 (64)
1945	43,121 (21)
1946	31,014 (55)
1947	45,102 (61)
1948	32,297 (40)
1949	34,052 (40)
1950	32,719 (33)
1951	33,542 (28)
1952	36,081 (71)
1953	35,046 (41)
1954	36,716 (44)
1955	29,392 (49)
1956	34,376 (46)
1957	37,610 (22)
1958	29,784 (55)
1959	35,842
1960	30,317

Mileage at 12/36: 57,118
Mileage at 31/12/50: 559,288

Sheds

Crewe	26/10/35
Springs Branch	7/12/35
Llandudno	15/10/38 (loan)
Springs Branch	3/12/38
Preston	4/5/40
Springs Branch	8/6/40
Patricroft	14/6/41
Bolton	15/9/62
Burton	27/5/63

Stored
1/10/62-3/12/62
11/3/63-8/4/63

Withdrawn w.e. 17/8/63

45199 on the turntable at its home shed, Patricroft. It was there from 1941 until September 1962 when it was transferred to Bolton; 45199 was withdrawn in w.e. 17/8/63. The AWS was fitted in April 1959 and the domeless boiler in August 1961; 45199 kept its original welded tender throughout. Photograph www.Rail-online.co.uk

45200

Built as 5200 at Armstrong Whitworth 21/10/35
Renumbered 45200 w.e. 26/2/49

Improvements and modifications

22/8/38	Removal of vacuum pump
6/12/45	Steam sanding
10/11/56	Modernisation
4/12/61	Fitting BR ATC equipment

Repairs

2/2/37-16/2/37	LS
11/8/37-17/9/37	HO
18/1/38-22/8/38	HG
26/12/39-8/1/40	LS
21/9/41-17/10/41	HG
27/10/42-28/11/42	HS
9/9/43-9/10/43	LS
4/4/44-22/4/44	LO
12/8/44-26/8/44	LS
5/12/44-9/12/44	LO
17/5/45-7/6/45	LO
19/11/45-6/12/45	HG
31/3/47-12/5/47	LS
1/8/47-29/8/47	LO
28/1/49-22/2/49	HI
20/12/50-22/1/51	HG
22/9/52-24/10/52	LI
28/3/53-7/5/53	LC(EO)
13/12/54-11/1/55	LI
19/9/56-10/11/56	HG
25/10/58-27/11/58	LI
29/6/59-10/7/59	LC(EO)
23/1/61-2/3/61	LI
23/12/63-4/3/64	HG

Boilers

New	8980
22/8/38	9003 from 5223
17/10/41	8987 from 5032
6/12/45	8981 from 5052
22/1/51	8675 from 5044 (domed)
10/11/56	8835 from 45132

Tenders

New	9304
3/11/63	10442
26/1/67	10636 (part-welded)

Mileage/(weekdays out of service)

1935	6,936 (22)
1936	50,003 (109)
1937	52,333 (83)
1938	59,613 (73)
1939	53,311 (71)
1940	43,597 (55)
1941	41,081 (55)
1942	44,499 (72)
1943	57,601 (51)
1944	42,221 (68)
1945	42,713 (53)
1946	49,927 (43)
1947	24,915 (115)
1948	34,592 (57)
1949	31,424 (61)
1950	33,840 (50)
1951	37,019 (56)
1952	30,383 (65)
1953	37,418 (51)
1954	25,454 (58)
1955	36,793 (45)
1956	33,967 (80)
1957	51,864 (30)
1958	41,206 (60)
1959	50,481
1960	36,537

Mileage at 12/36: 56,939
Mileage at 31/12/50: 668,306

Sheds

Bank Hall	2/11/35
Trafford Park	21/12/35
Bank Hall	1/36 (loan)
Trafford Park	18/1/36
Southport	14/12/40
Huddersfield	12/10/46
Southport	18/10/47
Blackpool	3/3/51 (loan)
Southport	5/5/51
Blackpool	9/6/51 (loan)
Southport	16/6/51
Accrington	29/3/52
Blackpool	19/9/53
Stockport	19/2/66
Newton Heath	11/5/68
Carnforth	6/7/68

Stored
25/11/35-19/12/35
13/1/36-18/3/36
17/4/36-15/5/36

Withdrawn w.e. 20/7/68

45200 at its home shed Stockport Edgeley with a painted 9B shed plate. It was there from February 1966 until it went to Newton Heath in May 1968 when the shed closed. It has a domeless boiler, a part welded tender acquired in January 1967 and the AWS was fitted in December 1961. Photograph G. Harrop.

45201

Built as 5201 at Armstrong Whitworth 22/10/35
Renumbered 45201 w.e. 5/3/49

Improvements and modifications

8/3/38	Removal of vacuum pump
?	Steam sanding
27/9/56	Modification
15/12/61	Fitting BR ATC equipment

Repairs

28/10/36-1/12/36	LS
20/8/37-17/9/37	LO
30/9/37-13/10/37	LO
8/2/38-8/3/38	HG
20/4/39-1/6/39	HS
26/3/41-19/4/41	HG
19/8/42-18/9/42	LS
26/10/43-8/11/43	LS
5/8/44-24/8/44	HG
26/9/45-13/10/45	LS
29/8/47-28/10/47	HG
31/1/49-2/3/49	LI
16/5/50-14/6/50	HI
31/12/51-9/2/52	HG
31/12/53-26/1/54	HI
21/8/56-27/9/56	HG
28/8/58-2/10/58	HI
28/11/60-7/1/61	HI
29/11/61-15/12/61	NC
2/2/62-3/3/62	LC
10/9/63-16/10/63	HG

Boilers

New	8981
21/2/38	9021 from 5091
1/6/39	9021 from 5201
19/4/41	8998 from 5218
24/8/44	8680 from 5021 (domed)
28/10/47	8918 from 5189
9/2/52	8966 from 45135
27/9/56	8967 from 45095
10/63	8833 from 45056

Tenders

New	9305
1/6/39	9569
?	9164 (riveted)

Mileage/(weekdays out of service)

1935	4,903 (29)
1936	59,178 (73)
1937	58,043 (78)
1938	64,829 (68)
1939	44,058 (109)
1940	44,071 (50)
1941	49,194 (44)
1942	46,344 (50)
1943	42,955 (38)
1944	54,034 (50)
1945	43,830 (56)
1946	40,072 (45)
1947	28,430 (87)
1948	54,137 (41)
1949	42,764 (85)
1950	40,756 (90)
1951	29,129 (40)
1952	39,548 (62)
1953	29,740 (50)
1954	33,663 (47)
1955	28,082 (82)
1956	35,253 (63)
1957	49,337 (30)
1958	42,179 (70)
1959	45,157
1960	27,917

Mileage at 12/36: 64,081
Mileage at 31/12/50: 717,598

Sheds

Bank Hall	9/11/35
Trafford Park	21/12/35
Bank Hall	1/36 (loan)
Trafford Park	18/1/36
Southport	14/12/40
Newton Heath	25/3/44
Southport	8/4/44
Low Moor	3/11/45
Wakefield	3/11/51
Bank Hall	16/6/56
Blackpool	8/2/58
Speke Jct	21/3/64

Stored
9/12/35-19/12/35
11/9/39-18/9/39

Withdrawn w.e. 27/4/68

45201 at Crewe on 24 June 1961 still has the pre-1957 emblem on its welded tender even though it had completed two Heavy repairs in 1958 and January 1961. It was always domeless apart from one boiler change between 1944 and 1947. 45201 was a long time Central Division engine and was at Blackpool from February 1958 until moved to Speke Junction in March 1964. The large chalked train descriptions were for an express working to Birmingham. Photograph D. Forsyth, Colourrail.co.uk

45202

Built as 5202 at Armstrong Whitworth 21/10/35
Renumbered 45202 w.e. 11/12/48

Improvements and modifications

11/4/38	Removal of vacuum pump
25/4/39	Steam sanding
19/10/40	BTH speed indicator
31/8/55	Modification
28/4/62	Fitting BR ATC equipment

Repairs

4/1/37-3/2/37	LS
20/9/37-21/10/37	LO
5/2/38-11/4/38	LS
8/3/39-25/4/39	HG
27/9/40-19/10/40	LS
21/3/42-11/4/42	HS
28/2/43-19/3/43	HG
28/8/43-24/9/43	LO
28/3/44-27/4/44	LS
25/1/45-17/2/45	LS
6/12/45-5/1/46	LS
8/5/46-17/5/46	LO
5/9/47-7/11/47	HG
18/11/48-11/12/48	HO
22/11/49-20/12/49	LI
16/7/51-25/8/51	HG
21/9/53-15/10/53	HI
4/8/55-31/8/55	HG
10/5/57-11/6/57	HI
20/8/59-6/10/59	HG
3/3/60-11/4/60	NC(EO)
5/4/62-28/4/62	LI
22/6/65-10/7/65	HI
27/9/65-16/10/65	NC

Boilers

New	8982
25/4/39	8650 from 5111 (domed)
19/3/43	8908 from 5072
7/11/47	8935 from 5129
25/8/51	9037 from 5067
31/8/55	8949 from 45139
6/10/59	8671 from 45196 (domed)

Tenders

New	9306
13/6/64	10559

Mileage/(weekdays out of service)

1935	7,000 (24)
1936	45,994 (121)
1937	51,788 (96)
1938	57,967 (68)
1939	44,818 (90)
1940	44,109 (54)
1941	46,743 (40)+
1942	54,679 (51)
1943	52,308 (71)
1944	46,527 (74)
1945	43,547 (73)
1946	40,100 (60)
1947	28,147 (89)
1948	33,012 (47)
1949	34,056 (60)
1950	37,519 (52)
1951	35,269 (75)
1952	35,704 (43)
1953	25,606 (59)
1954	38,336 (52)
1955	31,263 (68)
1956	45,111 (43)
1957	38,718 (66)
1958	39,998 (42)
1959	35,580
1960	37,430

Mileage at 12/36: 52,994
Mileage at 31/12/50: 668,314

Sheds

Bank Hall	2/11/35
Southport	14/12/40
Bank Hall	9/12/44
Newton Heath	9/11/46

Stored

25/11/35-19/12/35
1/1/36-18/3/36
21/4/36-15/5/36
11/9/39-18/9/39

Withdrawn w.e. 29/6/68

5202 fresh out of the works after a Heavy General completed in April 1939 fitted with domed boiler no. 8650. This was originally built with a 14 element superheater at Vulcan Foundry and was rebuilt with a dome and 24 element superheater in 1938, after which it was fitted to 5111.

45203

Built as 5203 at Armstrong Whitworth 28/10/35
Renumbered 45203 w.e. 6/8/49

Improvements and modifications

19/9/38	Removal of vacuum pump
2/5/44	Steam sanding
15/11/55	Modification
6/3/62	Fitting BR ATC equipment

Repairs

2/3/37-19/3/37	HS
13/12/37-2/2/38	LO
30/8/38-19/9/38	LS
12/7/39	TRO
28/3/40-19/4/40	HG
4/12/41-27/12/41	HS
15/4/43-8/5/43	LS
12/4/44-2/5/44	HG
1/3/46-23/3/46	LS
16/10/47-6/12/47	HG
29/6/49-3/8/49	LI
12/9/51-18/10/51	HG
27/10/53-14/11/53	LI
5/1/54-28/1/54	NC
6/10/55-15/11/55	HG
7/3/56-21/3/56	LC(EO)
3/2/58-25/2/58	HI
29/5/58-14/6/58	LC(EO)
30/5/61-1/7/61	HG
20/2/62-6/3/62	NC
8/6/64-23/7/64	HI
27/6/66-31/8/66	LC

Boilers

New	8983
19/4/40	8836 from 5019
2/5/44	8835 from 5178
6/12/47	9019 from 5044
18/10/51	8985 from 45137
15/11/55	8674 from 45188 (domed)
30/6/61	9029 from 45035

Tenders

New	9307
14/11/53	9254
21/3/56	9289

Mileage/(weekdays out of service)

1935	7,781 (14)
1936	49,100 (117)
1937	61,755 (72)
1938	54,439 (101)
1939	53,180 (73)
1940	44,364 (54)
1941	34,465 (84)
1942	47,030 (24)
1943	49,699 (40)
1944	33,693 (54)
1945	36,923 (46)
1946	31,860 (75)
1947	28,197 (80)
1948	42,111 (28)
1949	34,229 (74)
1950	32,969 (61)
1951	32,539 (51)
1952	43,012 (42)
1953	34,125 (59)
1954	35,032 (52)
1955	33,683 (75)
1956	41,095 (56)
1957	36,589 (54)
1958	40,231 (62)
1959	34,271
1960	31,599

Mileage at 12/36: 56,881
Mileage at 31/12/50: 641,795

Sheds

Bank Hall	9/11/35
Southport	14/12/40
Newton Heath	9/10/43

Stored

9/12/35-19/12/35
1/1/36-18/3/36
17/4/36-15/5/36

Withdrawn w.e. 29/6/68

45203 pictured in the late 1950s had a domed boiler between November 1955 and June 1961. It was shedded at Newton Heath from 1943 until withdrawn in June 1968.

45204

Built as 5204 at Armstrong Whitworth 28/10/35
Renumbered 45204 w.e. 20/8/49

Improvements and modifications

11/5/39	Steam sanding
?	Removal of vacuum pump
25/1/61	Fitting BR ATC equipment

Repairs

7/4/37-7/5/37	HS
17/1/38-26/2/38	HS
17/4/39-11/5/39	HG
26/5/41-19/6/41	HS
1/9/42-19/9/42	HS
8/5/44-23/5/44	LS
17/9/45-29/9/45	HG
20/2/48-31/3/48	LS
12/4/48-13/4/48	NC
15/7/49-19/8/49	LI
8/6/50-28/6/50	HG
28/7/52-30/8/52	LI
11/10/54-13/11/54	HG
27/11/56-29/12/56	HI
16/9/57-5/10/57	LC(EO)
3/11/58-11/12/58	LI
7/12/60-25/1/61	HG
23/9/61-20/10/61	LC
19/8/63-13/9/63	LI
15/11/65-4/12/65	UNSCH

Boilers

New	8984
11/5/39	8964 from 5180
19/6/41	8661 from 5135 (domed)
29/9/45	8909 from 5191
28/6/50	8641 from 5195 (domed)
13/11/54	8954 from 45211
25/1/61	8672 from 45028 (domed)

Tenders

New	9308

Mileage/(weekdays out of service)

1935	7,951 (7)
1936	54,572 (63)
1937	41,654 (99)
1938	54,185 (79)
1939	43,109 (76)
1940	32,392 (44)
1941	32,203 (54)
1942	32,195 (53)
1943	32,378 (32)
1944	28,980 (63)
1945	30,033 (50)
1946	29,838 (68)
1947	23,705 (64)
1948	27,495 (83)
1949	24,697 (99)
1950	35,688 (71)
1951	28,867 (39)
1952	30,543 (58)
1953	30,322 (62)
1954	27,489 (70)
1955	33,262 (60)
1956	31,873 (66)
1957	36,539

Mileage at 12/36: 62,523
Mileage at 31/12/50: 531,075

Sheds

Wakefield	9/11/35
Farnley Jct	30/4/55
Neville Hill	1/3/64
Holbeck	6/9/64

Stored
11/9/39-18/9/39

Withdrawn 9/1/67

45204, ready to leave Skipton, received a domed boiler and AWS during a Heavy General completed on 25 January 1961. It was always shedded in the North East, at Wakefield from 1935, Farnley Junction from 1955, Neville Hill in March 1964 and finally Holbeck in September 1964 from where it was withdrawn in January 1967. Photograph www.transporttreasury.co.uk

45205

Built as 5205 at Armstrong Whitworth 28/10/35
Renumbered 45205 w.e. 19/6/48

Improvements and modifications

19/1/39	Steam sanding
19/1/39	Removal of vacuum pump
8/4/61	Fitting BR ATC equipment

Repairs

6/4/37-5/5/37	HS
11/10/37-19/11/37	HO
19/12/38-19/1/39	HG
25/6/40-9/7/40	LS
1/9/41-25/9/41	HS
3/3/43-23/3/43	HS
28/11/44-9/12/44	HG
27/9/46-7/11/46	LS
21/5/48-18/6/48	LS
19/7/49-31/8/49	HG
11/4/51-7/5/51	HI
22/9/52-25/10/52	HI
12/2/54-9/3/54	HG
8/10/56-31/10/56	LI
18/8/58-18/9/58	HG
27/5/59-25/7/59	LC(EO)
20/2/61-8/4/61	HI
6/12/62-5/1/63	LC
26/9/63-5/11/63	LI

Boilers

New	8985
19/1/39	9032 from 5102
25/9/41	9020 from 5001
9/12/44	8931 from 5081
31/8/49	8830 from 5094
9/3/54	8995 from 45093
18/9/58	8930 from 45186

Tenders

New	9309
29/1/52	9239

Mileage/(weekdays out of service)

1935	6,182 (19)
1936	50,042 (62)
1937	37,631 (129)
1938	49,657 (87)
1939	43,801 (71)
1940	28,763 (53)
1941	27,134 (56)
1942	31,755 (26)
1943	30,138 (33)
1944	31,850 (72)
1945	32,091 (54)
1946	29,587 (73)
1947	31,890 (80)
1948	30,459 (70)
1949	28,701 (81)
1950	38,508 (40)
1951	30,441 (77)
1952	34,685 (76)
1953	50,659 (64)
1954	45,540 (77)
1955	30,298 (73)
1956	30,840 (86)
1957	39,411 (58)
1958	37,323 (74)
1959	34,502
1960	37,787

Mileage at 12/36: 56,224
Mileage at 31/12/50: 528,189

Sheds

Wakefield	9/11/35
Accrington	15/9/51
Rose Grove	14/11/53
Newton Heath	12/2/66

Stored
11/9/39-18/9/39

Withdrawn w.e. 29/10/66

45205 on a local freight working at Stockport 3 July 1961, shortly after a Heavy Intermediate repair during which it received AWS equipment. It was always domeless and was allocated to Rose Grove from November 1953 until moved to its final shed, Newton Heath, in February 1966. Photograph D. Forsyth, Colourrail.co.uk

45206

Built as 5206 at Armstrong Whitworth 5/11/35
Renumbered 45206 w.e. 13/8/49

Improvements and modifications

2/6/38	Removal of vacuum pump
8/8/39	BTH speed indicator
28/6/45	Steam sanding
17/11/61	Fitting BR ATC equipment

Repairs

21/11/36-14/12/36	LO
24/5/37-10/6/37	HS
20/4/38-2/6/38	HG
20/7/39-8/8/39	HS
19/9/40-18/10/40	HG
20/11/42-9/1/43	HS
15/7/44-29/7/44	LS
11/6/45-28/6/45	HG
12/8/47-4/10/47	HS
8/7/49-12/8/49	LI
11/5/50-1/6/50	LC
23/11/50-6/1/51	HG
11/11/52-2/12/52	LI
21/5/54-24/6/54	HI
19/5/56-22/6/56	HG
15/9/58-15/10/58	LI
18/1/61-11/2/61	LI
7/11/61-17/11/61	NC
18/2/63-15/3/63	HG
30/9/65-6/11/65	LI

Boilers

New	8986
17/5/38	8656 from 5039 (domed)
18/10/40	8639 from 5052 (domed)
28/6/45	9038 from 5094
6/1/51	8914 from 45217
22/6/56	8662 from 45131 (domed)
15/3/63	8683

Tenders

New	9310
?	10470

Mileage/(weekdays out of service)

1935	4,090 (24)
1936	42,643 (115)
1937	58,720 (41)
1938	51,724 (62)
1939	46,483 (54)
1940	26,005 (73)
1941	33,612 (34)
1942	25,045 (78)
1943	36,121 (26)
1944	29,076 (69)
1945	26,175 (62)
1946	21,616 (49)
1947	21,653 (110)
1948	33,308 (41)
1949	33,654 (74)
1950	26,293 (92)
1951	40,133 (40)
1952	34,355 (57)
1953	30,403 (53)
1954	29,712 (70)
1955	29,482 (66)
1956	30,584 (70)
1957	32,425 (60)
1958	27,815 (71)
1959	32,584
1960	28,164

Mileage at 12/36: 46,733
Mileage at 31/12/50: 516,198

Sheds

Low Moor	9/11/35
Wakefield	@14/12/36
Accrington	15/9/51
Fleetwood	16/8/52
Newton Heath	10/7/65
Carnforth	6/7/68

Stored

24/11/35-19/12/35
1/1/36-16/3/36
2/11/36-9/11/36
11/9/39-18/9/39
30/5/66-1/9/67

Withdrawn w.e. 3/8/68

Fleetwood's 45206 on 13 May 1960 at Stockport still has the early BR crest on its original welded tender. It is carrying its third domed boiler, fitted in June 1956, and reverted to a domeless example in 1963. It was always on the old Central Division, apart from the last month before withdrawal at the end of BR steam in August 1968. Photograph D. Forsyth, Paul Chancellor Collection.

45207

Built as 5207 at Armstrong Whitworth 5/11/35
Renumbered 45207 w.e. 4/12/48

Improvements and modifications

14/8/39	BTH speed indicator
14/8/39	Steam sanding
?	Removal of vacuum pump
1/3/56	Modernisation
?	Fitting BR ATC equipment

Repairs

16/2/37-11/3/37	HS
2/2/38-12/3/38	HS
17/8/38-13/9/38	LC
7/3/39-8/3/39	LO
26/6/39-14/8/39	HG
25/2/41-18/3/41	LS
27/11/42-2/1/43	HG
14/2/44-10/3/44	LS
12/9/44-16/9/44	LO
8/8/45-31/8/45	LS
19/3/47-28/4/47	HG
1/11/48-30/11/48	HS
25/4/50-11/5/50	LI
31/10/50-1/11/50	Weighing Only
24/11/50-28/11/50	Weighing Only
5/11/51-13/12/51	HG
15/10/53-5/11/53	HI
19/1/56-1/3/56	HG
21/4/58-15/5/58	LI
4/11/60-12/11/60	NC(EO)
7/10/61-9/11/61	GEN
7/10/65-6/11/65	INT

Boilers

New	8987
14/8/39	8906 from 5126
2/1/43	9002 from 5193
28/4/47	8963 from 5130
13/12/51	8942 from 45035
1/3/56	8649 from 45182 (domed)
9/11/61	8654 from 45199 (domed)

Tenders

New	9311

Mileage/(weekdays out of service)

1935	4,089 (23)
1936	46,636 (99)
1937	56,518 (54)
1938	47,795 (91)
1939	42,001 (85)
1940	41,422 (37)
1941	39,408 (43)
1942	32,901 (57)
1943	45,813 (40)
1944	39,091 (72)
1945	35,100 (68)
1946	35,531 (41)
1947	40,916 (80)
1948	33,984 (89)
1949	45,173 (51)
1950	40,854 (72)
1951	29,504 (63)
1952	49,954 (42)
1953	33,315 (65)
1954	40,458 (43)
1955	25,428 (75)
1956	40,964 (62)
1957	39,500

Mileage at 12/36: 50,716
Mileage at 31/12/50: 627,223

Sheds

Low Moor	9/11/35
Mirfield	20/8/61
Wakefield	20/5/62
Low Moor	17/6/62
Royston	8/9/63

Stored
24/11/35-19/12/35
1/1/36-27/3/36

Withdrawn w.e. 11/9/66

45207 at its home depot of Low Moor on 13 July 1952, where it had been shedded since delivery in 1935. It was one of several Central Division engines stored in the first year of delivery and was out of traffic for almost four months only three weeks after it arrived from Armstrong Whitworth. 45207 kept its original welded tender throughout and was domeless until March 1956.

45208

Built as 5208 at Armstrong Whitworth 5/11/35
Renumbered 45208 w.e. 6/11/48

Improvements and modifications

?	Steam sanding
?	Removal of vacuum pump
31/10/56	Modification
7/2/61	Fitting BR ATC equipment

Repairs

23/2/37-12/3/37	HS
29/11/37-23/12/37	LS
6/12/38-13/1/39	HG
1/6/40-18/6/40	LS
5/10/41-7/10/41	TRO
27/12/41-16/1/42	HG
16/8/43-31/8/43	LS
24/5/45-7/6/45	HG
6/3/47-29/3/47	HS
28/11/47-13/12/47	LO
18/9/48-1/11/48	HG
25/4/50-16/5/50	LI
18/6/51-9/7/51	LI
2/12/52-24/12/52	HG
23/10/54-19/11/54	LI
19/9/56-31/10/56	HG
22/10/59-5/12/59	LI
19/1/61-7/2/61	NC(EO)
6/1/62-15/2/62	GEN
29/1/66	NC

Boilers

New	8988
13/1/39	9055 from 5070
11/1/42	8951 from 5086
7/6/43	9039 from 5107
1/11/48	8974 from 5219
24/12/52	9051 from 45015
31/10/56	8914 from 45206
15/2/62	9050

Tenders

New	9312

Mileage/(weekdays out of service)

1935	4,260 (18)
1936	47,106 (100)
1937	50,532 (80)
1938	53,859 (61)
1939	33,832 (127)
1940	39,825 (47)
1941	33,869 (48)
1942	36,609 (41)
1943	43,454 (50)
1944	38,767 (66)
1945	40,399 (52)
1946	34,940 (53)
1947	39,328 (97)
1948	24,077 (84)
1949	51,013 (46)
1950	44,159 (72)
1951	38,212 (49)
1952	34,088 (58)
1953	53,012 (47)
1954	33,604 (88)
1955	43,788 (49)
1956	31,944 (70)
1957	48,551

Mileage at 12/36: 51,366
Mileage at 31/12/50: 616,029

Sheds

Low Moor	9/11/35
Mirfield	20/8/61
Wakefield	20/5/62
Low Moor	17/6/62
Mirfield	12/4/64
Low Moor	13/11/66

Stored

3/12/35-19/12/35
1/1/36-16/3/36
11/5/36-27/5/36
23/1/39-20/3/39
27/3/39-6/4/39
17/4/39-5/5/39
8/5/39-22/5/39

Withdrawn 1/10/67

45208, with domed boiler, departs from Wigan Wallgate with a Southport-Manchester Victoria train. All the recorded boilers on the History Card for this locomotive were 21 element domeless. The Engine Record Card was however marked to show a 24 element, i.e. domed boiler, fitted sometime in the 1950s, although the boiler numbers written alongside are the same domeless ones as on the History Card. 45208 was shedded at Low Moor from 1935 to 1961 and the shedplate is clearly 25F which was changed to 56F in September 1956. Hence the photograph is prior to that. Best guess, maybe, is that the wrong boiler number has been recorded on the History Card at the 24/12/52 change. The human touch! Photograph D.J. Greenwood.

45209

Built as 5209 at Armstrong Whitworth 4/11/35
Renumbered 45209 w.e. 21/5/49

Improvements and modifications

18/5/39	Steam sanding
?	Removal of vacuum pump
3/3/61	Fitting BR ATC equipment

Repairs

13/1/36-13/2/36	LO
27/1/37-12/2/37	LS
28/9/37-29/10/37	HS
24/4/39-18/5/39	HG
20/8/40-7/9/40	LS
26/9/41-18/10/41	HS
1/7/43-14/8/43	HG
4/11/44-18/11/44	LS
4/6/46-22/6/46	LS
16/8/47-23/10/47	HG
30/4/49-31/5/49	LI
8/5/51-1/6/51	LI
30/8/51-30/8/51	LC(TO)
12/5/52-5/7/52	HG
7/7/54-17/8/54	HI
6/9/56-11/10/56	HG
4/2/59-12/3/59	LI
31/7/59-24/8/59	LC(EO)
19/1/60-24/3/60	LC
17/2/61-3/3/61	NC(EO)
18/1/62-17/2/62	HG
1/6/65-28/6/65	LI

Boilers

New	8989
18/5/39	8992 from 5212
14/8/43	9023 from 5050
28/10/47	8677 from 5188 (domed)
5/7/52	8970 from 45076
11/10/56	8646 from 45062 (domed)
17/2/62	9037

Tenders

New	9313

Mileage/(weekdays out of service)

1935	5,605 (13)
1936	55,583 (58)
1937	51,039 (84)
1938	54,026 (52)
1939	43,039 (81)
1940	37,293 (55)
1941	32,602 (55)
1942	41,613 (39)
1943	33,090 (84)
1944	47,508 (44)
1945	40,558 (45)
1946	46,447 (39)
1947	29,343 (98)
1948	48,849 (56)
1949	35,102 (74)
1950	29,847 (68)
1951	34,704 (73)
1952	40,414 (83)
1953	43,136 (50)
1954	39,740 (65)
1955	30,979 (66)
1956	28,615 (70)
1957	39,436 (49)
1958	45,303 (43)
1959	39,093
1960	34,407

Mileage at 12/36: 61,188
Mileage at 31/12/50: 636,144

Sheds

Low Moor	9/11/35
Bank Hall	15/5/48
Southport	30/10/48
Wakefield	1/1/49
Accrington	15/9/51
Rose Grove	6/9/52
Accrington	12/9/53
Rose Grove	14/11/53
Hellifield	2/2/63
Carnforth	22/6/63
Lancaster	7/12/63
Carnforth	18/4/64

Stored
2/12/35-16/12/35
11/9/39-18/9/39
19/4/66-15/6/67

Withdrawn w.e. 29/6/68

45209 poses in the spring sunshine at Stockport on 27 May 1960. It was shedded at 24B Rose Grove from November 1953 until sent to Hellifield in February 1963. The domed boiler, which was fitted in October 1956, has blanking plates on the firebox shoulders indicating it is a 24 element rebuilt type. 45209 has the pre-1957 BR crest on its original welded tender. Photograph D. Forsyth, Colourrail.co.uk

45210

Built as 5210 at Armstrong Whitworth 12/11/35
Renumbered 45210 w.e. 20/11/48

Improvements and modifications

7/10/39	BTH speed indicator
?	Removal of vacuum pump
16/6/45	Steam sanding
20/10/61	Fitting BR ATC equipment

Repairs

1/12/36-23/12/36	LS
1/9/37-12/10/37	LO
11/2/38-12/4/38	HG
28/8/39-21/9/39	LS
3/1/41-21/2/41	HG
12/8/41-30/8/41	LO
11/3/42-4/4/42	HS
6/3/43-27/3/43	LS
6/9/44-20/9/44	LS
3/5/45-16/6/45	HG
16/7/47-22/8/47	HS
18/10/48-19/11/48	HO
24/8/49-21/9/49	LO
2/12/49-24/12/49	HG
28/2/50-9/3/50	NC
8/6/51-4/7/51	LI
27/8/51-30/8/51	Weighing Only
7/5/53-6/6/53	HI
16/6/55-23/7/55	HG
26/10/56-14/11/56	LI
14/4/58-10/5/58	HI
16/7/59-27/8/59	HG
15/7/60-2/9/60	LI
3/10/61-20/10/61	NC(EO)

Boilers

New	8990
21/2/41	8642 from 5056 (domed)
16/6/45	9058 from 5196
24/12/49	9047 from 5113
23/7/55	8928 from 45088
27/8/59	9002 from 45017

Tenders

New	9314
16/6/45	9233

Mileage/(weekdays out of service)

1935	5,333 (3)
1936	51,409 (81)
1937	48,337 (74)
1938	46,903 (97)
1939	41,744 (84)
1940	37,752 (29)
1941	36,428 (84)
1942	42,690 (46)
1943	42,530 (62)
1944	33,979 (42)
1945	40,985 (74)
1946	28,131 (90)
1947	28,434 (84)
1948	28,559 (86)
1949	32,808 (106)
1950	41,248 (36)
1951	35,357 (46)
1952	31,413 (40)
1953	33,697 (55)
1954	35,490 (48)
1955	32,787 (72)
1956	40,716 (44)
1957	51,836 (27)
1958	50,941 (50)
1959	44,839
1960	46,436

Mileage at 12/36: 56,742
Mileage at 31/12/50: 587,270

Sheds

Low Moor	16/11/35
Newton Heath	13/5/50
Huddersfield	21/10/50 (loan)
Low Moor	9/12/50
Farnley Jcn	12/4/52 (loan)
Low Moor	17/5/52
Bank Hall	8/9/56
Aintree	17/3/62
Carlisle Kingmoor	11/5/63
Blackpool	1/8/64
Lancaster	15/8/64
Rose Grove	21/11/64
Carlisle Kingmoor	7/8/65

Stored
20/4/36-22/12/36
28/11/38-22/12/38
2/1/39-6/2/39

Withdrawn w.e. 2/4/66

45210, under the coaling stage at Willesden on 28 April 1962, was from 27B Aintree where it had been transferred the previous month from Bank Hall. The AWS was fitted in November 1961 but the domed boiler was not recorded on its Engine History Card. Photograph www.rail-online.co.uk

45211

Built as 5211 at Armstrong Whitworth 11/11/35
Renumbered 45211 w.e. 4/6/49

Improvements and modifications

?	Removal of vacuum pump
29/3/44	Steam sanding
26/11/60	Fitting BR ATC equipment

Repairs

20/1/37-8/2/37	LS
2/9/37-16/9/37	LO
4/3/38-21/4/38	HG
11/3/39-12/4/39	LS
20/2/40-20/3/40	HG
30/8/41-20/9/41	HS
29/10/42-28/11/42	LS
6/3/44-29/3/44	HG
8/10/45-26/10/45	HS
12/6/47-28/7/47	LS
19/4/49-3/6/49	HG
19/6/50-25/7/50	LI
7/4/52-3/6/52	HI
7/1/53-4/2/53	HC
12/5/54-21/6/54	HG
20/4/55-18/5/55	LC(EO)
5/6/56-2/7/56	LI
2/5/58-28/5/58	LI
2/5/60-10/6/60	HG
17/11/60-26/11/60	NC(EO)
6/1/62-7/2/62	LC
6/12/64-9/1/65	INT

Boilers

New	8991
20/3/40	8671 from 5041 (domed)
29/3/44	8905 from 5111
3/6/49	8954 from 5055
21/6/54	9040 from 45180
10/6/60	8996 from 45147

Tenders

New	9315
28/11/42	9305

Mileage/(weekdays out of service)

1935	6,751 (3)
1936	56,635 (43)
1937	53,784 (79)
1938	60,817 (68)
1939	50,656 (62)
1940	40,397 (49)
1941	30,029 (72)
1942	40,422 (47)
1943	48,460 (37)
1944	41,146 (78)
1945	40,681 (57)
1946	41,819 (29)
1947	36,889 (66)
1948	26,694 (80)
1949	42,910 (79)
1950	40,989 (84)
1951	37,128 (50)
1952	31,640 (49)
1953	34,074 (63)
1954	38,630 (76)
1955	31,148 (97)
1956	38,022 (62)
1957	35,730

Mileage at 12/36: 63,386
Mileage at 31/12/50: 659,079

Sheds

Low Moor	16/11/35
Bank Hall	13/5/50
Newton Heath	28/10/50
Farnley Jct	9/12/50
Holbeck	12/1/64
Stourton	2/10/66
Holbeck	15/1/67

Withdrawn 17/5/67

45211 pictured at Ashton, probably during 1960, was at 55C Farnley Junction from 1950 until transferred to Holbeck in January 1964. It was always domeless apart from 1940-44 and received AWS in November 1960.

45212

Built as 5212 at Armstrong Whitworth 12/11/35
Renumbered 45212 w.e. 9/10/48

Improvements and modifications

10/3/39	Steam sanding
10/3/39	Removal of vacuum pump
16/6/54	Modernisation
19/1/62	Fitting BR ATC equipment

Repairs

8/1/37-28/1/37	LS
23/8/37-15/9/37	LO
16/12/37-7/1/38	LS
12/4/38-27/4/38	LO
6/2/39-10/3/39	HG
24/7/40-13/8/40	LS
6/6/42-26/6/42	HS
22/11/43-8/12/43	HG
7/7/45-11/8/45	LS
12/6/47-2/8/47	HS
20/9/48-8/10/48	LO
10/6/49-30/7/49	HG
19/12/51-15/1/52	LI
17/5/54-16/6/54	HG
24/1/56-18/2/56	LI
18/8/58-18/9/58	HI
9/9/59-30/10/59	HC(EO)
1/5/61-23/5/61	LC(EO)
4/1/62-19/1/62	NC
2/11/62-30/11/62	HI
7/1/63-26/1/63	LC
20/12/65-29/1/66	HI

Boilers

New	8992
15/3/39	8678 from 5061 (domed)
8/12/43	9025 from 5045
30/7/49	8998 from 5091
16/6/54	8666 from 45185 (domed)
?	9010
?	8682 (domed)

Tenders

New	9316

Mileage/(weekdays out of service)

1935	5,650 (4)
1936	56,484 (40)
1937	50,390 (69)
1938	56,422 (55)
1939	36,932 (112)
1940	35,327 (48)
1941	34,506 (28)
1942	42,308 (48)
1943	31,879 (65)
1944	46,909 (49)
1945	32,497 (90)
1946	33,367 (70)
1947	24,983 (79)
1948	27,292 (75)
1949	25,036 (76)
1950	31,308 (33)
1951	26,034 (47)
1952	31,049 (54)
1953	26,529 (84)
1954	28,276 (71)
1955	32,131 (56)
1956	30,846 (63)
1957	31,880 (46)
1958	25,603 (93)
1959	26,904
1960	25,648

Mileage at 12/36: 62,134
Mileage at 31/12/50: 571,287

Sheds

Low Moor	16/11/35
Fleetwood	29/11/47
Carnforth	3/10/64
Speke Jct	6/3/65
Carnforth	26/6/65
Carlisle Kingmoor	25/9/65
Lostock Hall	6/1/68

Stored

27/3/39-6/4/39
17/4/39-5/5/39
8/5/39-22/5/39
15/3/67-17/5/67

Withdrawn w.e. 3/8/68

On ex-LNER territory at Bridlington 45212 with an excursion train of LMS stock on 12 February 1959. It was at 24F Fleetwood from November 1947 until moved to Carnforth in October 1964. It had a domed boiler from June 1956 and was a late recipient of AWS in January 1962. 45212 survived until the bitter end of BR steam, working one of the last two steam hauled service trains before being preserved. Photograph N. Skinner.

45213

Built as 5213 at Armstrong Whitworth 18/11/35
Renumbered 45213 w.e. 3/4/48

Improvements and modifications

?	Removal of vacuum pump
3/10/40	BTH speed indicator
12/7/47	Steam sanding
?	Fitting BR ATC equipment

Repairs

13/1/36-27/2/36	LO
22/6/36-5/8/36	LO
5/1/38-7/2/38	HG
15/5/39-27/5/39	LS
10/9/40-3/10/40	HG
15/5/42-6/6/42	HS
25/4/43-15/5/43	LS
22/3/44-15/4/44	LS
28/10/44-15/11/44	LO
10/12/45-19/1/46	HG
3/2/47-11/3/47	LS
25/2/48-3/4/48	LS
22/7/48-18/9/48	LO
24/8/49-8/10/49	G
11/1/51-21/2/51	LI
1/5/51-3/5/51	NC
14/8/51-6/9/51	LC
28/11/51-8/12/51	LC(EO)
19/12/51	LC(TO)
7/8/52-26/9/52	LI
20/4/53-30/5/53	G
15/6/53-20/6/53	NC(EO)
21/7/54-1/9/54	HI
25/1/56-17/2/56	HI
5/7/56-10/8/56	LC(EO)
31/12/56-12/1/57	LC(EO)
15/6/57-11/7/57	G
20/9/58-4/10/58	LC
14/7/59-20/8/59	HI
29/7/61-9/9/61	LI
6/4/62-16/4/62	LC(EO)
31/8/63-7/12/63	G
13/3/64-10/4/64	LC
14/8/64-11/9/64	NC
18/12/64-23/12/64	NC

Boilers

New	8993
21/1/38	9203 from 5093
3/10/40	8916 from 5029
19/1/46	8828 from 5006
8/10/49	9021 from 5175

Tenders

New	9317
?	9601
30/5/53	10684 (part-welded)
17/2/56	10685 (part-welded)
10/8/56	9545
11/7/57	9487
11/4/64	9285
2/12/64	10510

Mileage/(weekdays out of service)

1935	7,105 (2)
1936	43,847 (122)
1937	55,637 (89)
1938	60,362 (72)
1939	50,878 (80)
1940	41,553 (79)
1941	39,242 (28)
1942	43,787 (45)
1943	50,177 (81)
1944	41,165 (76)
1945	35,627 (93)
1946	47,457 (60)
1947	53,664 (76)
1948	40,114 (117)
1949	47,785 (74)
1950	55,998 (21)

Mileage at 12/36: 50,952
Mileage at 31/12/50: 714,398

Sheds

Bank Hall	23/11/35
Rose Grove	14/12/40
Low Moor	18/10/41
Perth	22/11/43
Inverness	29/1/44
Polmadie	1/7/44
Perth	27/7/46
Stirling	6/8/55 (PE)
Ayr	11/6/66 (PE)
Motherwell	5/10/66

Withdrawn 31/12/66

45213 on 11 August 1951 with a long freight at Newtonmore, south of Aviemore. It was shedded at Perth from July 1946 until transferred to Stirling in 1955. It has a domeless boiler, large cab numbers and brackets under the bufferbeam and holes in it for attaching a snowplough. Photograph www.rail-online.co.uk

45214

Built as 5214 at Armstrong Whitworth 18/11/35
Renumbered 45214 w.e. 2/10/48

Improvements and modifications

27/7/38	Removal of vacuum pump
?	Steam sanding
2/6/61	Sloping throatplate boiler
?	Fitting BR ATC equipment

Repairs

12/8/37-23/9/37	HO
20/6/38-27/7/38	HG
1/2/40-16/2/40	LS
21/2/41-25/3/41	HG
4/11/41-15/11/41	LO
11/1/43-6/2/43	HS
19/8/44-8/9/44	LS
24/5/45-6/6/45	LO
17/7/45-4/8/45	LO
13/4/46-7/5/46	HG
21/4/47-17/3/47	LO
3/9/48-29/9/48	LS
29/3/50-21/4/50	HI
21/5/51-19/6/51	HG
11/9/52-19/9/52	NC(EO)
6/10/52-8/11/52	HI
21/11/53	NC(EO)
4/2/54-26/2/54	HI
7/6/54-22/6/54	LC(EO)
14/9/54-23/9/54	LC(EO)
21/1/56-3/3/56	G
31/8/57-21/9/57	HI
25/11/58-3/12/58	LC(EO)
9/5/59-28/5/59	LI
19/5/60-4/6/60	LC
29/4/61-2/6/61	G
6/4/63-25/5/63	HI
5/2/65-9/3/65	LI
28/10/65-13/11/65	NC

Boilers

New	8994
12/7/38	9054 from 5124
25/3/41	9026 from 5100
7/5/46	8979 from 5186
19/6/51	8647 from 45039 (domed)
2/6/61	? (sloping throatplate)

Tenders

New	9318
6/2/43	9187 (riveted)
?	9190 (riveted)
26/2/54	9823
23/4/55	9107 (riveted)
3/3/56	9636
21/9/57	10618 (part-welded)
22/11/65	10510

Mileage/(weekdays out of service)

1935	7,003 (3)
1936	56,238 (69)
1937	53,998 (97)
1938	59,498 (89)
1939	57,822 (55)
1940	45,989 (50)
1941	27,008 (68)
1942	46,504 (28)
1943	43,015 (71)
1944	35,933 (55)
1945	35,811 (57)
1946	42,807 (46)
1947	31,582 (95)
1948	27,354 (80)
1949	29,450 (50)
1950	31,222 (56)

Mileage at 12/36: 63,241
Mileage at 31/12/50: 631,234

Sheds

Bank Hall	23/11/35
Rose Grove	14/12/40
Low Moor	18/10/41
Fleetwood	29/11/47
Blackpool	10/6/50
Fleetwood	14/10/50
Eastfield	8/9/51 (loan)
Eastfield	15/9/51
St Rollox	25/12/54 (PE)
Stirlling	19/9/55
Corkerhill	9/4/66 (PE)

Withdrawn 31/12/66

Pictured on 10 April 1954 at Eastfield, 45214 was allocated there from September 1951 until December 1954. The domed 24 element superheater boiler, its first, was fitted in June 1951. As with many of its shedmates it has large cab numbers and fittings for a bufferbeam mounted snowplough.

45215

Built as 5215 at Armstrong Whitworth 19/11/35
Renumbered 45215 w.e. 30/10/48

Improvements and modifications

24/5/38	Removal of vacuum pump
17/7/45	Steam sanding
23/11/54	Modernisation
29/12/61	Smith-Stone speed indicator

Repairs

21/10/36-24/11/36	LS
2/9/37-1/10/37	HS
3/1/38-21/1/38	LO
23/3/38-24/5/38	HG
21/11/39-5/12/39	LS
19/1/41-8/2/41	HG
9/5/42-12/6/42	HS
15/7/43-7/8/43	LO
1/1/44-20/1/44	LS
22/6/45-17/7/45	HG
25/6/47-15/8/47	LS
24/2/48-5/4/48	HO
5/10/48-29/10/48	LS
3/10/49-18/11/49	HG
20/6/51-27/7/51	LI
18/2/53-11/3/53	LI
15/10/54-23/11/54	HG
5/1/57-30/1/57	LI
1/6/59-27/6/59	HI
24/6/60-20/8/60	LC(EO)
25/11/61-29/12/61	HG
25/4/63-22/5/63	LC
13/10/64-28/11/64	LI

Boilers

New	8995
10/5/38	8960 from 5180
8/2/41	8915 from 5005
17/7/45	8642 from 5210 (domed)
18/11/49	9027 from 5065
23/11/54	9007 from 45147
29/12/61	8931 from 45105

Tenders

New	9319
18/7/65	10735

Mileage/(weekdays out of service)

1935	4,284 (10)
1936	57,298 (70)
1937	55,399 (85)
1938	50,020 (112)
1939	53,264 (71)
1940	42,259 (44)
1941	30,756 (80)
1942	33,097 (57)
1943	32,423 (66)
1944	37,544 (42)
1945	33,441 (63)
1946	42,371 (49)
1947	24,780 (77)
1948	31,987 (78)
1949	32,691 (79)
1950	36,674 (27)
1951	29,480 (59)
1952	36,962 (36)
1953	34,508 (78)
1954	31,739 (78)
1955	41,176 (41)
1956	43,748 (34)
1957	45,994
1958	28,620 (80)
1959	28,894
1960	31,329

Mileage at 12/36: 61,582
Mileage at 31/12/50: 598,288

Sheds

Bank Hall	23/11/35
Aintree	14/12/40
Agecroft	8/3/41
Bank Hall	11/5/46
Huddersfield	12/10/46
Sheffield	8/7/50 (loan)
Huddersfield	5/8/50
Leicester Central	8/11/58
Neasden	21/2/59
Annesley	18/6/60
Rose Grove	3/7/65 (loan)
Rose Grove	24/7/65

Withdrawn w.e. 7/10/67

One of Annesley's allocation 45215 in June 1961 before fitting with a Smith-Stone speed indicator in December of that year. It always had a domeless boiler except from 1945-49.

45216

Built as 5216 at Armstrong Whitworth 25/11/35
Renumbered 45216 w.e. 25/9/48

Improvements and modifications

?	Removal of vacuum pump
21/1/47	Steam sanding
15/2/61	Fitting BR ATC equipment

Repairs

21/1/37-8/2/37	LS
12/4/37-24/5/37	LO
29/8/38-4/10/38	HG
1/4/40-17/4/40	LS
27/9/41-22/10/41	HG
28/6/43-20/7/43	LS
24/2/45-24/3/45	LS
16/10/45-24/11/45	LO
6/1/47-21/1/47	HG
31/8/48-25/9/48	HS
20/1/50-9/2/50	HI
27/8/51-6/10/51	HG
11/12/52-2/1/53	HI
25/5/54-15/6/54	LI
21/11/55-17/12/55	HG
30/10/56-7/12/56	LC(EO)
10/12/57-4/1/58	HI
23/12/58-23/1/59	LI(EO)
29/8/59-30/10/59	LC(EO)
9/1/61-15/2/61	LI

Boilers

New	8996
4/10/38	8930 from 5150
22/10/41	8978 from 5034
21/1/47	8827 from 5010
6/10/51	8669 from 45088 (domed)
17/12/55	8964 from 45043

Tenders

New	9320
17/3/52	9246
23/1/59	9000 (prototype)
15/2/61	9557

Mileage/(weekdays out of service)

1935	4,520 (2)
1936	64,524 (48)
1937	51,244 (102)
1938	59,205 (73)
1939	55,991 (67)
1940	43,933 (63)
1941	20,585 (74)
1942	33,532 (26)
1943	36,698 (57)
1944	32,610 (25)
1945	27,198 (94)
1946	41,298 (81)
1947	44,689 (58)
1948	46,313 (56)
1949	54,934 (35)
1950	49,031 (62)
1951	41,279 (64)
1952	51,000 (54)
1953	45,896 (56)
1954	46,683 (42)
1955	42,540 (85)
1956	49,940 (59)
1957	47,639 (40)
1958	50,616 (55)
1959	45,495
1960	26,877

Mileage at 12/36: 69,044
Mileage at 31/12/50: 666,275

Sheds

Bank Hall	30/11/35
Southport	10/10/36
Bank Hall	7/11/36
Aintree	14/12/40
Agecroft	25/1/41
Bank Hall	11/5/46
Blackpool	7/6/47 (loan)
Bank Hall	28/6/47
Newton Heath	17/2/51
Bank Hall	21/4/51
Southern Region	23/3/53 (loan)
Bank Hall	27/6/53
Rose Grove	23/1/60

Withdrawn w.e. 12/2/66

45216, pictured on 5 March 1960 at Stockport Edgeley, had the Stanier prototype tender no.9000 from January 1959 until February 1961. It had been domeless since December 1955 and was not fitted with AWS until the following February. It had been shedded at Bank Hall from 1941 and was one of the engines loaned to the Southern Region in 1953; it had recently been transferred in January to its final shed, Rose Grove. Photograph D. Forsyth, Colourrail.co.uk

45217

Built as 5217 at Armstrong Whitworth 25/11/35
Renumbered 45217 w.e. 29/5/48

Improvements and modifications

21/3/39	Steam sanding
21/3/39	Removal of vacuum pump
15/3/57	Modification
30/3/61	Smith-Stone speed indicator
18/1/63	Fitting BR ATC equipment

Repairs

21/11/36-15/12/36	LS
31/5/37-28/6/37	LO
30/11/37-22/12/37	LS
22/2/39-21/3/39	HG
17/6/40-2/7/40	LS
16/9/42-1/10/42	HG
7/2/44-26/2/44	HG
1/1/46-26/1/46	LS
14/6/46-2/7/46	LO
7/10/47-25/11/47	HG
12/3/49-2/4/49	HI
6/9/50-24/10/50	HG
9/4/52-3/5/52	HI
21/1/53-12/3/53	HG
6/8/53-4/9/53	LC(EO)
20/9/54-22/10/54	LI
28/1/56-21/2/56	LI
18/2/57-15/3/57	HG
18/5/58-24/6/58	LC(EO)
29/6/59-12/8/59	HI
31/1/61-30/3/61	HG
20/12/62-18/1/63	LC
23/3/64-4/8/64	INT

Boilers

New	8997
21/3/39	9018 from 5088
26/2/44	8668 from 5188 (domed)
25/11/47	8914 from 5075
24/10/50	8833 from 5150
12/3/53	8974 from 45208
15/3/57	9008 from 45110
30/3/61	9038 from 45003

Tenders

New	9321
8/8/64	10538 (part-welded)

Mileage/(weekdays out of service)

1935	5,556 (3)
1936	63,198 (66)
1937	56,168 (90)
1938	65,990 (51)
1939	55,090 (69)
1940	45,568 (67)
1941	16,907 (189)
1942	31,850 (58)
1943	44,197 (23)
1944	34,143 (83)
1945	29,556 (53)
1946	36,138 (87)
1947	39,774 (84)
1948	57,015 (48)
1949	49,143 (69)
1950	44,270 (63)
1951	50,165 (55)
1952	37,891 (77)
1953	34,964 (116)
1954	33,722 (64)
1955	31,841 (64)
1956	40,251 (47)
1957	44,429 (48)
1958	40,723 (74)
1959	42,652
1960	44,742

Mileage at 12/36: 68,754
Mileage at 31/12/50: 674,563

Sheds

Bank Hall	30/11/35
Newton Heath	14/12/40
Agecroft	14/2/42
Fleetwood	28/10/44
Bank Hall	11/5/46
Blackpool	10/5/47 (loan)
Bank Hall	31/5/47
Crewe North	11/2/50 (loan)
Crewe North	11/11/50
Brunswick	24/3/51
Annesley	25/6/60
Carlisle Kingmoor	25/5/63

Withdrawn w.e. 26/11/66

Several Class Fives saw out the ex-Great Central line including 45217 which was at Annesley from June 1960 until May 1963. It was photographed at Rickmansworth on 7 September 1961, having recently been fitted with a Smith-Stone speed indicator in April, like some others in the Annesley allocation. It has its original welded tender which it kept until replaced by a part-welded example in 1964 and a domeless boiler.

45218

Built as 5218 at Armstrong Whitworth 26/11/35
Renumbered 45218 w.e. 3/7/48

Improvements and modifications

21/3/42	Removal of vacuum pump
6/3/45	Steam sanding
?	Fitting BR ATC equipment

Repairs

22/2/37-16/3/37	HS
14/2/38-9/4/38	HG
28/3/39-7/4/39	LO
30/6/39-8/9/39	LS
19/12/40-31/1/41	HG
27/6/42-18/7/42	HS
18/12/43-8/1/44	LS
12/2/45-6/3/45	HG
7/12/46-11/1/47	LS
7/6/48-3/7/48	HS
31/10/49-17/12/49	HG
26/9/51-27/10/51	LI
3/11/51-8/11/51	NC(Rect)EO
27/7/53-26/8/53	LI
31/8/53-5/9/53	NC(Rect)EO
24/9/55-22/10/55	HG
13/9/57-9/10/57	HI
13/6/58-1/7/58	LC(EO)
6/4/59-28/5/59	LC(EO)
29/4/60-9/6/60	LI
12/6/61-7/8/61	HG
17/7/63-9/8/63	LI

Boilers

New	8998
31/1/41	8993 from 5192
6/3/45	8910 from 5112
17/12/49	9045 from 5074
22/10/55	9006 from 45105
7/8/61	8948 from 45039

Tenders

New	9322
28/4/49	9290
6/6/61	10709 (part-welded)

Mileage/(weekdays out of service)

1935	5,033 (3)
1936	64,132 (49)
1937	59,913 (70)
1938	56,202 (89)
1939	42,659 (100)
1940	30,598 (88)
1941	32,799 (56)
1942	35,527 (43)
1943	32,863 (41)
1944	34,271 (59)
1945	33,716 (42)
1946	35,665 (54)
1947	39,524 (51)
1948	36,274 (66)
1949	33,591 (86)
1950	33,672 (16)
1951	27,081 (64)
1952	42,541 (45)
1953	26,576 (57)
1954	32,834 (51)
1955	23,851 (98)
1956	36,298 (33)
1957	37,157 (50)
1958	32,622 (59)
1959	30,852
1960	35,221

Mileage at 12/36: 69,165
Mileage at 31/12/50: 606,439

Sheds

Bank Hall	30/11/35
Agecroft	16/11/40
Newton Heath	29/3/41
Agecroft	14/2/42
Fleetwood	28/10/44
Bank Hall	11/5/46
Huddersfield	12/10/46
Farnley Junction	10/6/50
Huddersfield	30/9/50
Wakefield	7/2/53
Huddersfield	12/11/54
Wakefield	22/1/55
Southport	16/6/56
Carlisle Canal	12/1/63
Carlisle Kingmoor	22/6/63
Wigan (L&Y)	14/3/64
Springs Branch	18/4/64
Rose Grove	27/6/64
Fleetwood	19/6/65
Carlisle Kingmoor	18/9/65

Withdrawn w.e. 16/4/66

Southport's 45218 on 12 August 1961 at Stockport Edgeley shed was newly ex-works following a Heavy General completed five days earlier. It had acquired the part-welded tender the week before it went into the works 45218 was always domeless throughout; the fitting of the AWS was not recorded on its History Card. Photograph D. Forsyth, Colourrail.co.uk

45219

Built as 5219 at Armstrong Whitworth 29/11/35
Renumbered 45219 w.e. 5/6/48

Improvements and modifications

?	Removal of vacuum pump
1/3/41	BTH speed indicator
10/5/44	Steam sanding
?	Fitting BR ATC equipment

Repairs

16/11/37-8/12/37	HS
24/2/38-25/2/38	HO
20/2/39-28/2/39	LO
9/11/39-30/11/39	HG
10/2/41-1/3/41	LS
26/11/42-2/1/43	HS
25/4/44-10/5/44	HG
19/6/45-12/7/45	LS
26/11/46-18/12/46	HS
2/1/48-31/1/48	LO
28/4/48-4/6/48	HG
10/1/50-27/1/50	LI
6/11/51-28/11/51	LI
5/8/53-16/9/53	G
30/8/54-1/10/54	HI
15/10/56-15/11/56	LI
10/6/58-3/7/58	HG
4/12/59-18/1/60	HI
21/12/60-27/1/61	HI
1/6/62-29/6/62	HI
30/7/65-11/9/65	INT

Boilers

New	8999
9/11/39	8685 from 5067 (domed)
10/5/44	8974 from 5130
4/6/48	9056 from 5021
16/9/53	8678 from 45072 (domed)
3/7/58	8989 from 45101

Tenders

New	9323
7/5/48	10555 (part-welded)
25/5/55	10537 (part-welded)
15/11/56	10588 (part-welded)

Mileage/(weekdays out of service)

1935	2,588 (1)
1936	51,202 (50)
1937	46,361 (76)
1938	49,967 (74)
1939	42,620 (68)
1940	37,071 (40)
1941	34,825 (68)
1942	31,696 (75)
1943	46,140 (48)
1944	36,471 (52)
1945	34,760 (50)
1946	28,960 (76)
1947	38,527 (29)
1948	32,772 (75)
1949	38,869 (41)
1950	53,817 (55)
1951	18,857 (80)
1952	33,905 (28)
1953	34,824 (59)
1954	49,222 (62)
1955	37,019 (61)
1956	27,914 (64)
1957	45,093

Mileage at 12/36: 53,790
Mileage at 31/12/50: 586,646

Sheds

Low Moor	30/11/35
Farnley Junc	21/12/35
Blackpool	13/6/36
Bank Hall	17/10/36
Southport	7/11/36
Bank Hall	17/7/37
Southport	20/11/37
Newton Heath	4/6/38
Southport	1/10/38
Rose Grove	15/6/40
Accrington	18/7/41
Newton Heath	28/2/42
Bank Hall	28/3/42
Southport	10/10/42
Newton Heath	27/3/43
Agecroft	11/10/47
Newton Heath	10/4/48
Huddersfield	21/10/50 (loan)
Low Moor	25/11/50
Low Moor	3/11/51
Copley Hill	20/8/61
Low Moor	16/6/63
Royston	8/9/63
Holbeck	12/6/66

Withdrawn 30/9/67

45219 from Low Moor at York on 18 June 1960. It had been domeless since July 1958 and had a part-welded tender from May 1948. Although it has the later external steam lance pipework it had not yet received its AWS. Photograph J.T. Clewley, www.transporttreasury.co.uk

45220

Built as 5220 at Armstrong Whitworth 29/11/35
Renumbered 45220 w.e. 30/4/49

Improvements and modifications

23/9/38	Removal of vacuum pump
9/6/45	Steam sanding
28/6/56	Modification
3/11/61	Fitting BR ATC equipment

Repairs

25/1/37-10/2/37	LS
11/10/37-9/11/37	HO
18/2/38-23/3/38	HO
6/9/38-23/9/38	LS
1/6/40-22/6/40	HG
5/12/41-10/1/42	HS
4/4/42-9/5/42	LO
23/10/43-17/11/43	LS
10/5/45-9/6/45	HG
6/11/46-4/12/46	LS
22/11/47-24/12/47	HS
10/3/48-21/4/48	NC
23/3/49-28/4/49	LI
21/11/50-21/12/50	HG
17/11/52-6/12/52	LI
9/6/54-29/6/54	LI
29/5/56-28/6/56	HG
26/3/58-29/4/58	HI
5/8/59-16/9/59	LC(EO)
19/9/60-5/11/60	HG
25/10/61-3/11/61	NC(EO)

Boilers

New	9000
22/6/40	8643 from 5044 (domed)
9/6/45	8662 from 5180 (domed)
21/12/50	8972 from 5221
28/6/56	8968
5/11/60	8916

Tenders

New	9324
?	10566
2/11/63	9263

Mileage/(weekdays out of service)

1935	3,636 (-)
1936	48,211 (73)
1937	42,649 (83)
1938	42,570 (98)
1939	43,773 (58)
1940	31,814 (90)
1941	38,638 (53)
1942	29,415 (81)
1943	37,479 (73)
1944	36,216 (29)
1945	33,310 (58)
1946	36,765 (54)
1947	31,113 (70)
1948	29,516 (103)
1949	36,972 (61)
1950	26,062 (92)
1951	41,796 (32)
1952	29,693 (66)
1953	44,685 (39)
1954	32,267 (58)
1955	31,678 (71)
1956	31,504 (60)
1957	42,644 (44)
1958	32,631 (72)
1959	39,362
1960	30,572

Mileage at 12/36: 51,847
Mileage at 31/12/50: 548,039

Sheds

Low Moor	30/11/35
Farnley Junction	21/12/35
Blackpool	13/6/36
Southport	31/10/36
Newton Heath	4/6/38
Southport	1/10/38
Newton Heath	17/5/41
Blackpool	14/2/42
Newton Heath	22/1/44
Agecroft	11/10/47
Newton Heath	10/6/50
Trafford Park	22/2/64

Stored
19/10/36-2/11/36

Withdrawn w.e. 1/10/66

45220 from Newton Heath piloting Patriot 45550 through Lancaster on 6 September 1962. It was domed until December 1950 and was fitted with AWS in November 1961. Photograph www.rail-online.co.uk

45221

Built as 5221 at Armstrong Whitworth 29/11/35
Renumbered 45221 w.e. 28/5/49

Improvements and modifications

6/9/39	BTH speed indicator
6/9/39	Steam sanding
6/9/39	Removal of vacuum pump
6/1/61	Smith-Stone speed indicator

Repairs

8/2/37-21/2/37	LS
27/10/37-25/11/37	LO
12/5/38-30/5/38	HS
14/8/39-6/9/39	HG
27/3/41-16/4/41	HS
12/3/42-11/4/42	HS
11/2/43-9/3/43	LS
4/7/44-29/7/44	LS
26/6/45-13/7/45	LO
31/12/45-23/1/46	HG
28/8/47-11/10/47	HS
29/10/47-11/11/47	NC(Rect)
30/4/49-26/5/49	LI
11/9/50-10/10/50	HG
13/11/52-9/12/52	LI
5/10/53-27/10/53	HI
12/4/55-7/5/55	HG
27/12/56-19/1/57	LI
24/1/58-27/2/58	LI
16/2/59-18/3/59	LC(EO)
19/5/59-29/5/59	LC(EO)
2/10/59-6/11/59	HI
28/10/60-6/1/61	HG

Boilers

New	9001
6/9/39	8984 from 5204
16/4/41	8822 from 5090 (domed)
23/1/46	8972 from 5003
10/10/50	9013 from 5099
7/5/55	8661 from 45155 (domed)
6/1/61	9028 from 45033

Tenders

New	9325
23/1/46	9290
28/4/49	9322

Mileage/(weekdays out of service)

1935	4,294 (2)
1936	53,008 (49)
1937	48,193 (64)
1938	62,237 (49)
1939	44,503 (70)
1940	45,073 (32)
1941	36,686 (42)
1942	44,598 (44)
1943	46,974 (59)
1944	35,185 (84)
1945	28,087 (56)
1946	47,591 (54)
1947	30,542 (102)
1948	38,306 (73)
1949	31,122 (73)
1950	27,942 (65)
1951	45,270 (55)
1952	33,185 (64)
1953	40,102 (50)
1954	49,343 (30)
1955	39,027 (69)
1956	38,948 (56)
1957	38,516 (59)
1958	38,295 (70)
1959	29,287
1960	33,070

Mileage at 12/36: 57,302
Mileage at 31/12/50: 624,341

Sheds

Low Moor	30/11/35
Farnley Jct	25/4/36
Blackpool	13/6/36
Farnley Jct	7/11/36
Low Moor	8/5/37
Wakefield	23/9/39
Low Moor	16/12/39
Southport	2/10/48
Wakefield	1/1/49
Nottingham	11/11/50 (loan)
Kentish Town	2/12/50 (loan)
Leicester	17/1/51 (loan)
Leicester	2/2/52
Bedford	26/1/57
Nottingham	23/1/60
Derby	17/9/60
Saltley	4/3/61
Nottingham	6/4/63
Derby	23/11/63
Nottingham	27/6/64
Springs Branch	6/3/65
Warrington	26/6/65
Stockport	7/10/67

Stored
19/10/36-9/11/36

Withdrawn w.e. 30/12/67

45221 at Doncaster in June 1963 on an excursion headed for the east coast. It had a domeless boiler from January 1961 and was always paired with a welded tender. 45221 was originally a Central Division engine until 1950 when it moved to various Midland Division sheds. Photograph www.rail-online.co.uk

45222

Built as 5222 at Armstrong Whitworth 9/12/35
Renumbered 45222 w.e. 19/2/49

Improvements and modifications

29/7/38	Removal of vacuum pump
12/6/43	Steam sanding
13/6/59	Fitting BR ATC equipment

Repairs

3/2/37-23/2/37	LS
29/10/37-3/12/37	LO
17/6/38-29/7/38	HG
23/7/40-8/8/40	LS
30/1/42-21/2/42	LS
21/5/43-12/6/43	HG
27/11/44-21/12/44	LS
16/1/46-9/2/46	HS
30/10/47-24/12/47	HG
18/1/49-15/2/49	HI
8/6/50-4/7/50	NC
24/10/50-21/11/50	HI
4/12/52-1/1/53	HG
12/4/54-12/5/54	HI
8/11/55-26/11/55	HI
21/11/56-7/12/56	LC(EO)
15/3/58-23/4/58	HG
20/5/59-13/6/59	HI
24/5/61-20/6/61	LI
17/12/62-11/1/63	LI
17/12/64-30/1/65	HI
9/12/66-19/12/66	NC

Boilers

New	9002
30/6/38	8681 from 5064 (domed)
12/6/43	9013 from 5162
24/12/47	8941 from 5198
1/1/53	8910 from 45095
23/4/58	8685 from 45089 (domed)

Tenders

New	9326

Mileage/(weekdays out of service)

1935	2,356 (-)
1936	53,906 (37)
1937	42,441 (100)
1938	36,506 (127)
1939	27,315 (140)
1940	34,333 (47)
1941	37,740 (42)
1942	36,377 (57)
1943	34,440 (82)
1944	32,257 (61)
1945	37,118 (38)
1946	40,528 (61)
1947	27,563 (87)
1948	43,601 (36)
1949	38,178 (48)
1950	25,092 (105)
1951	40,679 (37)
1952	33,792 (58)
1953	40,786 (48)
1954	43,809 (56)
1955	37,929 (77)
1956	43,149 (52)
1957	33,865
1958	33,879 (65)
1959	35,813
1960	37,622

Mileage at 12/36: 56,262
Mileage at 31/12/50: 549,811

Sheds

Newton Heath	14/12/35
Huddersfield	9/12/50
Southern Region	23/5/53 (loan)
Huddersfield	27/6/53
Northampton	8/11/58
Bletchley	17/9/60
Northampton	5/11/60
Willesden	19/11/60
Rugby	9/9/61
Bletchley	14/7/62
Bescot	14/3/64
Banbury	1/1/66
Colwick	19/2/66
Newton Heath	12/11/66

Stored
17/10/38-22/12/38
2/1/39-3/4/39
17/4/39-17/5/39

Withdrawn w.e. 11/2/67

45222 ready for departure from Euston in the 1960s. The broken 1E shedplate denotes Bletchley where it was from July 1962 until March 1964. It received a domed boiler in April 1958 and AWS in June 1959. Photograph www.rail-online.co.uk

45223

Built as 5223 at Armstrong Whitworth 9/12/35
Renumbered 45223 w.e. 31/7/48

Improvements and modifications

22/7/38	Removal of vacuum pump
2/10/42	Steam sanding
23/2/55	Modification
7/3/61	Smith-Stone speed indicator

Repairs

26/1/37-12/2/37	LS
8/11/37-8/12/37	LO
15/6/38-22/7/38	HG
17/6/40-1/7/40	HS
4/9/42-2/10/42	HG
20/1/44-8/2/44	HS
20/12/44-13/1/45	LO
26/9/45-20/10/45	LS
24/2/47-22/3/47	HG
16/6/48-31/7/48	HS
8/4/50-24/5/50	HG
16/10/51-10/11/51	LI
2/2/53-6/3/53	HI
20/1/55-23/2/55	HG
29/11/56-10/1/57	HI (EO)
8/10/58-1/11/58	HI
2/1/61-7/3/61	HG
8/10/63-6/11/63	LI

Boilers

New	9003
24/6/38	9005 from 5075
2/10/42	9029 from 5101
22/3/47	9050 from 5143
24/5/50	8983 from 5093
23/2/55	8922 from 45028
7/3/61	8979 from 45137

Tenders

New	9327
22/12/56	9524
20/10/62	10799 (part-welded)
6/11/63	10787 (riveted)

Mileage/(weekdays out of service)

1935	2,488 (-)
1936	51,513 (31)
1937	44,035 (94)
1938	38,046 (119)
1939	29,818 (138)
1940	33,971 (54)
1941	34,555 (38)
1942	30,758 (68)
1943	43,286 (23)
1944	42,907 (37)
1945	26,672 (70)
1946	36,027 (49)
1947	35,530 (68)
1948	33,469 (64)
1949	33,408 (56)
1950	37,508 (73)
1951	36,196 (49)
1952	35,799 (66)
1953	40,407 (58)
1954	36,826 (44)
1955	38,843 (52)
1956	35,546 (75)
1957	45,960 (29)
1958	30,023 (57)
1959	33,016
1960	31,366

Mileage at 12/36: 54,001
Mileage at 31/12/50: 553,991

Sheds

Newton Heath	14/12/35
Agecroft	11/10/47
Newton Heath	10/4/48
Southern Region	23/5/53 (loan)
Newton Heath	27/6/53
Agecroft	9/2/57
Leicester GC	12/9/59 (loan)
Leicester GC	7/11/59
Annesley	9/1/60
Woodford Halse	9/9/61
Leicester GC	17/3/62
Cricklewood	9/3/63
Bangor	25/5/63
Holyhead	19/6/65
Speke Jct	5/2/66

Stored
17/10/38-22/12/38
2/1/39-3/4/39
17/4/39-17/5/39

Withdrawn w.e. 10/12/66

45223 from Newton Heath at Wigan Springs Branch in the 1950s. It was one of the Central Division engines stored before the war, spending six months out of service between October 1938 and May 1939. It was always domeless with a welded tender until 1962. The domed covers from the firebox shoulders have gone missing. 45223 was loaned to the Southern Region in 1953 when the Bullied Pacifics were temporarily taken out of service with axle problems. Photograph www.rail-online.co.uk

45224

Built as 5224 at Armstrong Whitworth 10/12/35
Renumbered 45224 w.e. 21/8/48

Improvements and modifications

7/6/38	Removal of vacuum pump
2/12/44	Steam sanding
27/7/61	Fitting BR ATC equipment

Repairs

17/2/37-22/3/37	HS
26/5/38-7/6/38	LS
1/4/40-25/4/40	HG
2/10/41-23/10/41	LS
7/5/42-15/5/42	LO
5/10/42-24/10/52	HS
26/2/43-19/3/43	LO
6/11/43-27/11/43	LS
6/11/44-2/12/44	HG
25/5/46-15/6/46	LS
29/12/47-31/1/48	HS
14/7/48-18/8/48	LO
4/2/50-16/3/50	HG
18/10/51-14/11/51	LI
1/7/52-7/8/52	LC(EO)
4/5/53-29/5/53	LI
9/2/55-7/4/55	HG
3/12/56-19/1/57	LI
11/4/58-8/5/58	LI
9/11/59-7/1/60	HG
22/1/60-20/2/60	LC(EO)
17/7/61-27/7/61	NC(EO)
19/3/62-14/4/62	HI

Boilers

New	9004
25/4/40	8821 from 5004 (domed)
2/12/44	8923 from 5004
16/3/50	9058 from 5210
7/4/55	8836 from 45133
7/1/60	8834 from 45180

Tenders

New	9328

Mileage/(weekdays out of service)

1935	1,614 (-)
1936	52,405 (38)
1937	47,225 (70)
1938	38,315 (105)
1939	33,801 (104)
1940	34,878 (58)
1941	33,637 (55)
1942	38,440 (46)
1943	35,992 (66)
1944	34,073 (56)
1945	38,867 (43)
1946	31,873 (62)
1947	32,990 (52)
1948	28,966 (90)
1949	24,769 (66)
1950	37,944 (58)
1951	32,265 (89)
1952	35,372 (74)
1953	35,659 (72)
1954	28,091 (56)
1955	33,342 (83)
1956	31,440 (80)
1957	36,690 (57)
1958	33,809 (50)
1959	22,842
1960	40,947

Mileage at 12/36: 54,019
Mileage at 31/12/50: 545,789

Sheds

Newton Heath	14/12/35
Bolton	20/12/62
Burton	25/5/63
Derby	14/8/65
Colwick	27/8/66

Stored

17/10/38-22/12/38
2/1/39-20/3/39
1/8/66-17/8/66
12/9/66-12/11/66

Withdrawn w.e. 12/11/66

45224 pictured in the 1950s at Polmadie was the final locomotive built with a vertical throatplate domeless boiler. It was shedded at 26A Newton Heath from new until December 1962, was always domeless apart from one boiler during war and kept its original welded tender throughout. It has an oval Crewe-built worksplate on the front frames, a legacy from an exchange of frames during a Heavy General repair at Crewe Works in February/March 1950. It received the frames from 45013 and donated its frames to 45006. Photograph www.rail-online.co.uk

Endpiece

On the final leg of the 1T57 '15 Guinea Special', 45110 poses for photographers at Rainhill on 11 August 1968.